PANDEMONIUM
TREMENDUM

JAMES E. HUCHINGSON

PANDEMONIUM TREMENDUM

CHAOS AND MYSTERY IN THE LIFE OF GOD

THE
PILGRIM
PRESS
Cleveland

The Pilgrim Press, Cleveland, Ohio 44115
www.pilgrimpress.com

06 05 4 03 02 01   5 4 3 2 1

Library of Congress Cataloging-in-Publication Data

Huchingson, James Edward, 1940-
    Pandemonium tremendum : chaos and mystery in the life of God /
James E. Huchingson.
      p. cm.
    Includes bibliographical references and index.
    ISBN 0-8298-1419-1 (pbk. : alk. paper)
    1. Philosophical theology. 2. Information theory – Religious aspects –
Christianity. I. Title.

BT40 .H83 2001
210 – dc21   2001018533

Contents

Preface   vii

1. The Transformative Machine   1

2. God-Talk and the Case for Cosmology   22

3. In Defense of Metaphysics   42

4. A Primer of Communication and Systems Theory   66

5. The Pandemonium Tremendum   96

6. The Source of Abundance   116

7. An Outspoken God   139

8. The Mighty Throng of Creatures   159

9. In the Image of God and the World   178

10. The Joyful Noise of Providence, Judgment, and Revelation   202

11. Evaluating the Model   219

Index   224

Preface

⬛ THIS BOOK IS AN EXERCISE in synoptic vision. It is a study of the way things go and how they hang together and sometimes fall apart. These things are not limited to the vast multitude of things, both inanimate and animate, that inhabit our worldly neighborhood—planet earth, the Milky Way, and the cosmos itself. They also include the things of heaven—God and the adjunct realities that may inhabit that transcendent neighborhood. Of course, a study about every particular thing seems overly ambitious unless it is clearly understood that what is being sought is an account of the totality of things in their deepest associations, that is, a general description of the *system* of reality. But, as we shall attempt to show, the telling clue to the life of God does indeed lie in the *particularities* of the vast throng of beings constituting this system of creation.

Still too ambitious? Certainly. That is why help is sought from numerous brilliant explorers, including Plato, Aristotle, Paul Tillich, Alfred North Whitehead, Gregory Bateson, and Claude Shannon, who stand out among the many others we consulted in the task. Plato and Aristotle are familiar, and many know of Tillich, Whitehead, and Bateson—but Claude Shannon? For the sake of this initial orientation and in anticipation of later discussion, a brief introduction is in order. Shannon is the father of communication or information theory. He was a mathematician whose work was primarily aimed at practical application: the improvement of the efficiency of communicating electrically over wires and electromagnetically through the air. Shannon's theories provided the foundations for the development of computers, which is why we measure a machine's power by its information-processing capacities, its speed and memory, in terms of bits and bytes.

The use of computer science to suggest theological models may seem to some to be ludicrous. Will the results of our inquiry be a digital deity and a computational universe, caricatures dictated by the logic of the computer metaphor? If communication theory were the only source for the models of God and world we hope to construct, then these distortions would be predictable. However, those, like Tillich and Whitehead, who advanced their own models, were brilliantly skilled in such projects. Their systems offer indispensable guidance on how to minimize the risk of distortion; we will draw upon them liberally. Also, "ludicrous" is derived from the Latin *ludus,* a play or game. In this sense our project is indeed ludicrous; it is carried out in the modest spirit of playful exploration just to see what happens, an "adventure of ideas," to modify slightly the title of one of Whitehead's books. This point is well made by F. E. Peters in the "Preliminary Note" of *Greek Philosophical Terms:*

> [The Greeks] trusted in names and their self-assurance was such that they could even afford to be playful about them. And when they came to devising strange new names that they themselves had wrought, they approached the task with both confidence and inventiveness.[1]

Admittedly, there is a tension here. Computer science gives the point of contact between this world of our senses and actions and some more encompassing whole in which God is included. Computers are not only metaphorically suggestive but also ontologically suggestive. The computer is a microcosm; exploring the theoretical foundations of its operations gives hints into the very nature of things, or so we will argue. It is with respect to these foundations and the "strange new names" they bring to theology that we will consult frequently with Claude Shannon and others who think like he does.

How can a highly technical scientific theory, especially one devised solely to address the workings of electronic machines, be applied at all to an accounting of God and world? Is the choice of communication theory arbitrary, and are the connections with God and world imaginary? These are questions that should be asked but not answered in a preface since one aim of this study is precisely to provide responses. Suffice it to say in preparation for what follows that all starting points in metaphysics or metaphysical theology are arbitrary in that each is a path chosen from a number of possible paths, perhaps from insight or inspiration alone. The justification and rewards come from discoveries along the way. Also, the imagination is important here, just as it is in any creative project.

---

1. F. E. Peters, *Greek Philosophical Terms: A Historical Lexicon* (New York: New York University Press, 1967), ix.

Without creative associations or images, we would never advance beyond sense experience or an occupation with the present moment. And certainly the imagination is indispensable when we speculate about realities that cannot be made available for our immediate inspection.

A theology that considers the implications of the computer-driven conceptual revolution is necessarily a work in progress, not pretending to be complete. The foundations that this book provides for a constructive theology of God rely on the following premises. The computer is contributing to a new understanding scientifically of how things go in nature. This understanding questions the prevailing worldview of the Enlightenment about the universe and our place in it. Consequently, the construction of a new worldview incorporating these most recent discoveries is underway. The idea of God or the sacred that prevails in any cultural epoch is determined in large measure by the dominant worldview or cosmology. Thus, we need to look at the doctrines of God and the creation so as constructively to build upon them in terms provided by the electronic revolution and the worldview it informs.

For the sake of orientation, we should begin with a brief survey of the chapters that follow. By illustrating the deeper influence of electronic machines on modern culture, chapter 1 explains why the computer offers a crucial and provocative clue for the task of theological construction. In chapter 2, we argue for the need to recover the important but neglected connection between theology and cosmology. This argument is carried further in chapter 3 with a justification of metaphysics as a necessary discipline for both theology and cosmology—a difficult assignment, given the prevailing intellectual and popular disdain of metaphysics or "large ideas." Chapter 4 is a primer on Shannon's communication theory and systems theory that prepares the way for their application in constructive theology. The primordial chaos of Genesis takes center stage in chapter 5, where we use Shannon's ideas to explore the strange realm of this book's title concept, the *Pandemonium Tremendum*. Models of God are introduced in chapter 6 by building on the connection between divinity and this *Pandemonium Tremendum*. With this framework and working vocabulary in place, we turn in chapter 7 to the creation to explicate the role of God, who stands between chaos and cosmos, employing the power of the one to generate, sustain, and direct the other. Chapter 8 moves from the creation to its creaturely inhabitants and describes how variety, the stuff of chaos, is the generative and nourishing abundance for all complex systems. The special complex system of the human person is the subject of chapter 9, where we give attention to the irreducible historical character of our species as a self-reflective and open system. Every attempt is made to work theological concepts into the themes of each chapter. In chapter 10, however, we give the doctrines of providence, judgment, and revelation center stage. In the final chapter, we evaluate the model that has been constructed, based on criteria against which metaphysical proposals may be tested.

This project, then, is an exercise in constructive theology. It is a conceptual simulation focusing initially on the primordial chaos, God, and the creation and then zooming down, first to describe creatures in general and then to specify the human creature—all within the framework of a systems-informational cosmology and metaphysics.

Ideas, however novel, are never created by fiat, spontaneously arising from a vacuum. They are, rather, the consequence of thought applied to insights given by others, even if the contributions are made unawares. This being so, I can only acknowledge some of the many contributors to this book. They include John Eagleson and Robert Maccini, whose wonderful editing skills considerably reduced my labors, and Timothy Staveteig and George Graham at The Pilgrim Press for their impressive professionalism and guidance through the entire production process. I also deeply appreciate the support provided by colleagues in the Department of Religious Studies of Florida International University. Most of all, I am indebted to my spouse, Dr. Olga Craven Huchingson, to whom I dedicate this book, for her continuous encouragement and unwavering confidence in me during the entire project, but especially for her enduring love.

– 1 –

The Transformative Machine

AT FIRST GLANCE, any connection between theology and computers appears remote at best. Theology is concerned, by definition, with divine realities. Its focus and intention are to articulate visions of revelation and salvation, of God's loving will enacted in history through events of divine reconciliation. Computers are machines with souls consisting of long strings of 0's and 1's in a magnetic medium and wills made of software programs. As efficient augmentation to the computational powers of the human brain, they are tools capable of accomplishing prodigious practical tasks but nothing of transcendental significance. Only a rich imagination could conjure a connection, surely artificial, between the divine and digital domains. Further glances, however, bring things more into focus to reveal what is actually the profound effect of computers directly and indirectly upon theological thought. The intention of this chapter is to demonstrate through a series of such glances that these information-processing devices bear considerable promise for constructive theology.

MACHINES AND SOCIETY

The Consequences of Cars

As any student of the mutual interaction of technology and society knows, a new machine is not introduced into history arbitrarily, nor does its presence have only immaculate effects in intended ways without collaterally altering the social and cultural context. Inventions affect society at several levels. The automobile, for example, has immediate consequences for transportation, successfully taking people speedily and comfortably to their destinations. Secondary effects of cars, however, are often neither positive nor intended. Millions of automobiles crowded into metropolitan areas create massive problems in traffic and pollution. Exclusive reliance upon

1

a single form of transportation increases a nation's vulnerability in supplying the fossil fuel that powers the car. Cities take on new designs with their citizens living in sprawling suburbs and slowly commuting along clogged roads to their workplaces. The economic well-being of a nation becomes heavily reliant on the productions of cars, a situation that places considerable power in the hands of large oil companies and automobile manufacturers. Recall the slogan of fifty years ago, partially accurate even today, that "What is good for GM is good for America."

In addition to the primary and secondary consequences of an invention, there is a tertiary level of effects on social and cultural attitudes, social values, self-identity, and even worldviews. Certainly, the automobile exerts a profound impact on American culture. Its presence reinforces the public philosophy of radical individualism that is one of the major defining characteristics of American society. The automobile ("self-mover") meshes nicely with our nonnegotiable sense of autonomy. The car is an unprecedented symbolic extension of that identity and a literal amplification of the power inherent in it.

It can be further argued that the automobile culture has theological consequences. For one thing, it reinforces the Protestant notion of the individual and recommends an approach to faith as a consumer choice to be made on a comparative basis in the competitive market. Ford or Toyota, Methodist or Unitarian—we shop around.

More important than this is the attention theology pays to moral and social issues of the automobile culture. An example is found in automotive production. The condition of the American worker was changed forever with Henry Ford's introduction of mass production. Workers, like automobile parts, became standardized and interchangeable. The cherished individual freedom encouraged by the automobile was ironically denied to the worker on the assembly line. The automated process of production envisioned in the Taylor system of efficient physical action included human units whose robotic movements would be completely repetitive. Such conditions robbed workers of any sense of pride or control of their labor and provided the best illustration of the Marxian notion of the alienation of workers from their labor. The role played by theology in this account of the impact of the automobile is primarily in moral theology involving religious institutions as advocates of social justice in the workplace and of equal participation of individuals and communities in the economic benefits of society.

In ways other than these important concerns for justice, the effect of this invention on the worldview or prevailing philosophy of American life and theology has been minimal. The automobile has magnified the values of the modern world, already dominant for three centuries, but it has modified them only slightly.

Information and Identity through Computers

This cannot be said for the computer and its contribution to the "Information Revolution." The very foundations of the economy and material society have come to rest as much on the infrastructure of information technology as on the roads and expressways upon which we drive our automobiles. In parallel to the consequences of the automobile on the common life, the impact of the computer is equally profound, but in our estimate, carries much further into worldviews and theology.

In its primary effects, the computer has given us tremendous power to store and retrieve vast amounts of information from massive databases almost instantaneously. Every sector of society—government, the military, offices, hospitals, banks, schools, and individuals—has seen its productivity and the accompanying convenience rise dramatically as a result. With the instantaneous transfer of information and money from one end of the globe to the other, e-commerce is a full-fledged revolution. Progress in electronic technology means that computers become ever smaller and smarter. Tiny microprocessors make any device accommodating and portable. Pocket-sized mobile devices accompany the wearer anywhere. For better or worse, we are never out of touch. More and more, their diminutive size and increased intelligence qualify these machines to serve as our personal assistants, guiding our daily activities.

The secondary impact of computers on social attitudes and ideals is proportional to its impact on material culture. In a "wired" world, the workplace, education, and personal interaction are in dramatic transformation. These are not without their risks. Intrusive surveillance threatens privacy. Power follows knowledge; nations may soon be divided into the haves and the have-nots with respect to access to the skills and contact required to be competitive in a world progressively saturated with information. The entire information system, so fully integrated and immensely complex that knowledge of the intricate details of its operations is beyond anyone, is vulnerable to disabling accidents and terrorist acts of sabotage.

Theology's response to this revolution is wide-ranging. As with the automobile, it includes traditional concerns for social justice and the fair distribution of benefits as befitting the inherent dignity of all persons. Theology is also concerned with some of the more radical, if not esoteric, tertiary consequences of computers and cyberspace. These include questions about the deconstruction and reconstruction of personal identity on-line with the capability of providing flexible, imaginative persona—self-constructed electronic masks—while communicating with invisible strangers who likewise may not be real. This alone is a threat to the fundamental modern notion of the indivisible self. What happens, then, to "the soul in cyberspace?"[1] Is it possible to create a worshiping community on the World Wide Web? Or is there a "soul *of* cyberspace?"[2] And finally, is the very notion of a closed canon of scripture imperiled by the fluidity of the written word in cyberspace and the power of hypertexting that allow the reader to amend, recompose, and extend any text merely with a click of the mouse?[3]

In addition, of course, there are theological questions in the burgeoning science of artificial intelligence. Machines that truly think strongly suggest that persons are merely thinking machines. What have such developments to say about human nature and the inherent dignity traditionally imputed to it? Will flesh and blood persons be reduced to electronic identities, or will intelligent machines be welcomed as equals into the community of self-conscious and responsible human agents? These questions are, of course, not nearly as simple as they sound. And theology neglects them only at great risk.

Theologians have an investment in these and similar issues because questions of human identity, the nature and structure of reality, and God's relation to both of these are the business of theology. We should also recognize that the posture taken by theologians regarding the philosophical and religious implications of new technology is not that of defensive vigilance, as appropriate as

---

1. See Douglas Groothuis, *The Soul in Cyberspace* (Grand Rapids: Baker Books, 1997), for a thoughtful and somewhat critical analysis from a conservative perspective.

2. In his book of interviews by that same name, Jeffrey Zaleski is somewhat more optimistic than Groothuis about the religious possibilities of the computer revolution. See *The Soul of Cyberspace: How New Technology Is Changing Our Spiritual Lives* (San Francisco: HarperEdge, 1997).

3. See Stephen D. O'Leary, "Cyberspace as Sacred Space: Communicating Religion on Computer Networks," *Journal of the American Academy of Religion* 64, no. 4 (1996): 781–808.

this stance may be at times (e.g., nuclear weapons or environmental destruction). Rather, theologians welcome opportunities to take constructive hints from imaginative new developments. The remainder of this chapter will illustrate and assess several theologically relevant contributions of information technology as an overture to the constructive system to be laid out in subsequent chapters. We begin with a brief outline of the computer's place within the broader taxonomy of technological instruments as a way of emphasizing its radical distinctiveness and, hence, novel potential.

COMPUTERS AND OTHER MACHINES

A Typology of Machines

Machines are devices for doing work, and work is the transfer of energy. Along with matter, energy is one of the fundamental constituents of the physical world. Machines are fundamental instruments for the transformation of that world into one of our own making. Lewis Mumford, a brilliant student of the role of technology in history, offers a classification of instrumental devices that includes tools, machines, and automata.[4] *Tools* are implements that extend human capabilities by augmenting or amplifying body movements. Tools range from the primitive club or knife to eating utensils and even to writing implements—the pen or pencil. *Machines* may be classically simple (e.g., the screw, lever, or inclined plane), or they may be impressively complex, as with the internal combustion engine. Unlike tools, machines do work by employing primarily their own sources of energy, including wind, water, gravity, and fossil fuel. Machines require human direction, and this is what distinguishes them from *automata,* which either have their directions built into their very structure or are capable of responding to their immediate environment. Many automatic machines perform repetitive tasks in the manufacture of standard products. More advanced cybernetic systems are coupled with sensitive devices to modify the machine's performance by adjusting to changing circumstances. The home heater or air conditioner regulated by a thermostat is a simple representative of this group of machines.

---

4. Lewis Mumford, *Technics and Civilization* (New York: Harcourt Brace, 1934), 9–12. For a full discussion of Mumford's ideas, see Carl Mitcham, *Thinking through Technology: The Path between Engineering and Philosophy* (Chicago: University of Chicago Press, 1994), 161–91.

Some complex artifacts are difficult to fit neatly into this simple taxonomy because they are combinations of several categories. The automobile, for example, integrates the simple lever (the steering wheel) with a highly complex engine and drive system and, in contemporary cars, includes dozens of microprocessors that adjust the performance of various parts to optimize efficiency. And, of course, people drive automobiles. Even this may change, however, for future automobile technology includes the automation of most driving tasks.

Where does the computer fit along this spectrum of machines? Computers resemble tools in some of their application; when used as a word processor, the computer replaces the pen or quill. Computers serve as automated devices. They may be programmed to carry out mathematical operations in repeated sequences at incredible rates of speed, some greater than billions of calculations each second. And, as indicated earlier, in the form of a microprocessor, the computer monitors and adjusts the performance of large, dumb machines with fine precision.

Despite these obvious similarities with other machines, the computer is actually a radical device that either extends the range of the machine taxonomy into entirely new territory or eludes it altogether. In fact, the ease with which the computer satisfies the definition of tool, machine, and automaton is a clue suggesting that it is as much none of them as all of them. The utter distinction in the nature and character of the computer is to be found in its virtually unlimited ability to imitate or model any machine whatsoever. Computers may "act" as mechanical clocks and typewriters, machines rendered completely obsolete with the invention of microprocessors. To employ a traditional theological concept, the computer "transcends" all other instrumental artifacts by occupying a category that includes them all. Computers are concrete abstractive devices of nearly unlimited power. They are more plastic, more protean, than other devices in their ability to transform, even self-transform. In this sense they transcend traditional machines in their uniqueness, inclusiveness, and potential.

Simulation and Isomorphism

Computers "simulate" objects, environments, and other realities. "Simulation" means literally "looking or acting alike." The process of modeling other realities within an electronic environment has taken its place operationally in the scientific method as a new kind of indirect experimentation with empirical consequences and important epistemological issues.[5] However, computer simulations are not always faithful visual images of the realities being simulated. The computer is a virtual laboratory wherein the processes of complex natural systems—for example, weather systems—consisting of numerous interactive variables are replicated according to mathematical rather than physical structure. The final results are a series of moving curves on the monitor screen indicating patterns of relationships between these variables in visual but often abstract form.

In systems sciences, such shared features between apparently dissimilar objects are known as *isomorphies,* from the Greek *isos,* meaning "equal," and *morphe,* meaning "form." Systems of any sort—conceptual, physical, social—are said to be isomorphic if they share some deep structural and process uniformities. Systems that are similar in pattern or that display corresponding relationships in their operations may be utterly different in their material makeup, organization, and forms of energy. For example, a traditional spring-wound watch, with its cogs, levers, and wheels, is very different from a digital timepiece powered by a small battery and governed by a simple electronic chip. Dismantling each to inspect their materials and compare the shapes and fit of their respective parts would not go very far toward identifying aspects in which they are alike. Yet, the operations of both systems may be described by the same sets of mathematical equations. They are isomorphic. Deep formal correspondence may relate vastly different concrete systems and processes, from the decay of radioactive atoms and certain financial transactions.[6] Of course, these may be simulated as well.

Isomorphism may be found widely employed in human thought. As we will see in more detail in chapter 3, metaphorical speech, so important in everyday discourse, derives its power by articulating surprising connections between objects that are apparently very different. Metaphors work (in less formal ways than mathematics, of course) because of real underlying and shared features of a systemic nature. These features, when recognized, give rise to novel disclosures. The difference is that while metaphors work primarily through insight and intuition, isomorphic systems often carry the framework of their own disclosure.

5. See, for example, Terrell Ward Bynum and James H. More, eds., *The Digital Phoenix: How Computers Are Changing Philosophy* (Oxford: Blackwell, 1998).

6. Ludwig von Bertalanffy, *General System Theory: Foundations, Development, Applications* (New York: George Braziller, 1968), 33–34.

Metaphors are exceedingly powerful linguistic devices for shaping human thought at the highest levels of philosophical and theological speculation. One has only to note the root metaphors used in describing the universe that are found in the various cosmologies of history. At different times, the world has been likened to a living organism or a vast machine or a river of process. Religious and cultural attitudes of a society are greatly influenced by the logical consequences of some prevailing world metaphor. How much more influential, then, would be a ubiquitous machine, the computer, in providing deep isomorphic structures that suggest new images of the world, humankind, and even God for the society it serves? Examples of this profound influence are not difficult to find. We now turn to several for the purpose not only of arguing the claim represented by this rhetorical question but also of providing concrete insights to be used later in the development of a theological model of God and world.

TECHNOLOGY AND THE BIRTH OF A NEW AGE

Postmodernism

The period that includes the past three hundred years, roughly from the Protestant Reformation, the Scientific Revolution, and the Renaissance until the latter decades of the twentieth century, is widely recognized as the age of modernism in the West. Its ideals, articulated best by the philosophers of the Enlightenment, remain in effect today. But the mood has changed, and the beliefs held by the modern world concerning humankind, the natural world, and even God are seriously questioned by those who would modify and even replace them and thereby introduce a new age. Unfortunately, this incipient age has only the vaguest of identities and even lacks a distinctive label. The best we can do at the moment is to refer to it as "postmodernism," a term that defines it not by its distinguishing beliefs and attitudes but by reference to its predecessor, whose attitudes and assumptions its proponents seek drastically to modify, reject, or dismantle.

Some philosophers have tried to give substance to the label by arguing that the Western worldview is undergoing a significant transformation that will have genuine real-world consequences. J. Baird Callicott, an environmental philosopher, has attempted to give positive content to a postmodern worldview, especially with respect to the idea of the place of the human species in nature. Callicott deconstructs two modern ideas. The first is that humankind is "spiritually and intellectually unique and thus discontinuous with nature."[7] The other is that nature itself is static and unchanging. The postmodern replacement for the first idea emphasizes our continuity with nature. Humankind is just another species; we are "precocious to be sure but just big monkeys, nevertheless." Since our works "are no less natural than those of termites and elephants," Callicott concludes, "We are therefore part of nature and not set apart from it."[8] The second modern idea, that nature is static, is replaced with the postmodern notion that nature is constantly changing and evolving "in every frequency—diurnal, meteorological, climatic, geological, astronomical."[9]

Callicott's intention is not simply to identify postmodern beliefs; he also includes a call "to begin a genuine symbolic integration of man with nature."[10] At this point technology enters the picture. He argues that the dominant worldview of a society communicates normative imperatives on how its citizens should live, and, reciprocally, the unquestionable authority of the worldview is reinforced by these everyday actions. The modern mechanistic age reflects the worldview of the Newtonian world machine. "The longer ordinary people lived in an increasingly mechanized world...the more widespread and deeply ingrained the mechanical worldview became."[11] Given these premises, the conclusion must be that wholesale changes in the forms and spirit of technology are needed to reshape the modern worldview.

Computers and Systems Experience

It is no surprise, then, that Callicott embraces information technology as the major cultural force moving us into the postmodern age with its goal of integrating humankind into restless nature. He recognizes that computers are far more than intelligent extensions of the classical machines that provided the fundamental metaphor for the mechanistic worldview, which, in turn, fed back into an age of machines. He is hopeful that our experience with computers will actually teach us to relate to the natural world in new ways:

7. J. Baird Callicott, "La Nature est Morte, Vive la Nature!" *Hastings Center Report* 22, no. 5 (1992): 17.
8. Ibid., 18.
9. Ibid.
10. Ibid., 20.
11. Ibid.

Think about your old Smith Corona typewriter. One key-stroke, one mark on the paper. The typewriter with its linked rods transferring the motion of the finger to the motion of the rods to the motion of the metal letter is a mechanism par excellence. With the PC, one keystroke can dramatically and instantaneously change the whole configuration of a paragraph or a spreadsheet or a graphic. Here we have a technological analogue of an ecosystem in which the extirpation of a single species can produce cascading reverberations throughout a biological community. People who use computers have grown accustomed to systems experience. The present generation of kids, who grow up with computers in their bedrooms, will think systematically—including, we hope *eco* systemically.[12]

The very reason that the computer experience reflects the post-modern integrative ecological age is that as a dynamic system it embodies principles that apply to natural systems, including amplification causality or the tendency of a delicately balanced system to respond dramatically and as a whole to small perturbations. In its more practical utilization, the electronic computer is a partial microcosm of nature; that is, its operations are isomorphic with those of natural systems. Kids who develop friendly relations with their computers are naturals to develop equally friendly relations with the natural world.

Despite the important role of an intellectual elite in its formulation, a worldview is neither constructed in nor imposed from the ivory tower. Callicott takes the position of the philosophical pragmatist that actions implement beliefs and even justify them. This contention may apply not only to worldviews but also to the theologies that rely upon them. The connection between models of divinity and cosmologies will be traced in further detail in chapter 3. But the point to be taken here is that theology, even more than philosophy, is responsive to shifts in cultural epochs and therefore to changes in the technological spirit that often accompany and hasten such shifts. Those children who grow up with computers may well require a model of God that reflects their postmodern experience rather than the experience of their modern grandparents.

---

12. Ibid., 22.

UNIVERSES OF INFORMATION

Three Universes and Their Gods

The computer is a powerful instrument for several reasons. One is that it allows us to store massive amounts of information in databases and retrieve them nearly instantaneously. Information—data, facts, and knowledge—is more than a commodity. How we value and appropriate it depends on how we, as a society, organize our world of information. It is possible to speak of "universes of information." These are characteristic ways that a culture organizes the totality of its experience and knowledge and hence are very significant in any discussion of worldviews.

According to Magorah Maruyama, a noted systems theorist, there are many ways for a society to organize its totality of information.[13] Several approaches described by Maruyama are especially germane to our discussion of the potential of computer technology for theology. He says that information may be organized according to three principles: classificational, relational, and relevantial; and a universe can be constructed from each. Any model of a universe implies some corresponding image of God. While Maruyama does not speculate on the model of deity that governs each of his universes, we will extend his discussion by suggesting our own.

The *classificational universe* is familiar because it represents the traditional or commonly held view of the universe in the West and is deeply indebted to Greek philosophy, especially that of Plato and Aristotle, for it origin. Classificational thinking arranges reality into enduring substances (Plato called them "forms") that may be divided downward into categories and subcategories. These categories are based on similarities between particular objects that permit them to be gathered upward into classes, giving rise, logically, to "higher," more abstract and inclusive superdivisions. Anyone who has consulted the organization of *Roget's Thesaurus* or studied Linnaeus's taxonomy of life forms is familiar with the classificational universe.

The classificational universe is governed by a distinctive deity whose attributes are logically derived from the nature of the universe. Maruyama observes, "The classificational universe, with its hierarchical structure, has the compulsion to rank order." Individual essences are slotted into rungs of a familiar hierarchy, the classic

---

13. Magorah Maruyama, "Metaorganization of Information," *Cybernetica* 4 (1965): 107–15.

"great chain of being," according to some ontological standard of greater being or greater rationality, with the "higher" rungs declared "superior." The categorical ascent and valuation must end somewhere, and, of course, the highest reality is God. God is perfect (i.e., the self-actualized being in whom there is no nonbeing, nothing missing or merely potential). The classificational deity is truly immobile for two reasons. The first is that God has no potential, nothing to be actualized, nothing to move toward or fulfill. The second is that God has created the nearly perfect world machine with profound consequences for providential involvement. The cosmos whose components, from standard atoms to standard galaxies, are arranged hierarchically is subject to predictably repetitive movements governed deterministically by intrinsic principles known as laws of nature. When confronted with such a perfect production, God is left with nothing to do.

Maruyama's *relational universe* is event rather than substance oriented. In a classificational universe, relationships between concrete individuals are mere accidents or surface modifications of some enduring and fundamental form. In the relational universe, form gives way to context. Relationships are dynamic and defining. Even polar opposites, such as war and peace, male and female, are understood as mutually defining; remove one, and the other vanishes. Any accounting of a particular object is incomplete without reference to its situation, which may vary significantly from the situation of another object that would be considered identical in a classificational scheme. Maruyama explains with a concrete illustration:

> Let us take a flower in a garden. In the classificational universe, it belongs to a certain species of plant which is a subcategory of some larger division. In the polycritical [categorized by essential characteristics] classificational universe, it gets additional descriptions as to size, location, etc. In the relational universe, it decorates a garden, it was planted by the daughter of the house, it is a part of the esthetic composition together with the bush behind it, it attracts insects which attract birds which please the old lady next door, etc. The relations are many-sided, mutual, situational, and not governed by the principle of subordination, superordination, and paraordination. The relational universe does not establish hierarchy.[14]

---

14. Ibid., 110.

One could argue that in a garden or a meadow, the flower remains the same discrete and enduring individual. But this is not the case. The very essence of the flower and its defining characteristics were not assigned to it as an entry in some original cosmic encyclopedia. They are instead the final harmonious arrangement of biological capabilities derived over millions of years in the grandest context-generating process of all—evolution. The precursors of the flower were shaped and defined through environmental interaction. But the flower is not the merely passive recipient of the accidents of its genetic history. Its ancestors were active players in an evolutionary narrative of mutual causality. In the garden or the meadow, evolutionary relationships are "many-sided, mutual, situational." Maruyama's relational universe is our ecological universe in which context is supreme.

In our estimate, one well-qualified candidate for a model of deity that fits the relational universe is the God of process theology, the responsive, presiding God who, while remaining unsurpassable, grows and develops along with creatures in a context of mutual influence. In true relational spirit, Alfred North Whitehead, the founder of process philosophy, described God and world as embracing in a deep and defining partnership of cocreation in which neither party takes priority.[15] Hierarchy is no issue in such a system.

Thus far, Maruyama is reciting a fairly standard account of competing universes. But his discussion of the *relevantial universe* is original and suggestive. The "relevantial universe consists of the concerns of the individuals in the world."[16] Information is relevant when it addresses the existential needs of individuals. Relevance can be practical or trivial; I consult the phone book for the best place to buy tires for my car. It can also be personal and crucial; I will consult that same phone book to locate a physician to diagnosis worrisome symptoms. Maruyama observes that the most important relevantial information often comes from other individuals having themselves experienced the same need as seekers and for whom this information was at one time crucially relevant.

While relevantial information is a simple and intuitive concept, its particularity makes it difficult to access. Maruyama laments this difficulty. "At the present," he writes, "our libraries are very poorly equipped to handle such information. Yet such information is more

15. For a discussion of the process divinity, see Alfred North Whitehead, *Process and Reality: An Essay in Cosmology*, ed. David Ray Griffin and Donald W. Sherburne, corr. ed. (New York: Free Press, 1978), pt. 5, ch. 2, "God and World."
16. Maruyama, "Metaorganization," 112.

vital to the well-being of the individual than the contents of all encyclopedias."[17] He has some doubts that such a "library" can be built. As we shall see, the future will prove him wrong.

Although it is true that certain emphases of Whitehead's vision of deity fit well in a relevantial universe,[18] we will focus on the theology of Paul Tillich, a significant twentieth-century theologian, for its insights.[19] Historically, the most relevant questions are often the most universal, those having to do with the human condition. "Who am I, and what ought I to do? Why do we suffer? Is there a point to life?" Tillich identifies these and similar questions as expressions of "ultimate concern" because they address the most basic issue of our being and nonbeing. Theologically, they are questions of salvation, the answers to which are variously given by the world's religions.

Again following Tillich's theological analysis of culture, the God suggested by the relevantial universe is any reality that sufficiently addresses the ultimate or most urgent concerns of the individual about the threat of nonbeing. In reality, we often get stuck with lesser gods, idols from our own hands that deceptively satisfy our ultimate concerns because of the power of their immediate relevance.[20] Since no finite and mortal creature, itself subject to the same threat of nonbeing, can deliver on the promise to secure itself and others against this threat, the seeker is driven to the very source or ground of being, the only true Ultimate, at least in theory.

The Electronic Diaspora: Conflictive Tendencies in Our Relevantial Universe

We mentioned earlier that Maruyama was not sanguine about the possibilities for developing a system that would deliver relevantial information. With the construction of the Internet, lamentation has

---

17. Ibid., 113.
18. Whitehead's God governs the world by communicating with its most fundamental constituents, tiny puffs of experience called "actual entities" or "actual occasions." God transmits a particular aim or goal—a "lure"—to each becoming actual entity in terms of its relevance. This lure is tailored for that unique entity in its special situation. By accepting and actualizing God's lure in its life, the actual entity achieves ideal fulfillment.
19. See Paul Tillich, *Systematic Theology,* 3 vols. in 1 vol. (Chicago: University of Chicago Press, 1967).
20. Another candidate, somewhat less ultimate, is found in primal polytheism. Here the divinities are specialized to provide services to individuals who approach them with particular problems. One god deals with problems related to love, another with fertility or health or war, and so on. The effectiveness of these divinities is a function of their nearness to the believer and the ease with which they can be addressed immediately within a local context.

turned to celebration. The relevantial universe has found its day. Thanks to the massive computational power of mainframe computers, made available through Internet search engines, the individual can specify and access a cornucopia of relevantial information on any subject with timely ease. Ironically, the system works because it is constructed according to the principles of the classificational universe. Data are stored in logical compartments labeled, for example, as people, places, or things. Things are divided into natural and artificial and further into plants and animals and inanimate objects or business, household, and transportation respectively. Different systems arrange these classes in different categories. The greater the number of categories, the more specific the information becomes. Searching through a vast sea of information is made possible through such detailed and cross-referenced classification systems. Classificational information becomes relevantial through specification and practical through the powers of search engines to deliver the information quickly and accurately.

Cyberspace is also relational. I can carry on textual conversations with any one of millions of logged-on individuals through e-mail. What is far more significant, however, is that I can locate individuals or groups who share any particular (or peculiar) interest and engage them in roundtable discussion in a "chat room" designated for that subject alone. These focused conversations extend across a range of Tillichian ultimacy, from comfort provided by support groups for those who are afflicted with specific diseases or other onerous conditions to fellow believers in a religious tradition or political philosophy. This account suggests that a form of situational polytheism dominates. Approximations of ultimacy are customized in highly specific basic beliefs and interests made possible by the nearly limitless options available in the religious bazaar of cyberspace. It is also, to some extent, gnostic, since the intention in seeking it is to locate the hidden knowledge that will lead to salvation, in whatever way it is defined.

In the areas of the individual and community, we are witnessing conflictive tendencies. The Internet offers unequaled opportunities for individuals to explore, learn, and improve their lives. Yet, it also aggravates cultural tendencies toward individualism, a philosophy espoused in radical form in our society. Americans are already guilty of a form of minimalism regarding commitment in their social and personal lives. Those Internet users who spend many hours "surfing" or exploring particular topics in great depth and passion risk growing isolation and further neglect of important personal relationships. Corresponding neglect of larger social involvement threatens the common assumptions upon which all civil discourse is based. Anonymity on the Internet may erode this sense of *civitas* or social responsibility. To characterize this phenomenon as an "electronic diaspora," the scattering of individuals amplified by information technology, involves only slight exaggeration.

These conflictive tendencies are found in communities as well. If the bonds of common interests, goals, or values are strong enough, a loose association of individuals with common interests may well become organized to the mutual benefit of all the participants. If the bonds of association are strong, the individual enters into what can be called a cyberspace "tribe" and is empowered through that membership. But the risk is that the tribe, true to the electronic diaspora, will become a highly insulated parochial community espousing a narrow and exclusive ideology reinforced by the shared beliefs and absolute loyalty of its members. In extreme instances, the result is a neurotic involution of thought and action that leads to a concentration bordering on solipsism, here understood as the experience of an individual or closed community whose world consists of only one kind of knowledge with which that person or community is self-identical. Clearly, such distorted versions of the individual person and true human community can only bring difficulty to the larger society in a further erosion of *civitas*.[21]

Every new age carries its conflicts and ambiguities, which is why anxiety is heightened. Ironically, anxiety, often accompanied by a sense of powerlessness, is enhanced by the information age with its unlimited choices and self-proclaimed candidates for ultimacy. The gods roam through cyberspace.

TOOL-DRIVEN REVOLUTIONS

Instruments and Scientific Progress

Our discussion of the ideas of Callicott and Maruyama is intended to demonstrate the claim that the computer, in its numerous applications, is a tool that drives novelty in the developing postmodern worldview. The primary role played by inventions in the transformation of the fundamental philosophical presuppositions of a society is not widely known or appreciated, despite the fact that historians of technology have recognized it for years. In this section

---

21. Tillich refers to these closed and destructive systems as "demonic." We discuss them in some detail in chapter 10.

we will examine the claim of a philosopher, Alfred North White-head, and a scientist, Freeman Dyson, that scientific progress is due as much to advances in instruments as to the creative theo-retical breakthroughs of brilliant scientists. Then we will suggest that, in like manner, theology may constructively profit from the tool revolution of electronic technology.

In his book *Science and the Modern World,* published in 1925, Whitehead was the first to see that "The reason we are on a higher imaginative level [in science] is not because we have a finer imag-ination, but because we have better instruments. In science, the most important thing that has happened in the last forty years is the advance in instrumental design."[22] The benefits are more than practical; "These instruments have put thought on a new level." Whitehead concludes, "The gain is more than a mere addition; it is a transformation."[23]

Freeman Dyson agues similarly,[24] beginning with the observation that the prevailing notion that scientific revolutions are primar-ily conceptual was successfully promoted by Thomas Kuhn in his famous book *The Structure of Scientific Revolutions.*[25] Kuhn de-scribed the revolution in theoretical physics in the first few decades of the twentieth century in which the Newtonian paradigm was re-placed by that of quantum mechanics. Thanks to Kuhn's work, the idea that scientific revolutions are driven primarily by transforma-tions in theoretical perspectives became the popular cultural myth. Dyson points out, however, that conceptual revolutions in science are rare. Indeed, he can discover only seven in the last five hun-dred years. They were inspired by Copernicus, Newton, Darwin, Maxwell, Einstein, Freud, and the physicists who brought in the quantum-mechanical revolution. But during this same period sci-ence has progressed through about twenty tool-driven revolutions. He mentions only two: "the Galilean revolution resulting from the use of the telescope in astronomy, and the Crick-Watson revolution resulting from x-ray diffraction to determine the structure of big molecules in biology."[26] One could speculate that the microscope and the particle accelerator would qualify for this list as well.

---

22. Alfred North Whitehead, *Science and the Modern World* (New York: Mac-millan, 1925), 114.
23. Ibid.
24. Freeman Dyson, "George Green and Physics," *Physics World* (August 1993): 33–38.
25. Thomas Kuhn, *The Structure of Scientific Revolutions,* 2nd ed. (Chicago: University of Chicago Press, 1970).
26. Dyson, "George Green and Physics," 33.

Unveiling Complexity

An outstanding candidate for induction into the scientific instrument hall of fame is the computer. Of course, computers perform countless tasks with accuracy and a lightning speed that far surpasses human capability. Their contribution is to make possible very complex instrumentation for science in all fields, from astronomy to neuroscience. But the computer also qualifies as a revolutionary instrument in its own right. The telescope and the microscope revealed dimensions of reality previously unsuspected. The computer carries this tradition forward. The telescope provided a window to the immensely large, the microscope to the immensely small. The computer is a window to the immensely complex.

The emerging sciences of chaos and complexity are genuinely new fields of scientific inquiry with tremendous potential for explanatory power in fields ranging from meteorology to sociology.[27] Given a theory of chaotic systems and instruments sufficient to model their behavior, it becomes possible to detect such systems throughout nature. The problem is this: chaotic systems are described mathematically by nonlinear equations and give rise to frustratingly complex behavior. Linear equations are easy to solve because, since they omit factors that vary with respect to one another, the behavior of the systems they describe is fairly easy to predict. This is not the case with nonlinear equations. In his popular introduction to the subject, *Chaos: Making a New Science,* James Gleick gives a particularly clear example of nonlinearity at work:

> Without [considering] friction, a simple linear equation expresses the amount of energy you need to accelerate a hockey puck. With friction the relationship gets complicated, because the amount of energy changes depending on how fast the puck is already moving. Nonlinearity means that the act of playing the game changes the rules. You cannot assign a constant importance to friction, because its importance depends on speed. Speed, in turn, depends on friction. That twisted changeability makes nonlinearity hard to calculate, but it also creates rich kinds of behavior that never occur in linear systems.[28]

27. For example, James Gleick, *Chaos: Making a New Science* (New York: Penguin Books, 1987); Robert John Russell, Nancey Murphy, and Arthur R. Peacocke, eds., *Chaos and Complexity: Scientific Perspectives on Divine Action* (Vatican City: Vatican Observatory Publications, 1995); Mitchell Waldrop, *Complexity: The Emerging Science at the Edge of Order and Chaos* (New York: Simon and Schuster, 1992).

28. Gleick, *Chaos,* 24.

Not only is this complex dance of variables a frustration to scientists who wish to predict accurately the future state of a dynamic system, but also the whole process is often subject to an exquisite sensitivity. This is because researchers are unable to specify the initial states of the system with the nearly infinite precision required to handle the sensitivity of the variables with respect to each other. The subsequent tiny fluctuations become amplified as the system runs it course, such that the end results appear entirely unpredictable.

The role of the computer, especially the high-speed parallel-processing computer, can hardly be overestimated in the study of complex, nonlinear systems. Computers simulate chaotic phenomena in ways that take account of the intricacies of interaction between several variables simultaneously. They allow for the replication of the sensitive dependence on initial conditions and then run the program rapidly forward to simulate consequences. The cascading calculations, millions per second, feed back upon each other with astonishing rapidity to give a faithful representation of the actual dynamical systems in full career. These detailed and complex simulations have revealed, despite their complete determination as described by the equations that govern their behavior, that natural systems are rife with novelty and unpredictable consequences. Indeed, such systems are often so rich in complexity that beginning a complex simulation program anew leads to outcomes that are different from those generated in a previous simulation.

We have spoken earlier about the uniqueness of computers with respect to other machines. Their uniqueness and power are based on their ability to simulate the behavior of objects or events by faithfully replicating their dynamic structures, primarily in logical and mathematical symbols and relationships. By simulating deep properties of a system in terms of a formal system that duplicates its features, the computer stands in for the real thing—a weather system, ecosystem, or biological system—to disclose knowledge that otherwise would be hidden or unavailable. Thus, the power and distinctiveness of computers is that they can be isomorphic with any natural system. This power is harnessed by scientists when they vary initial conditions in the model, or select different variables, or simply run a simulation over and over to assess the unpredictability of the outcomes. For the first time, scientists can experiment on large dynamical systems within the laboratory of the computer itself.

Matter or Messages

With this brief description of the role of computers in scientific research, it seems warranted to suggest that the computer indeed qualifies as the "tool" in an ongoing tool-driven revolution. Since such instruments, Whitehead claims, "put thought on a new level,"[29] we should explore the consequences of the computer revolution not only for scientific progress but also for the transformation of our philosophical, metaphysical, and, particularly, theological attitudes. Overall, the computer is an instrument facilitating and even transforming our understanding of the world by making us aware of a new dimension of dynamic complexity that was heretofore neglected for lack of such an instrument. The earlier worldview, based in large part on this neglect, cannot now be accurate. That worldview reflected the metaphysical concept that the universe is a great machine governed by the deterministic laws and the Newtonian equations that describe them. Nature is fixed and immutable, at least in its deep structural configurations. Cosmetically (from the Greek for "appearance")[30] it changes, but not spontaneously and certainly not fundamentally. While the basic metaphysical assumptions of mechanism still pertain—no one is willing to abandon the lawlike character and organization of the physical universe—this cosmetic dimension is now given a far more significant place in the understanding of how the governing principles are made manifest in the behavior of large complex systems. The metaphysics of strict causal determinism has been modified by a metaphysics of complex interdependence.

The deepest and most fundamental impact of the computer is in the way it is altering our understanding of reality itself. The power of the high-speed computer lies in its ability to process information rapidly and in great quantity—to "crunch" numbers by executing mathematical and logical operations with great rapidity. The result is a virtual world, isomorphically akin to the world of everyday experience, but made of bits rather than atoms. This world can be altered at will, simply by instructing the computer to signal changes. The prevailing belief about the material world, that it consists of inert and immutable matter, is replaced by a new plasticity. Matter melts into massive information to be molded not as clay in the hands

---

29. Whitehead, *Science and the Modern World*, 114.

30. F. E. Peters, in his lexicon, *Greek Philosophical Terms* (New York: New York University Press, 1967), 108, points out the distinction in Greek thought between the visible cosmos of appearance and the deeper invisible cosmos intelligible to the mind.

of the potter, but as signals transmitted by a programming agent. That *matter gives way to messages* is a central premise and ontological anchor of this study. Thus, the computer is not only a tool; it is the chief exemplar of the picture of reality it reveals.

CONCLUSION

Callicott, Maruyama, Whitehead, and Dyson illustrate the contention with which this chapter began, namely, that information sciences and technology exert profound influence on society that goes far beyond mere issues of application to include the basic framework of beliefs and attitudes about nature, ourselves, and God to which we collectively subscribe. Subsequent chapters will lay the necessary foundation for a constructive theology based on metaphysical principles taken from these same sciences.

– 2 –

God-Talk and
the Case for Cosmology

LET US SUPPOSE that our contention that electronic technology carries serious potential for informing and altering our worldview and theological perspectives along with it is accurate. Should we now launch into the project of exploring the foundations of information science for the purpose of determining something of weight and significance about theological realities, about God? Unfortunately, further preparation remains before we can begin this undertaking.

In fact, two major issues must be addressed before the real labor begins and its fruits are gathered. The first concerns the status of all discourse about God. In the contemporary social and cultural context, talk directed toward accounting for the reality and nature of God is reluctantly undertaken. The reasons for this reluctance, occasionally bordering on prohibition, cannot be blamed entirely on the overt secular character of Western society. Even contemporary theology contributes to the restriction of its own project. The task of this chapter is to address this reluctance and suggest new options for the renewal of serious God-talk. Even if talk about God is allowed, can it succeed? In other words, can theology legitimately construct models of deity that have any objective foundation whatever? This issue revolves about the possibility of metaphysics. Arguing for that possibility is the task of chapter 3. First, however, we must examine major sources for the resistance of talk about God and suggest a source for its renewal—cosmology.

CONSTRUCTIVE THEOLOGY: IT'S ALL ABOUT GOD

How is theology best done today? The question itself is so complex that its very asking is preceded by extensive qualifications. Do we mean academic or applied theology, conservative or liberal, exclusive or universal? Is our focus to be creation or redemption? Will the answer be christocentric or theocentric? And in what cultural idiom is the answer declared?[1] Indeed, a theology of theology is required before one can proceed to answer what, at first glance, appears to be a straightforward inquiry. Perhaps the seeds of an answer lie in such a prolegomenon.

These questions suggest a range of possible responses with the most simple to be found at the extremes of the range. The strategy at one extreme would be for the theologian to retreat into the familiar themes and systems of predecessors from previous historical periods and promote their assuring themes to a contemporary age that has no assurance and few firm foundations. At the other extreme, the theologian might simply abandon the tradition and plunge into the free flow of the times, where the rock of ages dissolves into so much fluid magma.

For the traditionalist who would empower the past, the task is nearly impossible. The claims of the many voices of the past two millennia in Christian doctrine are simply added to the growing sum of competing visions in our cultural or religious marketplace. Earlier theologians spoke to the particular issues of their times and employed conceptual frameworks taken from prevailing philosophical systems. Their conclusions no longer inform the basic assumptions and identity of this postmodern age. The fate of the other extreme, the strategy of accepting the common coin in an attempt to speak to culture in its own terms, is oddly similar. The theological message dissolves into the cacophony of voices, becoming lost because, with no distinctiveness or transcendental standpoint, it makes no difference at all.

And yet, each of these strategies has its strengths. Without a sense of tradition and the wisdom of earlier theologians who, even though speaking out of the peculiarities of their times, spoke of things that are universal for all generations, there would simply be nothing important to talk about. And without concern for the emerging wisdom (or if not wisdom, then insight) in the freshness and novelty of our own times, theology would simply miss the opportunity to sustain its vitality and freshness and even to learn something as well as teach something.

Combining these strengths while avoiding those dangers places

---

1. For an excellent survey of the contemporary situation in theology, see Lonnie D. Kliever, *The Shattered Spectrum: A Survey of Contemporary Theology* (Atlanta: John Knox Press, 1981).

the contemporary theologian in a place of excitement and risk. The best strategy, the one we will attempt to take, lies somewhere between the extremes. It is to take the world seriously if not selectively as a source of raw material for the doing of constructive theology.[2] Constructive theology is not an oxymoron. True, the fundamental issues of theology are perennial. They give continuity to the tradition. But, while the forms endure, the content changes. Questions about God, creation, sin, and salvation best find expression when articulated faithfully within the experience of a historical period. Constructive theology is the enterprise of articulating the truths of the tradition in a new and experimental way.

The implementation of the strategy of theological construction begins and ends with God. Particular theological systems may begin in other places, and with good reason, but they must eventually come down to the point of the enterprise—God. The point of all theology may be God, but the problem is God as well, or, more accurately, the image of God. For a number of reasons, talk about God is difficult in the contemporary situation. Prevailing attitudes from a number of sources converge on the conclusion that informed and speculative construction of models of God, however insightful and imaginative, are, at the most, only of limited value. They may be useful for the direction and orientation they provide for the community of faith, but in themselves they signify little else. This position holds that models of God, linguistically identified as metaphors, do not reflect the objective nature of deity. In a metaphorical discourse, models are justified because metaphors deliver insight but not necessarily knowledge. They are held playfully and dialectically; they claim to say yes and no to the perceived resemblance between the worldly model and the deity.[3] It is important to be clear that the idea of God we will be proposing is much stronger in that it audaciously posits an ontological resemblance between certain aspects of the world and God.[4]

---

2. See Gordon Kaufman, *An Essay on Theological Method* (Atlanta: Scholars Press, 1995).

3. Sallie McFague makes a similar point in *Models of God: Theology for an Ecological, Nuclear Age* (Philadelphia: Fortress Press, 1987), 33.

4. McFague (*Models of God,* 32) allows for the conceptual side of the theological task: "Their [theologians'] place, as understood by metaphorical theology, is an anomalous one that partakes of both poetry and philosophy: they are poets insofar as they must be sensitive to the metaphors and models that are at one consonant with the Christian faith and appropriate for expressing that faith in their own time, and they are philosophers insofar as they must elucidate in a coherent, comprehensive, and systematic way the implications of these metaphors and models." We should note that the theologian's task is to attend to the metaphors. McFague does

THE PROBLEM OF GOD-TALK

The Rise of Historicism and Anthropology

The word "theology" is derived literally from the Greek *theos logos*. *Theos* means "God," while *logos* means "word" or "speech." Hence, theology is a word about God or, as defined in colloquial terms by the philosopher John MacQuarrie, "God talk."[5] Based on this definition, early Christian theologians clearly understood their task. It was to articulate a comprehensive understanding of the reality, nature, and acts of God.[6] In subsequent development of doctrine this primary focus was lost as the theological task expanded to include many other matters of faith, particularly soteriology or salvation history. As long as the concept of God provided the cornerstone for a systematic integration of all the elements of faith, this enlarged task remained true to the original focus of theology. In contemporary culture, however, reflection on the very idea of God has been, for the most part, neglected, except, perhaps, by philosophy, and not always treated sympathetically within that circle.

The reluctance to speak directly and objectively about God as theology's primary focus is accompanied by considerable attention to other areas of inquiry. One such area is historicism, where an understanding of the nature of deity is derived inductively from evidence taken from human experience in the world and primarily in history.

The question is not the use of the word "God" or even the reality to which the word applies. No theological training is required to know that "God" refers to that supremely powerful and eminently benevolent personal being who created and directs the world with a loving will. For the believer, this knowledge is derived through faith in the witness of revelation, primarily scriptural, intended for salvation, and confirmed in human experience. The hermeneutical circle is closed. Scripture gives the essentials of the divine will that provide guides for acting in and understanding history. And the events of history are, in turn, sources for interpreting or confirming scrip-

---

not include attending to or speculating about the reality articulated by the metaphors—God. We would take a more integrated approach by employing metaphor as both disclosure and as a way to articulate in concrete images what philosophical conceptualizing has revealed.

5. John MacQuarrie, *God Talk: An Examination of the Language and Logic of Theology* (New York: Harper & Row, 1967).

6. For example, see Thomas Aquinas, *Summa Theologica,* "Treatise on God," pt. 1, q. 1, art. 7, "Whether God Is the Object of Science."

ture. In the contemporary theological situation, the two are often so inseparably linked that it appears little else can break through.

There is tremendous practical utility in this circle. We see history being made in daily news reports. The specific response of faith to these events is made possible by the application of principles of action primarily derived from the sensitive and sensible reading of scripture. It should come as no surprise that many contemporary theologies have turned away from speculation about God (*theoria*) and toward these concrete programs for action in the world (*praxis*). Consequently, God is mostly hidden and invisible with respect to details of the divine life that lie beyond generic descriptions derived from the events of holy history chronicled in scripture. In other words, the important thing is not God per se; rather it lies in what God requires, the intuition of the divine will. Power is derived from discerning the will of God and acting accordingly in contemporary situations that, in their analogical resemblance to events in the Bible, repeat history and call for similar responses.

Given this emphasis on history as the focus of theological construction, most of the essential elements in the expanded field of theology are secure and thriving. Again, the bold exception is the notion of God. The problem seems not to be with the "Word of God" but rather with the word "God." Ironically, the Word of God—revelation as understood the themes of scripture, tradition, and prophetic pronouncement—seems not to have been attenuated in its power and authority in the current spirit of praxis in theology. Rather, the very intelligibility of the source of this revelation, that is, a clear concept of the reality signified by the word "God," has become problematic on grounds other than the shifting sands of metaphorical similarity. Discussions of God are frequently vague. They drift along with the currents of historical events where they offer power to the moment in political and social causes. Beyond this notion of the God who acts in profane history consistent with divine action in sacred history (the events chronicled in scripture), not much emerges about the kind of God who is involved.

Challenges to God-Talk

That this shift is so is no mystery. Reasons for the predicament abound and are well documented. The emphasis upon praxis as the locus of responsible human action is a recent one; here are several others.

The Intimidation of Modern Philosophy. Deeply influenced by great modern philosophers such as David Hume and Immanuel

Kant, philosophers often reject any claims to truth that are not grounded in solid evidence (empiricism) or logic (analysis). The celebrated Enlightenment turn to the question of knowledge included the repudiation of all possibility of discovering metaphysical truth, including truths about God. A majority of philosophers reject even the possibility of doing philosophy that bases its arguments on realities or principles that are immune to confirmation or falsification by an appeal to matters in the world. That is, metaphysics, as it has been classically understood, is ruled out. Clearly, traditional theology was metaphysical. Consequently, theology of this sort was also ruled out as a legitimate form of inquiry. If God-talk is intended to describe a corresponding object, the referent for the label "God," then-God talk is literally nonsense, because God, being transcendent, has no earthly or creaturely referent and, indeed, is beyond the limits of possible experience.

In its reaction to these devastating criticisms, theology confirmed them. If God cannot be known through evidence and reason, God may still be known through direct and intuitive, if not private, insight. The influential nineteenth-century theologian Friedrich Schleiermacher set the stage for this turn inward with his definition of the knowledge of God as "the feeling of absolute dependence." The immediacy of this intuition is its own subjective confirmation, escaping the demands of evidence and logic while avoiding being labeled "metaphysical." And the intuition remains free to interpret the world of experience as evidence for the acts of God, especially in history.

The Infinite Distancing of God in Neo-orthodoxy. A second force that dampened any impulse to do pure theological reflection on God comes from theology itself. The influential Neo-orthodox school of Protestant thought, exemplified by Karl Barth[7] and often referred to as "dialectical theology," denies the very possibility of any account of God that is not based on the experience of revelation. As the "wholly other," God is entirely beyond human categories of thought. God cannot be captured and controlled by any system, nor must revelation conform to any merely human criteria. Certainly, God acts in history, and especially in "the strange world of the Bible," but the believer, confronted by the living word conveyed in the testimony of scripture, confirms revelation through the en-

---

7. Barth was a prolific writer, as exemplified by his thirteen volumes of *Church Dogmatics,* still unfinished when he died in 1968. A work central to his theology is *Anselm: Fides Quaerens Intellectum,* trans. Ian W. Robertson (London: SCM, 1960).

counter itself, immediately and on the spot. Absolute sovereignty or freedom in God means that humans possess no prior standards by which God's actions must abide for validation. Apart from God's definitive and gracious act of revelation through Christ we have nothing to go on. God's acts are simply unprecedented. Moreover, human endeavor is profoundly distorted by sin. All models of God are subject to this distortion and the fallen interests they serve. They cannot be trusted.

The Naturalistic Assumptions of Science. As a dominant authority and approach to knowledge, science raises additional important questions about a return to theology's original project, an objective account of God. At one with modern analytical philosophy, science is profoundly suspicious of claims of knowledge and truth that cannot be subjected directly to the canons and conditions of scientific methodology. Science is properly naturalistic in its working orientation.[8] That is, it assumes that the world or nature is all there is and that explanations for events in the world must come from empirical explorations of the patterned causes or inviolable laws of nature operating in the world. No appeal to an independent or transcendent influence is permitted. God is unavailable as evidence for anything going on in nature. In addition, God's capricious or anomalous intrusions would disrupt the autonomous and uniform laws of nature—a state of affairs that would render scientific predictions based on observations and the reproducible results of experiments untrustworthy. While those of faith, in good Schleiermachian fashion, may profess that God is the cause of everything (and this is the reason that our dependence is absolute), they are not allowed to extend this to claim further that God is the explanation of anything.[9]

The Dominance of Mechanism. The image of the cosmos as a great machine governed by immutable internal laws arose first as a suggestive metaphor for what early scientists were discovering about the orderly patterns of nature, especially in the heavens. Then, by subtle slippage, the metaphor became a metaphysic—an image representing a deeper claim about the nature of reality as a system of material objects interacting by physical contact and constituting altogether a great fixed and interacting system of parts. This vision, one that transcends the testimony of the evidence, is mechanism.

---

8. See Langdon Gilkey, *Creationism on Trial* (San Francisco: HarperCollins, 1985).

9. Malcolm A. Jeeves, *The Scientific Enterprise and the Christian Faith* (London: Tyndale Press, 1969), 103.

A major legacy of the historical tenure of mechanism lies in the fundamental conclusion it has bequeathed to us in theology and psychology. If there is no longer any place for a divine cosmic consciousness and will acting on a world of mortified matter, no room for a "ghost in the machine" of the cosmos, then the same exclusion is necessary for any beings in the cosmos who resemble autonomous mental agents, including human beings. Cartesian dualism abstracts mind from matter, leaving matter senseless, devoid of intention and responsiveness; mind is homeless or free-floating somewhere, one would assume, in the cranial cavity. Once the Cartesian program combined with the icon of the cosmic machine and successfully mortified matter, it turned its attention to the realm of the thinking subject. Under the objective scrutiny of physicalism, even mind lost its privileged status and came to be treated as a material phenomenon. As unexceptional creatures, persons are nothing more than electrochemical and protoplasmic machines—microcosms of the whole. Thinking, willing, and valuing are phenomena that are in principle reducible to physics and chemistry.

Despite the considerable progress resulting from neuroscience, this inevitable conclusion, based on the same mechanistic premise that banished God from the cosmos, has yet to take hold. Human self-understanding continues to be conflicted and dualistic. The ghost in the body machine has yet to be exorcised. One wonders if it can ever be, since the exorcist and the exorcised are one and the same!

The system of mechanism is so severe that we are left with but two options, each equally extreme. One is a reductionism in which lifeless parts explain the living whole without remainder. The other is a dualism that describes life and spirit somehow abiding in a material or corporeal casing with the connection between them a mystery. Holism, a mediating and unifying option, is disallowed by the stringent requirements of mechanism. In either case, the human subject, present to itself as the center of conscious decision, meaning, and value, does not vanish, but continues as an existential schizophrenic, best exemplified in Bertrand Russell's romantic account of the tragic cosmic hero raging against the "unconscious march of blind matter" that is destined to crush him.[10]

Rather than resolving the matter by confessing that we are entirely creatures and hence *bêtes machines,* modern men and

---

10. Bertrand Russell, "A Free Man's Worship," in *Why I Am Not a Christian* (New York: Allen and Unwin, 1957), 105–16.

women experience a profound alienation from nature. That is, if we reflected on the predicament, we might experience alienation. However, the prevalent historical response has been to compartmentalize, to separate ourselves from nature in a continuing project with ambiguous results to transform its resources into a protective and secure canopy beneath which we can carry out our lives with relatively little distraction. It is doubtful that the project of establishment environmentalism based on this project has done much to reconcile us to nature.[11] We continue to perceive wilderness, the sum of those limited plots of nature from which we voluntarily exclude ourselves, in a utilitarian perspective. They are precious primarily because they are objects of beauty to be enjoyed for our sake rather than for their own.

The existential human, exercising a selective modern perspective, reigns triumphant and supreme over nature, having chosen to see it as different and exploitable. It is not surprising, then, that citizens of the modern world define themselves essentially through institutions and self-referencing ideas rather than through associations with the cosmos. It is also not surprising that the actions of God are perceived to apply exclusively within the realm of society and politics. God is primarily the God of nations, with nature the mere backdrop or stage setting for the dramas of history.

The moral of this account of mechanism is that both God and the human person are excluded from nature. They have lost the essential cosmic connection. Thrown back upon ourselves, we have developed a deeply anthropocentric view that neglects nature in favor of the human species and the God of that species.

The Shift to Social Relativism. The application of science to social phenomena provides another source dampening theological inquiry into God.[12] The discovery is that most human knowledge, including the claims of religion and theology, is the product of historical conditions and social influence. Many theologians readily acknowledge that social and cultural forces extensively shape their ideas. How could it be otherwise? Every generation of theologians is responsible for speaking directly to its contemporaries, whose moods, attitudes, and perspectives may differ considerably from those of previous generations. This is certainly not to say that the

---

11. See William Cronon, "The Trouble with Wilderness," in *Uncommon Ground: Toward Reinventing Nature,* ed. W. Cronon (New York: W. W. Norton, 1995), 76–94.

12. See, for example, Peter Berger, *The Sacred Canopy: Elements in a Sociology of Religion* (New York: Anchor Books, 1990).

fundamentals of doctrine are historically relative. Rather, it is the claim that their reception by a community of faith is a matter of the prevailing cultural categories and framework of ideas that determine how anything, including doctrinal claims, is to be understood by the members of that culture.[13]

But this is not all that proponents of the social construction of knowledge and historical relativism claim. They go much further to conclude that the very idea of God (and not just models intended to articulate this idea) is itself the product of human dispositions introduced by cultural, historical, and even evolutionary and genetic influences. The prevailing attitude of relativism is aggravated by an awareness that much of what we do and think is the result of cultural assumptions and our own construction of reality. Religious, economic, and political systems, as well as science, are primarily human creations embedded in webs of assumptions and lacking substantial underpinnings. Meaning, authority, and the "indubitable" grounding of reason itself are relative to the constructive enterprise. Postmodernism subscribes to this position to the point of deriving its analytical method from its premise: anything that is the result of human construction may be "deconstructed"—taken apart—to reveal the sheer absence of underlying foundations.

The Emergence of Historicist Anthropology. This recognition leads to the discovery that the social construction of knowledge and value is frequently determined by the requirements of power that is directed not by universal and objective foundations of reason (the faith of the Enlightenment), but by gender, racial, and class distinctions. Theologies of liberation base an account of God on the experience of oppressed peoples—the poor and destitute of the world who are subjected to the sinful consequences of gender, racial, and economic distinction—in their unfree condition. God, therefore, is the one who acts in history to liberate the oppressed and bring justice to the downtrodden. Liberation theologians put social analysis and political praxis at the center of theological discourse, thoroughly repudiating any quest for transhistorical objective truth and certainty. Indeed, liberation theologians sometimes disdain academic or philosophical theologians because they abstract God from involvement in the world where evidence of the divine reality and will are to be exclusively found. Knowledge of God arises exclu-

---

13. Hence the neo-orthodox suspicion of "religion" as the institutional construct of humans who, in their fallen state, are predisposed to the distortion of sin in all their corporate activities.

sively out of the faithful actions of communities seeking justice and is relative only to their struggles.[14] It is no wonder that the only models of deity that prevail are those derived from human experience in accord with the scriptural themes testifying to the mighty acts of God on behalf of justice.

It is interesting to observe how beliefs of a waning worldview (mechanism) inform the beliefs of its emerging replacement. The critical consequence of mechanism was to alienate God and humankind from the cosmos. Theology then turned its attention to history and discovered important truths about revelation and divine will that require little reference to nature. Liberation theology is the beneficiary of this shift in attention made inevitable by the logic of the world machine.

COSMOLOGY AS A RESOURCE FOR THEOLOGY

Cosmology and Theology: A Necessary Connection

Until recently, connections between concepts of deity and views of the nature of the cosmos have been neglected, partially because they fall outside the hermeneutical circle of scripture and history mentioned earlier. But cosmology and religion have never been far apart. Each drives the other conceptually, and together they may dictate anthropology. Any survey of prominent cosmologies discloses the association of a culture's view of the cosmos and its view of the gods as imaginative symbionts. Each influences the other in some larger mutual system or framework of beliefs and values that includes the heavens, terrestrial nature, and the place of humankind in it.

In terms of monotheistic religions, the reason why theologies based on the prevailing cosmologies of any period carry preferred understandings of God is that they seek to be universal and comprehensive. God is the power overarching and undergirding all reality. How that power is understood must, in some sense, be continuous with a specific cosmology if the claims of divine creating, sustaining, governing, and directing are to make any sense at all. Otherwise,

---

14. José Míguez Bonino represents the position of liberation theology in this statement: "Theology, as here conceived, is not an effort to give a correct understanding of God's attributes or actions but an effort to articulate the action of faith, the shape of praxis conceived and realized in obedience. As philosophy in Marx's famous *dictum,* theology has to stop explaining the world and to start transforming it. *Orthopraxis,* rather than orthodoxy, becomes the criterion for theology" (*Doing Theology in a Revolutionary Situation* [Philadelphia, Fortress Press, 1975], 81.)

theology would be entirely dissociated from the best knowledge of the creation and sealed in its own compartment of limited relevance.

It is important to emphasize here that cosmology is far more than astronomy, the study of the universe or cosmos. An account of the totality of things includes some articulation of the fundamental foundations that underlie the unity or the basic character of the whole that accounts for its particulars. Mechanism, for example, subscribed to the belief that all reality is material and denominated in terms of irreducible atomic units. In contrast, process philosophy describes these simple elemental units as puffs of experience. The two positions are obviously incompatible, as are the views of the universe that each recommends. In each case, however, the resultant cosmology is founded on a *metaphysical* framework.

A Historical Survey

Ancestral societies located themselves in the world by reference to great narratives of origin. These etiological myths offered a satisfactory explanation for the very existence of the community, and they specified the nature and character of their deity or deities, the other creatures in their immediate environment, and the proper relationship of the people to this larger context. Their cosmos, a Thou rather than an It, was filled with spirits and dealt with through supplication, petition, and negotiation.

In ancestral societies the world of nature is saturated with a spiritual power that may be impersonal and manipulated by the processes of magic, or it may be personal and addressed in terms of spirits inhabiting animal bodies or objects or residing in sacred places. Whether these are individual and personal presences or whether the spiritual power is perceived as a diffuse, circumambient and impersonal energy is a question for students of primary cultures.[15] But the fact remains that beliefs about the character of nature and beliefs about religious subjects were highly integrated in what we might call an unselfconscious cosmology. The resulting insightful theism or pantheism gave the natural world beyond the confines of the tribal society its primary due and reverence.

The *ancient empires*—Egypt, Assyria, Babylon—paced their own corporate lives in tune with the deep pulses of the earth and the recurring sidereal motions of the heavens. In these state societies

---

15. For an excellent discussion of these thoughts with reference specifically to the Plains Native Americans, see Lee Irwin, *The Dream Seekers: Native American Visionary Traditions of the Great Plains* (Norman: University of Oklahoma Press, 1994).

the multiple divinities were fated by cosmic processes to play out their conflict repeatedly within the rhythmic cycle of the seasons. The great myths of Isis and Osiris, Tiamat and Marduk (whose epic intrigues reveal them to be the epitomes of dysfunctional families), gave profound dramatic tension to these orderly yet often fickle natural patterns and revealed the sense of utter dependence in these cultures on all of nature for their life sustenance.

Mythos gave way to *logos* in the discovery of rational thought by the *Greeks*. Between the seventh and fifth centuries B.C.E., Greek philosophers discovered the power of reason that sweeps beneath the surface of the things celebrated in myth. Plato's famous cosmological narrative, the *Timaeus,* is a perfect illustration of this profound shift in human inquiry. In this dialogue, Plato seeks to explain the origin of the world, the universe itself. This account can only be given in terms of a historical telling that shares the narrative structure of myths. But, rather than casting his characters in human form, Plato invents figures like the Demiurge, the Receptacle, the spherical Cosmos animated by a World Soul, and the realm of absolute ideas incarnated into recalcitrant matter by the Demiurge. These characters are connected not only by dramatic impulse but also by logical necessity. They share vestiges of animism and yet are defined by reason. The *Timaeus* is a hybrid tale, a combination of elements of *mythos* and *logos,* of story and reason. The gods have their place, but they are subject to a larger structured context that is itself primary and eternal.

For the Greeks, the cosmos is a finite and ordered system. Theology followed cosmology to be justified in terms of its contribution as a necessary component in a rational system. Indeed, in pursuing this program to its logical conclusion, the Roman Stoics dismissed personal divinities altogether in their identification of the World Soul as the divine *Logos* of the cosmos itself.

In the *Middle Ages* cosmology and theology were associated through teleology, the study of purposes, aims, goals, and intentions. While teleology was important in the thought of early Christian theologians primarily through Neoplatonic influence, the Greek philosopher Aristotle had earlier refined the notion. Building on the insights of Plato with great originality, Aristotle placed God in control of things. Each creature, including the human one, exhibits a "nature," an essence or fundamental form making it a member of a distinctive class or kind. The realization of one's nature or telos is the aim of life. But God, not the creature, is the source of the distinctive telos. Once supplied with the future form as pure potential, a particular being strives to satisfy the urge to actualize that form in the fullest possible way, and thus contributes to God's well-ordered cosmos. Aristotle concluded that the concept of God is a required ingredient in his overall theory of the world as the source and agent of all creaturely natures.

In the thirteenth century, Aristotle's philosophy was taken by Thomas Aquinas and ingeniously combined with the revealed doctrine of an original creation of the world to provide the philosophical underpinnings for a Christian theology of remarkable longevity. It can be argued, for example, that Aquinas's most influential contribution to the modern world is his Natural Law theory of ethics that is built on Aristotelian teleology. The proper role of science, as understood in the medieval period, was to support theology by providing it with illustrations of various creatures fulfilling their respective natures and thus contributing to the great functional order of the creation.

With the Renaissance and Scientific Revolution that introduce the *modern age,* Aristotelian classification and teleology were overthrown by a revived Platonism or, more accurately, Pythagoreanism, with its emphasis on the mystical notion of mathematical proportions. The goal of discovering God's intentions in nature was replaced with the task of discerning the divine plan for an orderly universe, one that operates in strict accord with laws given by God in some equivalent of the Mosaic Decalogue or Ten Commandments of nature. Because this divine legislation is composed not in human language but in mathematical relationships, measurement replaced classification as the method for discovering the divine patterning of nature.

Since this order included the heavens, it is no wonder that both Copernicus and Galileo endured considerable resistance from the church when their observations threatened to undermine this well-articulated medieval system. It should also be recognized that despite their refusal to acknowledge what the modern world considers as obvious in the persecution of Renaissance scientists, the deep concern of those church authorities was not misplaced. In the relatively brief period of two hundred years, the rich and complete medieval cosmology lay in pieces along with the cultural worldview that depended on it. The modern age was born.

Although its logic marched toward conclusions that assigned the deity to a remote location of excessive transcendence, the new modern vision of the cosmos based on science was not necessarily atheistic. During the Scientific Revolution it was not yet possible to eliminate the lingering effects of medieval cosmology and alto-gether dismiss God as the creator. The role played by God did, however, suffer a progressive diminishment. Explanation in terms of purpose, which required God, was replaced by explanation in terms of physical interactions between material atoms in accordance with fundamental and inexorable laws of nature, which did not.

This brief historical account is replete with irony. The scientific enterprise was originally informed by theological suppositions—that God was the author of an orderly and intelligible creation—and motivated by the impulse to discover divine revelation in that order. But it moved rather quickly to the denial of God's continuing in-volvement in the cosmos. The result was a form of operational atheism in which God was simply superfluous and therefore a negligible factor, a hypothesis, to paraphrase the words of the eighteenth-century astronomer Pierre Simon Laplace, for which scientists had no need.

God's involvement was subsequently limited to the original act of creation, after which, because the cosmos is so perfect, God simply was put out of a job. The great cosmic machine was independent of any requirement for a sustaining and guiding influence. With no current function, God was little more than an escort or superfluous adjunct of the cosmos.

The retreating God of Deism, as this theology came to be known, was essentially useless, unless, as Newton speculated, God was re-quired to make an occasional cosmic house call by miraculously intervening in the order of nature for some purpose of rescue or fine-tuning. Even the acceptance of these rare and extraordinary occasions, limited mostly to the distant past of biblical testimony, proved too much for scientific cosmology, since they represented an exception to the claim that nature works with absolute uni-formity. Without this faith in the consistency of nature, science as a universal enterprise would not be possible. God is permanently barred from acting in the autonomous (literally, *auto-nomos,* or "self-legislating") cosmos that is structured and governed by ele-gant laws whose origins are either unknown or the product of its natal stages. The most that could be conceded was that the laws of nature may have originated from the primordial act of a reced-ing *Deus,* but they gave rise to a world that is entirely closed and self-sustaining. Modern cosmology, based on scientific mechanism, has little need for a faraway God to carry out any plan, since ma-chines, by definition, do not have histories or natures that require actualization beyond their initial design and assembly.

Except for mechanism, none of these cosmologies—ancestral, ancient, Greek, medieval, and modern—began with an understanding of the absolute and central status of the human species as the "measure of all things." Certainly, because humans were constructing these worldviews, they necessarily played a major role in them and the language they used was decidedly anthropomorphic. But, only with the banishing of God from the official version of nature and the elevation of the human as the new superior being without apparent constraints did extreme anthropocentrism emerge to allow our species to "lord" it over the planet with uninhibited impunity. And even here, human superiority derived in great part its justification from the new and dominant cosmology of mechanism that did away with the immediacy of God, the organic character of a vital natural world, and any sense of human kinship to nature.

Does a comprehensive model for God give intelligibility to the cosmos, or does a comprehensive model for the cosmos give intelligibility to God? Theology often argues for the first emphasis: God makes the world finally comprehensible. Philosophy argues for the second: only a complete accounting of the world can determine even if a God has any explanatory role to play in it. These questions are reciprocal, not mutually exclusive. God gives intelligibility to the world and the world, the cosmos, allows us to speak of God intelligibly. The questions fold back upon one another in a loop, with inquiry into one taking account of the results of inquiry into the other. The emphasis placed on one or the other perspective is not so much a matter of priority or preference as of dialogical punctuation—whose turn is it to speak? As in any true dialogue, each party profits from the pronouncements of the other, even if the discussion is argumentative.

THE NEW SCENE

The Current Shift

"Happy the nation, fortunate the age, whose history is not diverting." This bit of wisdom from Benjamin Franklin's journal *Poor Richard's Almanac,* composed in the eighteenth century, accurately describes the beginning of the twenty-first.[16] It seems clear that modern culture is in the midst of another lurching shift in worldviews, including cosmology. The difficulties in living through one of these

---

16. Quoted in Ilan Stavans, *The Hispanic Condition: Reflections on Culture and Identity in America* (New York: Harper Perennial, 1995), 92.

somewhat sudden shifts in orientation include not only anxiety and uncertainty but also hope and anticipation. The current generation lives in two worlds. The first is the modern world with its consistent and admittedly powerful system of ideas and beliefs that have guided the West for over three centuries to a place of dominance. Ironically, this incredible success has given rise to the vision's own internal contradictions (e.g., both the embrace and the rejection of Cartesian dualism) now being felt. When combined with a natural instinct to fear an unknown and unpredictable future, these contradictions are the sources of our anxiety.

Still there is cause for hope. The second world is one whose principles and values are still vague and emerging or in the process of being tested for their pragmatic fit in life. As the power of this perspective grows, the uncertainty and disorientation in an age of great ambivalence situated between two worlds will diminish. Until then, the principles of the modern worldview continue to dominate, but in palpable tension with the nascent vision. This tension produces an uncomfortable insecurity that results in great creative energies, for the transformation from one age to another blesses the interim generation with a unique opportunity to imagine new worlds that they might actually realize.

Until this shift began, the overwhelming success of classical science in explaining and controlling nature had left the modern world with no competing alternative worldview. The twentieth century, however, saw science engage in a wondrous act of self-transformation. Without abandoning many of its classical suppositions, science has successfully entered into a new paradigm, a fundamental perspective for conducting its business. The story of this transformation has been told repeatedly. With revolutionary discoveries in the realm of the very small (atomic and particle physics), the very large (astrophysics), and the middle realm (biology), older ideas of the cosmos as a fixed and static machine consisting exclusively of material particles behaving blindly according to immutable laws have been modified almost beyond recognition. Particles are interchangeable with fields of force and energy. Atoms are centers of complex and harmonic vibrations. Space and time are knit together as a seamless fabric. Stars and galaxies are rife with dramatic change. The celestial universe as a whole emerged from the "flaring forth"[17] of an absolute moment of creation some twelve to

---

17. See Thomas Berry and Brian Swimme, *The Universe Story* (San Francisco: HarperSanFrancisco, 1992).

fifteen billion years ago to evolve or develop a structure. In the case of at least one planet, our own, the results include complex organic and self-conscious systems of life.

A Worldview of Self-Organizing Systems

In a second wave consisting of several disciplines that build on the perspectives of quantum physics, evolution, and the electronic revolution, mechanism's picture of a fixed and determinate universe is currently being significantly augmented, if not radically altered, by the emerging understanding of the world as a community of open, complex systems in constant dynamic interaction and evolutionary development. Nonlinear chaos theory, complexity studies, autopoietic systems theory, and information or communication theory are new disciplines that testify to these emphases. Mechanism continues to inform the natural sciences (chaos theory, for example, is as deterministic as any Newtonian would want). Nonetheless, these newer sciences open doors long closed by mechanism, especially regarding the reintroduction of freedom, novelty, and perhaps even purpose as legitimate subjects for scientific inquiry. And certainly they offer new possibilities for talking about the universe and God.

To reiterate the theme of chapter 1, this new perspective is deeply indebted to the information sciences and the tools that embody them. Computers not only provide windows to this new world but also incarnate the very principles upon which a distinctive theological metaphysic, inclusive of God and world, may be articulated.

The notion of complexity, the common object of study in several of these new sciences, is itself suggestive of a whole host of insights and concepts around which to build a new cultural paradigm, a cosmology or worldview founded in notions of interaction, interdependence, and diversity. If history repeats itself, this cosmology will likely lead to a new cycle of theological reflection concerning the nature of God and the creation as reinterpreted under the rubric of complexity.

If this new vision of the universe, along with a scientific approach tailored to its notions, is to be correlated with larger questions in theology, it should seek to contribute conceptually to a clear understanding of the creative acts of God, including God's original, sustaining, and culminating acts of creation. How does God act upon or interact with the creation such that the theological account of this activity corresponds to the emerging scientific account of the nature and structure of the creation itself? This is not a requirement that God be perceived as a mere appendage of the cosmos, nor is it a reduction of the reality of God to matters of science alone. Rather, the goal is the recovery of the sense of overall meaning and purpose to the cosmos by associating its reality with that of God.

Even though science has nothing official to say about God (and, when wrapped in the ideological garments of scientism, it has nothing *good* to say about God), theories derived from scientific inquiry may be properly appropriated by theology for the purpose of enhancing insight. The task of crafting a model of God and God's actions on the creation is both consistent with the theistic tradition and constructive in its insight and explanatory power. What is needed is a concerted attempt to construct a model of God that consistently employs the ideas, suppositions, and language of this new vision of the cosmos emerging from the information revolution and the scientific vision it drives.

If successful, benefits of the model would include a new source of theological articulation (God-talk), disclosure of novel and important insights for theological reflection, and the opportunity to correlate contemporary perspectives with the enduring claims of scripture and tradition.

CONCLUSION

The position we have taken in this chapter puts us in the minority. The prevailing assumptions, based on numerous arguments taken from philosophy, history, sociology, and theology itself, buttress the considerable opposition to constructive speculation about the nature and reality of God. In sum, the arguments conclude that objective discourse about God is a mistaken if not impossible project because language and conceptual thought refer to this world and none other, and because such discourse is always shaped entirely by the historical context out of which it arises. How can relative ideas faithfully reflect the absolute? Besides, talk about God is unnecessary and morally suspect. It is the abandonment of the dimensions of political and social praxis demanded by scripture and the tradition. Love for God and neighbor is expressed not in barren speculation, but in action.

This is a powerful platform, and those who persist in believing that God-talk is still legitimate need to accept the irreducible historical conditions that govern all efforts to construct models of God. While the project seems illegitimate when viewed exclusively from one dimension, history, it recovers its plausibility when seen in another, cosmology. On the one hand, for many liberation theologians, metaphysical speculation about God is the abdication of the primary responsibility to help the oppressed and powerless. On the other hand, failure to employ the best sources in scientific cosmology is the abdication of the responsibility to make the idea of God as intelligible and relevant as it might be in the postmodern age. Sources for the latter task, we suggest, lie in the emerging sciences of complexity. Still, further groundwork is required before construction of a model of God interpreted through these sciences can begin. This is the task of the next chapter.

– 3 –

In Defense of Metaphysics

BEFORE WE TURN to the task of laying the groundwork for a model of God and world derived from concepts taken from the new sciences, it is important to make the presuppositions about our method clear. These presuppositions include the possibility of metaphysics. Neither theology nor cosmology can remain content with a simple description of God and world. For this would mean that not only would the deeper questions about both realities go unanswered, but also that each would occupy a realm of its own detached from the other in terms of our understanding of how they relate. This understanding requires a clear grasp of the most fundamental features of God and creation such that the association between them can be deduced. It is therefore a metaphysical understanding.

THE QUESTION OF HOW GOD ACTS

The Impedance of Mechanism and the "Mighty Acts" of God

Recognizing this requirement, other cosmological periods in the West considered a proper metaphysical foundation as an essential and prerequisite for theology. Even when the metaphysical principles disallowed any significant relationship between God and world, at least the reasons were clear. For example, the metaphysical assumptions of the world machine leave no room for a supernatural agent acting upon an independent world beyond God's primal function as the miraculous originator of the machine itself, an enfeebled and fading *Deus ex machina*. The operational aspect of divine agency, that is, how the *Deus* could affect history without violating the integrity of creation, led to confused theologies. Given deistic assumptions, this unresolved issue is an imposing barrier for theism, which insists in all its traditions that God originates, sustains, and guides the creation. In terms of theistic religions, *what* God has done as revealed in the chronicles of sacred history and *why* God did it (ultimately to redeem a fallen creation and to bring justice to the land) are not in question. The *how* of divine activity is very much in question, and this, in turn, requires construction of theories about God's very nature that are consistent with both tradition and the prevailing cosmology of mechanism. In the philosophy of mechanism, this "how," or operational aspect of the divine economy—as God's actions in the creation are known—is considered to be a wrongheaded question. Because it has no place for divine governance of the creation, mechanism, a powerful paradigm for scientific progress, is impotent as a resource for theological progress.

Progress in bridging this gap between God and world may be possible only after the claim of Thomas Aquinas that cause and effect must share something in common is taken seriously.[1] This would mean a fundamental metaphysical reappraisal of the nature of God and the creation to identify shared features. Such an appraisal would extend the range of God talk in making possible some articulation of the causal efficacy of providence. Langdon Gilkey makes this point clearly:

> For those of faith [an act of God] must be objectively or ontologically different from other events. Otherwise, there is no mighty act, only our belief in it.... Only an ontology of events specifying what God's relation to ordinary events is like, and thus, what his relation to special events might be, could fill the now empty analogy of mighty acts, void since the denial of the miraculous.[2]

One of our tasks, taken up in later chapters, is to construct a system of God and world, including their shared features, that will address this issue of the mighty acts of God.

Monism, Dualism, and Theism

Another stumbling block to a coherent notion of divine action lies with traditional assumptions about the nature of God and world. The model of God and world proposed by theism is held in common by the three Abrahamic religions of Judaism, Christianity, and

---

1. See Etienne Gilson, *The Philosophy of St. Thomas Aquinas,* trans. Edward Bullough, ed. A. Erlington (Freeport, N.Y.: Books for Libraries Press, 1937), 137.

2. Langdon Gilkey, "Cosmology, Ontology, and the Travail of Biblical Language," *Journal of Religion* 41 (1961): 194–205; reprinted in *God's Activity in the World,* ed. Owen C. Thomas (Chico, Calif.: Scholars Press, 1983), 37.

Islam. This model attempts to mediate between the two extremes of monism and dualism. *Monism* is the understanding that there exists only a single absolute and ultimate reality that is subject to no limitations whatsoever, is completely simple (without defining and limiting features), and is infinite and eternal, creating and encompassing all space and time. The world of human experience and of nature are secondary or derived realities, having no independent status or substance and, when compared to the one ultimate reality, are quite nearly nothing at all.

Monism is best represented by the *Advaita* (nondualistic) philosophy of Hinduism.[3] Brahman is absolute reality, while the world of multiplicity and matter is the realm of *maya* and little more than an illusion. Monistic models of the divine collapse into pantheism in that they claim that ultimate reality is the ground and very stuff of our ephemeral mundane world. If we were in our right minds—that is, fully awake—we would know that deep within all things is a single, simple divine substance that unites them in its own undivided self.

The other extreme, *dualism,* holds that reality comes in two completely independent and distinctive substances. Each is absolute in its own right, but is so different from the other that no mutual influence is possible. Dualism has an ancient pedigree, but, as discussed earlier, its current influence is derived primarily from the philosophy of Descartes, who opposed mind and body as two fundamental substances. Efforts to reknit these sundered elements of reality led either to idealism with its emphasis on the primacy of ideas, mind over the material world, or to materialism, which reversed the priority. In each case the strategy was to repair the dualism by reducing it to a monism consisting of one or the other of these exclusive realities.

Deism arose in part from the inability of Cartesian philosophy to reconcile mind and matter. Just as mind is the ghost in the body machine, so God is the ghost in the world machine. The problem of how one absolutely distinctive and autonomous substance (mind) can influence another absolutely autonomous and independent substance (matter) presents obvious logical and metaphysical contradictions that clearly are without solution. This predicament is a tale of heaven and earth, and there is no way to get from one to the other. Similarly, the mind is left with no means for influencing

3. See Eliot Deutsch, *Advaita Vedaanta: A Philosophical Reconstruction* (Honolulu: East-West Center Press, 1969).

the body, which it certainly does, or of being influenced by the body, which it certainly is. So, God, who is more like mind than matter, is left with no means for influencing the creation, except, perhaps, through the exercise of the powers of miracle. But, of course, the appeal to miracle is itself no explanation at all.

Between these two untenable positions the classic forms of theism attempt to retain the distinct reality of both God and the creation while providing meaningful interaction between them, usually by balancing the categories of divine immanence and transcendence. In its concern to protect the transcendence, and hence the sovereignty of God, theism tends to err on the side of dualism. Theologies of immanence bring God perilously close to the creation in an intimacy that differs from monism or pantheism only by degree. Monism is surely not an option; yet, a comprehensive account of just how God interacts with the creation remains a large problem as long as dualistic assumptions remain. For God to govern the world, both must participate in some general system of conditions. To insist otherwise would be to admit that a complete theological cosmology (the understanding of God's interaction with the creation) is at the end unintelligible and, hence, impossible.

METAPHYSICS

Metaphysics Defined

Theology requires metaphysics if its aim is to articulate a satisfactory model of deity within a general system of conditions allowing for interaction between creator and creation. However, given the repudiation of metaphysics in much of contemporary philosophy and its rejection by many theologians, it is necessary to make a case for the unavoidability of metaphysics in theological inquiry.

Metaphysics seeks the most general traits, principles, or characteristics that apply without exception to any existing thing and to the world of all existing things, "an all-inclusive survey of reality at large."[4] It even seeks to account for the reality of the possibility of things. Metaphysics is concerned with the nature of existence. It is the study of what it means to be at all, of what the characteristics are of anything that is something or could possibly be something, and how its identity is determined. Metaphysics differs from science. Science seeks to understand this particular world or

4. Wolfhart Pannenberg, *An Introduction to Systematic Theology* (Grand Rapids: Eerdmans, 1991), 28.

cosmos in terms of the most general explanations that apply uniformly as laws or patterns of nature. Metaphysics searches for the most general principles that apply to any possible universe or set of universes, such that no world can conceivably exist without satisfying these principles (although it might exist without satisfying the particular conditions of *our* world). Hence, unlike scientific hypotheses, metaphysical hypotheses are not necessarily empirical or technically testable in the sense required by science.

This does not mean, however, that metaphysics may be pursued with closed eyes as if, by pure thought alone, it could gain access to a transcendental world, high or deep, that is detached from our own. Metaphysics is not some attempt to check out the plumbing in the basement of the cosmos. Rather, like science, it seeks to interpret the facts of experience within the most inclusive theoretical framework. Thus, nothing is irrelevant.

The most general question concerning metaphysics is the one framed by the philosopher Leibniz and rephrased by the twentieth-century philosopher Martin Heidegger: "Why is there something rather than nothing?" In hopes of responding to the challenge of this most universal of all mysteries, metaphysicians attempt to discover those conditions necessary for anything whatsoever to exist. For those of us with some existential sensitivity, it follows that the fundamental ontological question applies also to *me* as I recognize with some shock that I am included in the category of "something." The wonder provoked by this insight is one motivation for doing metaphysics. There are others.

Motives for Doing Metaphysics

Constructive projects in metaphysics are pursued for many reasons. A primary motive is the quest for a full and satisfying explanation of the world, provoked by a sense of curiosity that compels all creatures but is sought for its own sake only in a few species. Another is the creative urge, the aesthetic impulse to build a beautiful system or to tell a good story, as Plato does in the *Timaeus*. Completion of the telling is accompanied by a sense of beauty, of harmony and balance.

Theology also provides a motive for metaphysical inquiry. Faith seeks understanding, but always within assumptions of finite human capacities for understanding. Theological metaphysics almost always takes place within a situation of faith where God is both object and recipient of the results. Anselm, for example, offered his famous ontological argument as a prayer addressed to the very being whose existence it was intended irrefutably to establish.

Finally, there are practical reasons for building general theories intended to account for the total world system. Plato wanted to establish a sure and certain source of values and ideals, of beauty, goodness, and justice that would provide guidance for those who would govern the *polis* with a discerning integrity by avoiding the corrupting tendencies inherent in moral relativism. His realm of ideas does just that. Another pragmatic employment of metaphysics is to present a corrective alternative to prevailing theories of the world that are inadequate, harmful, or just plain wrong. By offering thoughtful competition to traditional philosophies of mechanism, process cosmologies perform this task admirably. Dominant metaphysical schemes and the worldviews they spawn are called into question when historical conditions change so extensively that their principles no longer give adequate guidance for life. Thus, the final reason for metaphysical inquiry is to meet the deeper needs of a budding historical epoch whose participants cannot trust the older system but, as yet, have none of their own to replace it. Besides, the raised consciousness that is prerequisite to any metaphysical project is likely possible only in a historical environment that permits or encourages it.

The Repudiation of Metaphysics

Not surprisingly, as a field of philosophical inquiry, metaphysics has fallen into disrepute. Many witnesses have testified against metaphysics, beginning perhaps with Abelard's embrace of nominalism in the medieval period, proceeding through the still-powerful arguments of Hume and Kant, to more contemporary skeptics such as A. J. Ayer (in his disdain of the "dummy entities" of metaphysics[5]). Philosophers are not the only ones rejecting metaphysics; our prevailing sensate culture is also deeply suspicious of "large ideas."[6]

Ours is an age of empirical inquiry and smaller questions. Claims of knowledge must be adjudicated before the court of evidence, which means primarily scientific evidence. Propositions that do not appeal to some immediate factual grounding for their authority are held in deep suspicion as being about realities that are not so real,

5. A. J. Ayer *Metaphysics and Common Sense* (Boston: Jones and Bartlett, 1994), 99.

6. Robert Cummings Neville, *Eternity and Time's Flow* (Albany: State University of New York Press, 1993), 68.

perhaps the figments of an overactive metaphysical imagination. We have little patience for questions that lead nowhere in terms of providing us with immediate cash benefits. Metaphysics, and its off-spring discipline, ontology (the study of being or existence), are both irrelevant and impractical; we should "be wary of such grandiosities of philosophical fancy."[7]

Science is operationally naturalistic. As an approach to truth, science rejects all metaphysical speculations as just that, speculations that escape the rigorous testing required of all hypotheses through processes of verification, falsification, and public reproducibility of results. Metaphysical propositions are a priori and not subject to empirical tests; scientific propositions always are. The two modes of inquiry are therefore incommensurable.

But is it fair to reject metaphysics on the basis of standards that do not entirely apply to the approach? Science seeks broad and inclusive generality. But science differs from metaphysics in that it limits its inquiry to the strictly empirical and potentially testable and generalizes from its success with limited experience to the whole of reality. Metaphysics tends to speculate further and seeks the foundations of a world that possesses the features revealed by science. Metaphysics is more adventurous, exploratory, and speculative in that it realizes that strict empirical testing of its claims is not possible in the same way that claims in science can be tested. Accordingly, metaphysics is more general than science and yet inclusive of the insights of science. Perhaps the two are not incommensurable after all.

Moreover, metaphysics denied is metaphysics insidiously affirmed. Even the philosopher A. J. Ayer, an avowed opponent of metaphysics, admitted that, in some situations, "the man who is ready to prove that metaphysics is impossible is a brother metaphysician with a rival theory of his own."[8] No theoretical discipline is without its implicit metaphysics, here understood as those foundational principles upon which it bases its method, offers it conclusions, and justifies its goals. Where would science be without its basic assumptions about the nature of the world (the totality of existing things) that makes it worthwhile to explore fruitfully (e.g., the principle of uniformity or epistemological reductionism)? These principles transcend the very method that they ground. They

---

7. John Polkinghorne, *The Faith of a Physicist: Reflections of a Bottom-Up Thinker: The Gifford Lectures for 1993–94* (Princeton, N.J.: Princeton University Press, 1994), 24.

8. A. J. Ayer, *Language, Truth, and Logic* (New York: Dover, 1952), 34.

are, by definition, metaphysical and constitute the faith of science understood as the acceptance of propositions about science that science itself is in no position to confirm. We are all metaphysicians unaware.

METAPHYSICS AND THEOLOGY

The Metaphysical Character of Theology

Theology does not escape implication in the rejection of metaphysics by the modern mind. In some religions metaphysical inquiry is not especially important and may be altogether absent. With its heritage of Greek philosophy, Christianity is clearly not one of them. The great theoreticians of the church, from the early medieval period through the twentieth century, relied heavily upon the tools of reason to explore questions of metaphysics for their authority. It would seem, therefore, that Christianity would have much to lose by eschewing metaphysics.

However, many theologians are deeply suspicious of any attempt to draw conclusions about God that are not directly inferred from traditional sources of revelation due to the very nature of divinity as a reality, an infinitely creative and determinative power that completely transcends our creaturely abilities. Even scripture testifies that "No one has ever seen God" (1 John 4:12). God is infinite, and finite minds cannot comprehend the infinite. Even though this is itself a metaphysical claim, it apparently bars further inquiry into the divine nature.

Still, metaphysics remains a useful form of theological inquiry. God, after all, is understood to be the answer to the questions of why and how things are and therefore an appropriate object for metaphysical speculation. While it may be entirely possible to construct metaphysical systems that do not require a concept of God for their completion, theology, by definition, strives to include God as the foundation and aim of its systematic speculations. Such theology is in the business of making the world ultimately intelligible through an appeal to a coherent model of God that includes general truths about creator and creation. Gordon Kaufman makes this point nicely:

> Much of theology is basically "metaphysical" in character, in that it addresses itself to the formal analysis and clarification of an understanding of reality or the world, and the ultimate point of reference for that understanding. But theol-

ogy is metaphysics with a special commitment and orientation,
namely, to grasping that ultimate point of reference specifically
as *God* and thus setting out a picture of reality and the world,
which focuses in God.[9]

The definition of the God of theism is itself metaphysical in the
absolute generality of its language. Candidates for a definition of
deity are not hard to find. Wolfhart Pannenberg says that "using
the word 'God' [in the singular] implies as its semantic minimum
the idea of power on which all finite reality depends."[10] He continues, "The idea of God determining all finite reality involves that
no finite reality can be understood in its depth without reference
to God."[11] Hans Küng refers to God as the "origin, support, and
goal" of all things.[12] Gordon Kaufman defines God as "our 'ultimate point of reference,' that in terms of which everything else is
to be understood, that beyond which we cannot move in imagination, thought, or devotion."[13] And, of course, the most pronounced
and unabashed metaphysical theologian in Protestant theology is
Paul Tillich, whose definition of God is "the ground of being" or
"the power of being," "Being itself."[14] So, while no one has seen
God, many able minds have *thought* about God in a manner that
irresistibly pushes them into metaphysics.

God: "The Metaphysical Individual"

Schubert Ogden is another theologian whose dedication to philosophical theology enables him to articulate his commitment to
metaphysics with clarity and passion. In his book *On Theology*[15]
Ogden discusses the task of philosophical theology, which he says
"is integral to philosophy's central task as metaphysics" and required "so to understand our common faith as to answer the basic
question of the reality of God." By claiming that "God's reality
is the ultimate presupposition of religion" and that " 'God' is its
'constitutive concept,' analogous, say, to the concept of 'physical

9. Gordon Kaufman, *An Essay on Theological Method* (Atlanta: Scholars Press, 1995), 19.

10. Pannenberg, *Introduction to Systematic Theology,* 8.

11. Ibid., 9.

12. Hans Küng, *Does God Exist? An Answer for Today,* trans. Edward Quinn (Garden City, N.Y.: Doubleday, 1980), 548.

13. Kaufman, *Essay on Theological Method,* 24.

14. Paul Tillich, *Systematic Theology,* 3 vols. in 1 vol. (Chicago: University of Chicago Press, 1967), 1:164.

15. Schubert Ogden, *On Theology* (San Francisco: Harper & Row, 1986).

object' in science or of 'obligation' in morality," Ogden asserts the irreducible metaphysical dimension of talk about God.[16]

He continues by making this assumption overt:

> If the doctrines of developed religion aim at metaphysics, the question of God's reality, which religion poses for philosophical understanding, is in its logic a metaphysical question. This is simply to be confirmed by the concept "God" itself.... Where God is conceived radically, as in monotheistic religions such as Judaism and Christianity, God is clearly understood as metaphysically real and so as not even possibly the object of strictly empirical modes of knowledge.[17]

And further:

> As "the Father almighty, Maker of Heaven and Earth, and of all things visible and invisible," God is the ultimate creative source of anything that is so much as possible, and hence God is to be in the strictest sense necessary, not merely a being among others, but in some way "being-itself." In fact, the God of theism in its most fully developed forms is the one metaphysical individual, the sole being, whose individuality is constitutive of all reality as such and who, therefore, is the inclusive object of faith and understanding.[18]

God is this "one metaphysical individual," the singular being who must exist if this universe, or any universe at all, for that matter, is even to be possible. That is, God is the one individual with strictly universal functions. As such, God is the one individual for whom reason alone can account, although further speculation about the particular character of God requires reference to our world as we find it. For this reason cosmology is relevant. So, theology, as reasoned and imaginative discourse about God, has an obligation to pursue its reflective and rational responsibilities to their conclusion.[19]

---

16. Ibid., 78.
17. Ibid., 79.
18. Ibid.
19. Historical religious traditions specify their claims about the nature and conduct of God through narratives of revelation and subsequent governing doctrines and creeds derived from them. It is, of course, not necessary to understand the metaphysical consequences or foundations of one's beliefs to be numbered among the faithful in such traditions. This is the task and vocation of theologians, the theoreticians of a tradition. Their responsibility is to ground the creedal confessions in a conceptual system that will provide plausible and coherent understanding of these beliefs.

TESTING METAPHYSICAL ASSERTIONS

Although it is true that metaphysical propositions are not subject
to empirical verification, anyone who would advocate metaphysics
is responsible for proposing the criteria that an accounting of
the world and God should satisfy if it is to contribute meaningfully to the fundamental task of theology. These requirements may
be grouped into three categories: internal coherence, mundane or
worldly relevance, and pragmatic application.

Internal Coherence

All parts of any worthwhile theory must mesh logically, with every
part related to the whole in some systematic way. The set of concepts
that constitute a metaphysical system must do just that—contribute
to the systemic and rational coherence of the entire scheme. Nothing should be superfluous, inconsistent with or contradicting any
other element. There should be no gaps, no conflict, no arbitrary .
inclusions. The articulation should be powerful enough to allow for
the orderly and progressive elucidation of all important themes and
concepts. That is, the set of concepts and arguments constituting
the system should be mutually clarifying and supportive. Ideally,
the system should be so tightly argued that any interested inquirer
could cut the pie of the whole at any place and proceed to all other
places from there.

Another criterion for internal coherence is that all important
ideas or claims should be sufficiently clear and vivid, that is, distinct
and unambiguous. Certainly, detail is surrendered in discussions
that are so general or synoptic that they apply in some sense to
anything whosoever. Nonetheless, the vagueness of the idea itself
should be reduced to a minimum, lest that vagueness be interpreted
as intentional obscurantism and mystification, charges frequently
leveled against theology in the past.

Mundane Relevance

Metaphysical claims, because they are about all possible worlds,
cannot be directly tested. But they must in some intuitive and logical way reflect the real world. This condition is similar to that
of pragmatic workability. The metaphysical system should be able
to account for all important categories of existing objects, events,
and relationships. Significant omissions would suggest an inherent
weakness in the whole system.

Pragmatic Application

The metaphysical propositions should have real-world consequences. They should make a difference or be applicable. They
should make sense out of experience, advance the solutions of
other issues, and contribute to a program of direction for individuals and society. While metaphysics is reputed to be an exercise
carried out in ivory towers by slightly drowsy academicians (and
therefore merely "academic"), those who would do metaphysics
in the twentieth century are often fully alert to the consequences
of their ideas. So a general scheme of ideas must be workable in
the world. When understood clearly, it should shed light on and
clarify rather than obscure the basic issues of life, history, and
nature that concern a particular period. As with great theories of
science, an adequate metaphysics should be fruitful and suggestive.
It should contribute to genuine progress in understanding, not as
an interesting sideshow but as a powerful source for genuine explanation. This is why not all metaphysical systems are equally
workable in a particular historical context even if they are equally
coherent internally. Worldview theory is concerned with this aspect
of metaphysics.

Technically, metaphysical theories are not strictly empirical and
therefore unfalsifiable. Since they are designed to be so general as
to satisfy any possible situation or case that might be used to test
them, they cannot be compared judged accordingly. Nonetheless,
some metaphysical theories are clearly superior to others in accord
with these and other criteria. A robust and vital metaphysical system
may therefore be quite relevant to the world, and we may have
growing confidence that it really reflects the nature of that world in
a reasonable and useful way.

The standards that apply in the evaluation of any metaphysics
also apply in the evaluation of a specifically theological metaphysics.
Other special criteria apply as well. One criterion is the requirement that the metaphysical system be commensurable with (that
is, consistent with) the basic sources and authorities of the particular tradition to which it is being applied, including scripture and
doctrine. Another criterion is that the metaphysical system should
enhance faith and worship in a meaningful and existential way.
Worship, after all, requires the involvement of the whole self, the
mind as well as the heart and soul. Ideally full participation requires
some clear understanding of and appreciation for the elements of
the rituals and ceremonies, the meaning of the creeds recited by the

worshiping community, and, obviously, some minimal idea of who God is.

THEOLOGY AND SCIENCE

Science as a Source for Theology

If metaphysical inquiry is a legitimate pursuit and theological metaphysical inquiry a necessary one, the next issue to be addressed concerns the advisability of taking theories from contemporary science as sources for models of divinity and their metaphysical foundations.

A case can be built advocating that theology pay attention to science as an important source for its task of constructing adequate models of God. One important argument has been developed in chapter 2. It is a historical fact that theologies often follow cosmologies, using the authority of established views of the nature of the universe to adjust views of God and accounts of how God relates to the universe. And reciprocally, cosmologies often reflect major influences of theology. Ian Barbour documents these precedents.[20] In understanding the world, the Greeks contributed notions of rationality and intelligibility of the cosmos, while the Hebrews contributed notions of contingency. The world is the free creation of God; its existence is not logically necessary. Therefore, reason alone cannot provide an explanation for the universe. The characterization of the universe as a "brute fact" is an expression of this insight into the radical contingency of all things found first in Hebrew thought. The contingency of the universe means that scientists have something to learn through empirical inquiry. The intelligibility of the universe means that they can be confident of some success. Also, God is the source and sustainer for a divine order reflected in nature. A major impulse for early science was a self-understanding of its vocation, namely, that attempts to discover mathematically expressed patterns within nature are efforts "to think God's thoughts after him," to quote an early astronomer, Johannes Kepler. Even today, the success of this enterprise has lead scientists from Albert Einstein to Paul Davies to the intuition that some sort of greater intelligence, not necessarily personal, lies within, beneath, or behind

20. Ian G. Barbour, *Religion in an Age of Science* (San Francisco: Harper & Row, 1990), 17.

the order revealed by scientific inquiry as the necessary condition and perhaps conclusion of its achievements.[21]

A second set of justifications for using scientific models in metaphysical theology is that by doing so, the inherent explanatory power of science can be turned to the advantage of theology. Science is an empirical and logical field. Its findings are subject to rigorous and repeated interrogation. Theology, if it is to be ultimately relevant to the world, should take advantage of science as one of the surest sources for knowledge about reality. More importantly, science is a fruitful source of concepts and vocabulary. Granted, the special sciences are often encumbered by their own special jargon leading to the construction of closed communities of discourse and specialization. But beyond this tendency toward babel, there is a common system of terminology that transcends these technical languages, and each discipline within science also has its standard terminology that makes the basic concepts available to the interested and persistent layperson. Otherwise, chemistry, physics, and biology would be impossible to teach in public schools. These concepts can provide powerful sources for insight to theology. Successful theories in science are fertile. They shed light on fields where connections and relationships were previously undetected. They also lead to new insights, disclosures that are both subtle and unexpected, through the playful association of ideas with the logic of deduction. Both metaphysics and theology require disciplined imagination if they are to progress. Science provides material and insight for this progress.

Finally, insofar as science reveals the world in depth and detail, theology has an interest in its discoveries. Each of the monotheistic religions teaches that God reveals something of the divine nature in and through the created order. If God is the author of this order, then it follows that that order is a reflection of God's intentions. Also, how the world works suggests how God works in the world. Those places where God initiates actions affecting the world must also be those places where God may be inferred as the source of the actions. This is not to advance a stronger claim that God initiates or causes certain specific effects in space and time, but simply in a weaker sense to suggest that the structures and processes of the creation allow theologians to construct accounts of God's actions

---

21. See Albert Einstein, *Ideas and Opinions* (New York: Crown, 1954); Paul Davies, *The Mind of God: The Scientific Basis for a Rational World* (New York: Simon and Schuster, 1992).

that would be specific to and consistent with these structures and processes.

Theology as Imaginative Science

Theology is a science, even in its metaphysical dimension. The critical justifications for its claims lie both in reason and the appeal to experience. But the science of theology is concerned with all reality and not just with the religious part. It does not aspire to become an all-embracing science of sciences to which the practitioners of any particular science would have to go for the final resolution of any problem. Since its accounts are all-embracing in their generality, no datum can be either determinative (since God is compatible with any possible worlds or state of affairs) or irrelevant (since God is the power that determines and directs all things).[22] Pannenberg exposes the logic of this position clearly: "If God is to be understood as the all-determining reality, everything must be shown to be determined by this reality and to be ultimately unintelligible without it."[23]

While theology is characterized as a science, it also, like most sciences, makes ample use of the imagination. Great discoveries in science are often the result of sudden leaps of intuition, insight, and creativity that break through after extended periods of concentration on a problem. The resulting insights are subsequently confirmed through empirical testing and through their rich suggestiveness that leads to further advances in theory. In theology the imagination is employed to identify images for God that speak to the current historical context. Metaphysics provides the rational grounding for the justification of the particular images. To avoid arbitrariness or an appeal to some self-affirming historical zeitgeist or charismatic individual as the source and confirmation of the image, some deeper connection is responsibly sought. Although existential confirmation and relevance are important criteria for all constructive theology, pragmatic applicability alone is insufficient justification for powerful theological claims unless (a very large "unless") one's theology allows historical experience exclusively to count as revelatory evidence for God's nature and intentions.

Granted, *mythos,* narrative imagination, precedes *logos,* justification through the search for ultimate grounds using critical thought. But one requires the other. Without the creative and often spon-

---

22. Hans Küng, *On Being a Christian* (New York: Doubleday, 1976), 88.
23. Wolfhart Pannenberg, *Theology and the Philosophy of Science* (Philadelphia: Westminster Press, 1976), 302.

taneous application of imagination, rational analysis has nothing
to start from or work with. But without further critical justification, images created by the imagination float freely about subject
to exploitation by power and authority. Concrete images of God
created by the disciplined imagination are masks that represent the
structures of some deeper and fundamental reality.

CONTINUITY BETWEEN GOD AND WORLD

Faces in the Clouds?

Metaphysics tends toward abstractions, and necessarily so, since its
aim is to discover strictly general principles that apply to all possible worlds. The strength of these abstractions is that they offer the
most inclusive understanding for the way things are. The weakness
is that they are woefully lacking in concrete details.[24] This poverty
applies also to God, that strictly metaphysical individual; metaphysical theology has little to add about the specific character of divinity.
Where is one to go for specific content?

Previous discussions prepared the way for a fundamental conclusion about the relation of God to the world that would allow for
this content to be articulated. It is simply this: God and world share
general metaphysical features. These features provide a "buttoning-
on-place" between the creator and the creation that permits specific
models for divinity to be imaginatively constructed.

The sources for these models are numerous and include history,
personal experience, and science. Even within these categories considerable selection must be made. Whose history? What sort of
personal experience? Which scientific concepts? At this point, the
investigator is thrown back upon the basic skills of the creative and
critical imagination. And the results of the construction of a model
of divinity based on a specific reading of history, a fundamental
sort of human experience, or a particular science must be secured
and defended by an appeal to the criteria discussed earlier. The best
ideas about the world can provide a framework for a discussion
of God so long as the resulting propositions are tested by the adequacy of their consequences for providing unity and meaning in
human community; they meet the criterion of pragmatic adequacy.

---

24. Pannenberg (*Introduction to Systematic Theology,* 29) concurs: "Ontological
language about being or beings does not get very far in relating the concept of God
to the concrete nature of the universe we know."

At least to this extent, the weak claim that God and world some-how share similar aspects is justified. The success of such projects makes stronger metaphysical claims more plausible.

It follows that science is a legitimate contributor of material for the construction of a model of God. The contribution is not only metaphorical and pragmatic (although it shares characteristics with both). It is based also on the condition of essential similar-ity or shared features. It is entirely possible, even necessary, for metaphysics to employ the concepts and theories of science. By generalizing on particular theories, constructive speculation car-ries them to their logical limits, where they approach metaphysical status; that is, they become principles of the explanation and elucidation of all reality.

The intelligibility of a theological system that does not include such mutual conditions would be questionable since its coherence would be broken from the outset. Any action God would take to-ward the world providentially would be arbitrary and inexplicable. The model of God arising from theological inquiry must include some continuity with the creation if it is to be intelligible. Kierke-gaard's requirement of an "infinite qualitative difference" between the infinite (God) and the finite (creation) is existentially and, to some extent, theologically defensible, but it is earned at the cost of the intelligibility of the idea of both God and the creation. If the interaction between a "strictly general" (Ogden) deity and any pos-sible world is intelligible or beyond appeal to magic and miracle alone, it follows that God and world share some of these features in common at the highest levels of inclusiveness and generality. Such levels are perhaps best identified and described by science and extrapolated by additional metaphysical speculation.

Are these correlations between a known reality, the world or cosmos, and an unknown reality, God, just another example of fallacious projections, of seeing "faces in the clouds"? Is anthro-pomorphism replaced by a more refined "cosmomorphism"? In some ways, the answer is yes. But here the projections are intended and conscious. This is not the case with traditional analyses, such as those of Feuerbach and Freud, where personal and corporate projections of a God upon the cosmic screen are unconscious acts of profound self-deception. That is, to paraphrase a statement at-tributed to Karl Barth, to say "God" is to say "man" in a very loud voice. Also, the validity or strength of the resulting images of God from disciplined metaphysical speculation is justified by reasonable argument, by appeal to standards that are independent of the particular model. This cannot be true of unconscious projection.

God, World, and Isomorphism

Recalling the discussion in chapter 1, the deepest isomorphic structures are also the most general since they apply to a vast range of systems. This very generality approaches the inclusiveness of metaphysics and may be extended to include discussion of God as well. The tacit assumption of metaphysics is that isomorphies exist. Otherwise, how could distinctive entities be compared?

The aim of this study is to identify and hopefully articulate deep isomorphic principles that might account for and give understanding to the relation of God and the creation. The source of these ideas will be the systems and informational sciences. While the intention is obviously metaphysical, the project may be read as an exercise in constructive metaphorical theology. All the elements are there: an appeal to the current historical situation and the need for an adequate model of God; use of images drawn from the world to liken to and illuminate divinity and allow for articulation; and insistence on the provisional character of these models. Or it may be read as an exercise in constructive, imaginative metaphysics: the emphasis on rational-empirical criteria for the justification of the models; commitment to the premise that general systematic parallels or isomorphies exist between God and creation permitting metaphysical extrapolation from the world to God to take place.

We will draw substantially from Claude Shannon's theory of communication. The selection is not arbitrary, but neither is it dictated by irresistible logic. We will argue in subsequent chapters that the theory can be generalized to describe not only the power of computers and communications systems, but also the world at large in terms of its ontological foundations. These foundations are really isomorphies or broad structural principles found universally, and perhaps even applying to every possible world. The thought process that moves from a specific theory of communication with limited intentions and application to a cosmological framework is certainly an act of constructive speculation.

Without a doubt, in the process the scientific character of Shannon's theory vanishes as his ideas are transmuted into metaphysical and theological principles. It should be made very clear that this promotion of a theory from scientific status to a metaphysical and theological status means that the elements or objects it describes are not identifiable worldly realities. That is, the God described in accordance with communication theory is not in the same category as Newton's *sensorium dei,* where divine omniscience is equated with the reality of absolute space. The expropriation of concepts is justified by the claim, held provisionally until argued successfully, that there exist real structural similarities between God and world such that the use of terms taken from communication theory to speak correspondingly of both realms is justified.

This approach is to be found in all philosophers and theologians who propose specific models of God. It is certainly true of Whitehead in his account of God as actual in the same sense as any concrete individual in the world is actual. It even applies to Tillich in his description of God as the "ground" of being. Tillich is correct in insisting that the image of "ground" is symbolic. But it is not arbitrary. That is, this particular symbol is selected from the range of countless other candidates because it uniquely reveals a specific structural arrangement that best allows for the articulation of the character of being. The symbol is driven by the isomorphy.

To approach the issue of methodology from another angle, numerous theologians have concluded that if God is creator, then it is not possible to understand the processes of nature without reference to God. Now, is the converse to this statement also true? Is it possible to understand God without references to the processes of nature? One response, resulting in a resounding "no" to the suggestion, is that the universe, being contingent, represents one of countless possible universes that might easily have existed instead of our own. These worlds differ in almost every respect that interests science, particularly in the laws that govern their processes. Thus, the discoveries of the particular laws and processes of our universe cannot be generalized into theological discourse to explore the consistent nature of a God who would be present to all possible universes.

Even so, say others who would respond "yes" to the question, all possible universes must share deep common structures and processes, including the presence of God to them, permitting their inclusion as members of the class "universe." The various worlds are individual instantiations of such necessary properties. Inhabitants of our universe or other universes engaging in science would discover that the unique laws that apply to their particular universe are not necessarily the laws that apply to other universes. But, by generalizing through reasonable speculation about the character of lawful universes, they might arrive at principles of correspondence that likely hold between their universe and other possible universes.

Metaphysics is in the business of getting at those deeper and truly universal correspondences. Our methodological leap of faith lies in the hypothesis that the elements of communication theory reveal the deep commonality in terms of isomorphic structures to be found in any possible universe.

METAPHOR, METAPHYSICS, AND IMAGINATION

All attempts to say something about God encounter a serious barrier. Theism and the monotheistic traditions subscribe to the understanding that God is *a se* (literally, "from oneself") and completely beyond the possibility of knowledge. Being utterly transcendent, God as such shares no common characteristic with the creation. God is known only through God's own gracious self-disclosure primarily in history (special revelation) and to some extent in the creation (general revelation). And even here human knowledge is both inferential and expressed in terms taken from creation, terms that are intended for use in the ordinary world but that are here stretched far beyond their original intentions to suggest something about extraordinary divine reality. Hence, we must be entirely suspicious of any univocal or literal application of words and concepts to account for God apart from God's actions in the world from which the specifics of God's will or intentions may be deduced. Indeed, perhaps all that one really knows about God that does not vary across historical periods, faith perspectives, and doctrinal systems is that God is will, and God wills to love.

This agnosticism that emphasizes the aseity and ineffability of God is very influential in current theology. In conjunction with the diminished reputation of metaphysics discussed earlier, this attitude results in extreme skepticism toward most theologies that contend to describe God's inner life. Further, those who promote such audacious attempts are, at least in good Barthian perspectives, guilty of a kind of arrogance, of hubris. In the face of such objections, speculations about the divine life have been overshadowed by metaphorical theology.

McFague's Metaphorical Theology

In several books, Sallie McFague has built a powerful case for doing theology constructively through the judicious use of metaphors.[25]

25. See Sallie McFague, *Speaking in Parables* (Philadelphia: Fortress Press, 1979); *Models of God* (Philadelphia: Fortress Press, 1987); *The Body of God* (Minneapolis: Fortress Press, 1983).

Through disciplined employment of their imagination within the framework of a tradition and sensitivity to the needs of their times, theologians undeniably construct "models" of God that give direction and provide insight but that do not claim to speak literally about the deity. Models are metaphorical; they draw upon familiar realities in human life to suggest something about the nature of God.

Without exploring such linguistic similarities between creation and creator, most God-talk would be impossible. McFague is also aware of the irreducible limits and provisional nature of such tools. "The essence of metaphorical theology," she says, "is precisely its refusal to identify human constructions with divine reality."[26] The value and fertility of metaphorical thought are unquestioned. But with most metaphors, the insight is the result of noticing similarities between two realities, both already known to some extent; one is just more familiar than the other. This kind of checkability is not possible with God, whose transcendence and complete otherness renders God's reality unknown in and of itself. The imaginative constructs that stand in for God allow theology to proceed, but the checkability to be found in mundane metaphor is absent with respect to God's unique and unapproachable reality.

Because of this missing degree of assurance of faithful correspondence, theological metaphors are always provisional. Given this agnostic posture regarding possible knowledge of God, McFague embraces a functional approach to the confirmation of particular metaphors of the divine. Agreeing with the constructive approach of Gordon Kaufman, she sees that the role of theology is to create community and inspire faithful dedication within the contemporary context. Metaphors of God are confirmed pragmatically when they promote the articulation of the tradition to the worshiping community and give direction on how to live responsibly in the world. In other words, the standard of verification is a type of functional anthropology. "God" functions to give a unified meaning to our common life. And functionalism has always found that the reality status of the object whose name and concept provide the unified meaning is secondary and even immaterial to its function.

Furthermore, McFague takes her insights from the contemporary situation. These include the importance of an ecological attitude that stresses wholeness and interconnectedness in the earthly community of all creatures, including the human creature. The model of

---

26. McFague, *Models of God,* 22.

God that is most fitting for these times is one for which this connect-
edness of all life is precious. Future historical epochs may, of course,
have fundamental requirements that do not include these particular
inductive metaphors with their ecological emphases. They are transitory in their importance, but no less significant because of that.
The best metaphors for God are just those that meet the deeper
needs of the human spirit and speak clearly to the issues of the
age. That they truly reflect the eternal nature of God is a secondary
concern, if a concern at all, since, according to skeptical proponents of functional metaphorical theology, it is impossible as well
as unnecessary for us to test the correspondence.

Understandably, McFague is not sympathetic to metaphysical
approaches to theology. Nonetheless, she is no exception to the
claim that every method has its metaphysics, its foundational principles that make claims that are not a part of the method itself.
She assumes, for example, that God is essentially unapproachable
by human reason. God is radically transcendent. Hence, all God-
talk is the result of constructive, imaginative efforts that say far
more about humans than about God and are consciously intended
to contribute to the betterment of human life.

Still, not all metaphors of God are equal. Some are assigned privileged status. McFague sees that the claim of divine personhood
is of great importance. "God is a person" may be a metaphorical
statement, but it occupies a place of great authority. Most other
metaphors must be tested against it. Thus, McFague's discussion
of the forms of divine love and the more specific human models
of Friend, Mother, and Lover are, in turn, based on this more
fundamental image of person. She is right, of course; monotheistic traditions would be unimaginable without the image of God as
a person. Nevertheless, while the claim remains metaphorical and
justified on pragmatic grounds, the image of God as the ultimate
personal individual approaches an indispensable status that is very
close to a metaphysical claim that transcends historical context.

In addition, it appears that something inherent can be inferred
about the nature of God, even in metaphorical discourse. God's love
can be profitably declared to be similar to the love of a mother or
friend. It apparently follows that the claim "God wills" is more
than simply a higher controlling metaphor. It is an essential and irreducible claim about God's nature. Remove the character of loving
will from the divine and the divine simply vanishes; "God" becomes
a vacant word, or at best a synonym for arbitrary power. The alternative to this univocal or nonsymbolic assertion that "God wills"

or that "God loves" is to imitate the gnostic teaching that there are two gods, the lesser and greater. In metaphorical theology, images of the lesser deity are constructed and historically relative while the true God who transcends it all remains unknown and unknowable. The Tillichian "God above God" cannot be spoken of, while the lesser metaphorical divinity is available to thought and theology. The only problem is that the lesser God alone provides us with meaning in life and context for worship. The higher original and unknowable divine being, a victim of excessive transcendence, is out of the picture and has nothing to do with it.

In order to avoid potential radical historical relativism and empty metaphorical discourse in theology, this study posits that some minimal knowledge of the divine character may in fact be articulated. Through this knowledge images of God can be held in tension with the functional needs of the age.

Metaphors and Isomorphies

Poetic devices such as metaphor and analogy are extremely useful and even necessary in the explication of theories, whether scientific or metaphysical. But in these cases inquiry is not directed by the poetic device and limited to its disclosures. Rather, metaphor and analogy are in the service of some larger structured system of thought where their purpose is to convey the claims of the system. Metaphor is an instrumental and didactic device, a powerful tool for expressing the abstract in terms of the concrete. And the images work because they are grounded in the isomorphic or structural realities of the system itself.

This practical realism is found not only in constructive theology but also in constructive physics. For example, the famous model of complementarity applied to the account of elementary particles is a combination of isomorphic correspondence between the behavior of a subparticle and certain mathematical expressions. But without metaphorical discourse, an electron, for example, remains invisible to the mind's eye. The image of the electron as particle and as wave are needed to concretize and enflesh the skeletal isomophisms. Equations tell the story, but they do not draw the picture. Formal structural resemblance and vivid image are required for the invisible to become visible in a humanly satisfying way. Metaphorical speech thickens the account.

Ian Barbour cites the work of Frank Brown on the relation between metaphoric and conceptual thought. Concepts are necessary, but abstract. But "metaphoric symbols are experientially rich and thus central in ritual and worship." Barbour concurs with Brown that "we have to move back and forth between metaphoric and conceptual models of thought." He recommends models as a tool for this task, "since they are more fully developed than metaphors and yet they are less abstract than concepts."[27]

Everyday conversation would be impoverished without metaphor, and religious discourse, reliant as it is upon the extension of ordinary speech to communicate extraordinary realities, would be reduced to mystical silence. We cannot pretend that metaphorical playfulness is not a powerful intuitive source for the articulation and enfleshment of metaphysical systems. This dependence upon various poetic devices is patent in the theological and metaphysical concepts developed in subsequent chapters. Their use is not an endorsement of the agnostic epistemology of metaphorical theology. Rather, it is recognition that without the animating power of metaphors, the bare isomorphic structures of the system would remain inert.

CONCLUSION

Science, theology, cosmology, and metaphor—the Olympian reach of our method is appropriate if the project is to construct a model of God, "Maker of Heaven and Earth." Indeed, if the major question is how God makes, sustains, and directs the creation, then no perspective or approach is superfluous or irrelevant. The unifying method of methods is metaphysical, that is, of absolute generality, and yet it finds its data in all human approaches to understanding life's activities. But one cannot say everything at once and hence must be guided by certain finite systems of thought as these are critically extrapolated to understand ultimate realities. This is what theological construction is all about. The remaining chapters are dedicated to this task. We begin by becoming familiar with the basics of the sciences of communication and systems since they will provide the ideas and framework for the promised model of God.

---

27. Barbour, *Religion in an Age of Science*, 46.

– 4 –

A Primer of Communication and Systems Theory

THE BROAD DESCRIPTION of postmodern cosmology fails to provide the specific directing principles, vocabulary, and detail that are required for the adequate construction of a reasonably coherent model of God. For that purpose we turn to a specific theory of contemporary science that represents this new cosmology, provides the precision we seek, is rich in insight and fruitful concepts, pervades the everyday social world, and is available for theological construction. The theory that satisfies all of these conditions is the communication theory of Claude Shannon.

In chapter 1 we tried to show that the computer-driven revolution offers resources for theological construction. That revolution is grounded in communication and information theory, which may be described without exaggeration as the ontology of electronic technology since they provide the structure upon which the "being" of computers is founded. And the computer, in turn, is the instrument that drives discoveries in the new cosmology of emergent complexity and the conceptual revolution that accompanies it.

In like manner, communication theory provides us with a framework for thinking through some of the major implications of an emerging cosmological picture for the idea of God. More importantly, this theory contributes to the construction of a model of deity that will assist in reconciling God to the world and potentially to ourselves as creatures in that world. It is exciting and certainly risky, provisionary yet strong in its ontological claims. However, before this project can progress to its theological chapters, we must initially lay out clearly what these concepts are. This chapter, then, is something of a primer of the basic ideas of communication theory and the notion of systems. These ideas, when taken together, offer a framework into which theological themes may subsequently be inserted and discussed.[1]

COMMUNICATION THEORY

Communicating "Communication"

Only rarely do major theories in science originate as solutions to engineering problems. Information or communication theory is one of them. Even as early as the Second World War, pioneers in the infant field of electronic technology realized that new developments in telephone technology, television, and electronic digital technology would be impossible without a sound theoretical understanding of communication itself. In 1948, an American electrical engineer, Claude Shannon, building on the contributions of his contemporary, the equally brilliant scientist Norbert Wiener, published his famous paper, "A Mathematical Theory of Information," laying out the foundations for such a theory.[2]

Although the article was intended for the engineer, the ideas it contained were to prove invaluable in many fields, ranging from cybernetics, computer technology, statistics, and cryptology to genetics, linguistics, psychology, and sociology. Success across this wide range of disciplines hints that the concepts of Shannon's theory may be more universal than he originally thought or intended. Indeed, communication theory, properly adapted, may prove fruitful for theologians and philosophers as well; our intention is to test this speculation. But before exploring the potential of Shannon's ideas in providing the conceptual structure for an intelligible model of God and God's relationship with the creation, the first step must necessarily be to introduce its major elements in terms that do not require the education of an electrical engineer to appreciate.

Communication covers far more than reading, writing, and reciting. Communication occurs when specific codes in the strands of DNA convey valuable instructions for the development of new cells and new organisms, when electrical impulses sent from the brain trigger impulses in the muscles toward the achievement of specific tasks, when the eyes see and the ears hear, when the thermostat controls the furnace, and when the artist takes the paint from the

---

1. Portions of this chapter and chapter 5 appear in "Chaos and God's Abundance: An Ontology of Variety in the Divine Life," *Zygon: Journal of Religion and Science* 32, no. 4 (1997): 515–24.

2. Claude E. Shannon, "A Mathematical Theory of Information," *Bell System Technical Journal* 27 (1948): 379–423, 623–56.

palette to the canvas. That is, communication occurs whenever an impulse originating in one place generates a response in another place through the transmission of signals.

As broad as it seems, even this definition was too narrow for Shannon's intention. He preferred a more comprehensive definition: communication is a decision process wherein a field or set of possibilities is reduced to some smaller number or even to a single possibility by the operation of a decision agency. To communicate is to rule out possibilities. Life, and in fact most events in the world, may be understood as the processes by which a range of possible states found in one moment is reduced to just one state in a subsequent moment through some general movement of specification or selection. Within this understanding it is entirely possible to see the flow of the world as a continuous stream of communication from potentiality to actuality. If communication can be defined so broadly, then it may be possible to extend the concepts of communication theory to include not only life and creation but also, isomorphically, the life of God.

Information

Theological applications were not among Shannon's intentions.[3] He, of course, was concerned with more mundane matters, especially the problem of how to transmit signals over wires and through space with the greatest efficiency and the least loss of information. Bell Laboratories employed him for just this kind of research. Shannon's major contribution toward these goals was to define a precise quantitative unit for the measurement of transmitted information. This mathematical derivation proved to be of incredible power in directing research in electronic technology. Now it became possible to measure precisely the amount of information carried by messages in a vast range of media.

Consider the following illustration of a complex sequence of communication events. From the stage of a performing arts center a conductor announces the next piece to be performed, a symphony by Brahms, then turns to the orchestra and raises the baton to begin. The music goes out to the world through television images relayed by satellites in geostationary orbit twenty-two thousand miles above the planet. In living rooms the electronic signal retransmitted by the satellite is converted into pictures and sound and

---

3. Throughout his life Shannon discouraged applications of information theory beyond its technical applications. He would not have approved of our expropriation of information theory to talk about, of all things, God!

received by the eyes and ears of the viewers before it is again converted to electrical nerve impulses sent to the brain to be processed into meaningful aesthetic experience. Each step in this complex sequence of transmission from performance to appreciation is a form of communication containing measurable information content.

The term "information," sometimes also referred to as "data," is perhaps an unfortunate choice of words for a technical idea. Information generally means facts or knowledge. Shannon's definition of the term is far more basic than this. The concept of information in communication theory is a measure of probability or improbability in response to the modest and decidedly nontechnical question, "What are the chances...?" What are the chances, for example, that a tossed coin will come up heads? Before a coin is tossed, the outcome is uncertain within the specified limits of heads or tails, or two possibilities. Probability is measured along a scale from 0 (the event is impossible) to 1 (the event is certain). Each of two equal possibilities would, therefore, be assigned a value of .5, or "50–50" in colloquial terms. Since these possibilities are equal for an unbiased coin, no one can predict what the outcome of a single toss will be; uncertainty prevails. Following the toss, this uncertainty is resolved when the coin lands either heads or tails up. Once and for all, the results settle the question.

The toss of a coin represents the unit of information devised by Shannon. It is a quantified measure of a decision that resolves the uncertainty between two equally probable events. The two possibilities represent a "variety" of two. Since only one toss is required to settle the question of which of the possible outcomes will be the case, the toss is said to contain one unit of information. This unit is known as a "bit" because it is expressed in binary digits, 0 and 1, that constitute the elementary letters of the mathematical language of computers.

The connection between the toss of a coin and the transmission of a message may not be obvious until one realizes that all communication involves making decisions that remove uncertainty. Toss a coin and you send a message the effect of which is to resolve the probabilities, to reduce the number of states that might occur to the one state that does occur. A message, then, is the result of the act of communication understood as a decision or selection process— the reduction of a set of possibilities to a single definitive instance. The decision may be intentional, as when I decide to stroke the "v" key rather than any one of the other fifty or more keys on my keyboard when spelling "variety." In this single act I send a message or "process" more than five bits of information. The variety of the fifty possibilities is converted to a logarithm to the base 2 and represents, intuitively, the number of yes-no decisions required to determine uniquely the letter "v" from this set of possibilities.[4]

Real-world communication is far more complex than this. In the musical performance described above, information is processed continuously. The conductor speaks to the audience by selecting words from a large set of possible sounds that count in human oral discourse. The conductor lifts the baton, a gesture chosen from a smaller set of possibilities and clearly understood by the members of the orchestra. The music itself is a complex pattern of sounds systematically selected from a field of possible notes, tones, meter, and other defining elements of music. Once converted into electronic signals, the sounds are beamed up to the satellite and then down to the television receiver as so much electronic data or massive "bytes" of information. The electronically reconstructed performance is conveyed to the senses of the viewer and through the nerves to the brain, an organ capable of converting vast amounts of discrete information into meaningful experience. In each step an immense variety or a range of possibilities is reduced to a single settled instance: a word, nod, electrical impulse or signal, firing neuron, and meaningful aesthetic event. And in each case something is resolved. In Gregory Bateson's whimsical terminology, a "muddle" becomes a "tidy."[5] Information is processed, a message is sent, and communication takes place.

Variety

In a communication event the amount of information contained in a single message depends on the variety of the set of possibilities that were excluded in its selection. If the sheer number of possibilities or options is great, the probability of any particular one being chosen (assuming that they are all equally probable) is low and the ignorance or uncertainty of the waiting receiver is great. Thus,

---

4. As Gregory Bateson notes when explaining this point, a Chinese ideograph would have to exclude several thousand alternatives. Hence, a message in the Chinese language contains more information that English (*Steps to an Ecology of Mind* [New York: Ballantine Books, 1972], 402). Information is the measure of the variety of a system defined as the number of distinguishable elements or possible states it contains. If this is N, then the number of bits contained in N is the logarithm of N to the base 2. In other words, variety is measured in powers of two. Ten bits of information is the measure of the variety of a set of more than one thousand states.

5. Bateson, "Why Do Things Get in a Muddle?" in *Steps to an Ecology of Mind*, 3.

when an information-rich message is finally sent from a large set of potential messages, it arrives unexpectedly, since the chances of predicting the arrival of just this or that message diminish substantially in proportion to the size of the set of possibilities from which it was chosen.

Niklas Luhmann puts it nicely. "What we have in the case of communication," he says, "is not the transfer of things, but the allotment of surprise."[6] While surprise is the existential response of the recipient to the arrival of the unexpected, it may also be understood objectively as the reception (by any receiver, human or not) of a signal chosen from a large, unbiased ensemble.[7]

Variety, then, is a keystone concept in communication theory, and its quantitative measure is information. The greater the information content of a message, the greater the variety of the set of possibilities from which it was uniquely selected. If the variety of the set is small, the uncertainty of the receiver will also be small, and any message representing that set will be of little interest and information content. If the variety is larger, the opposite is true. W. Ross Ashby, one of the founders of the science of cybernetics and a pioneer in information theory, provides a useful example.[8] Two soldiers are taken prisoner. Their wives receive the same message: "I am well." But one wife knows that her husband is allowed to choose from three messages: (1) "I am well"; (2) "I am slightly ill"; (3) "I am seriously ill." The other wife knows that her husband has no choice at all. His only possibility is "I am well."

It is obvious from the story, Ashby concludes, that, while both wives received identical messages, the first wife is better informed about her husband's health than the second. The one begins with significant uncertainty, not knowing which of three messages she will receive. The resolution of this uncertainty is meaningful knowledge. She learns a great deal. The other knows exactly what she will hear, but is worse off for that since, ironically, her certainty of the message guarantees her ignorance of its meaning. She learns nothing at all. Much may be learned if the receiver understands that the message is one of a large number of potential messages that might have been sent but were not. The variety so important for the power of a single message is found at the source of the message, in the set

---

6. Niklas Luhmann, *Essays in Self-Reference* (New York: Columbia University Press, 1990), 85.

7. For further discussion, see the section on revelation in chapter 10.

8. W. Ross Ashby, *An Introduction to Cybernetics* (New York: John Wiley & Sons, 1961), 124.

of possible messages that were excluded by its transmission. The point of Ashby's parable is clear: without variety, communication has no power to impart information, that is, knowledge. While there may be no necessary connection between information contained in a message and the meaning or sense it conveys, variety is the foundation for the transmission of existentially meaningful knowledge. Meaningful discourse, that is, rich and meaningful communication, is enhanced dramatically by the increase of information.

THE PROCESS OF COMMUNICATION

Variety and Disorder

Shannon conducted research on the frequency of letters of the alphabet as they appeared in normal human communication. The English alphabet contains twenty-six letters. These, along with the obligatory space between words and sentences, and several grammatical signs (e.g., comma, period) constitute a set with a variety of about thirty separate units. If the probability of each transmitted signal is the same as that for every other signal, then the information content of a single transmission is slightly fewer than five bits. Of course, we know that some letters are privileged. In English, the frequency of *s* and *e* is much greater than that of *x* and *z*. Because of this bias toward or against elements in a set of possible signals, the receiver has a head start in anticipating the transmission of some messages. This bias, known as "constraint," will be discussed in detail below. Presently, however, our concern is with a set of possible messages exhibiting no redundancy or constraint, one that is in a state of complete randomness. In such cases, the receiver has no idea what letter will appear next in an extended message. It is as likely to be an *x* as an *s*. Any attempt to anticipate or predict the next letter would be tantamount to guessing, and any guess would be as good as any other. In such cases, the uncertainty of the receiver is as great as it possibly could be; quite literally, the receiver doesn't have a clue. Since the chance of the transmission of any element is both identical and minimal (in each case $\frac{1}{30}$, or .033), the entire set is said to be in a state of maximum disorder, where disorder is to be understood as the absence of pattern, tendency, structure, or the faithful and predictable repetition of signals.

The relationship between information (as a measure of variety) and the degree of disorder in a set of messages is a simple one. They are identical. Complete randomness in the set of alphabetic elements means that the freedom of choice of the source to send any particular letter is as great as it could be. Any message that is sent will thus realize the greatest amount of information. However, if constraint were total, only one letter would be sent repeatedly. The receiver would have no uncertainty. Indeed, the receiver would be able to predict with absolute confidence that each subsequent message in a series would be the same as the last one. But this situation would also place the receiver in the same predicament as the prisoner's wife in Ashby's story. There is nothing to be gained with such an extreme reduction in variety, or its complete elimination. A set consisting of single elements has no variety at all.

Strangely, it appears that disorder, the absence of constraint, is a good thing in a set of possible messages. There are fewer inherent limits on the transmitting agent to conform to some pattern or set of rules dictating an increased frequency for some messages. Freedom of choice is maximized when the set is in a pure state of randomness or total disorder.

The oddity of the connection between disorder and information leads to intuitive dissonance. Information is derived from "inform," which implies the imputation of form or determinate orderly structure to a system. But disorder suggests *dis*-formation, the opposite of form or system and a synonym for chaos. For the sake of reducing the dissonance, we should perhaps conceive of the set of messages as mere potential awaiting realization and communication as the act of actualization of some portion of that potential. The richer the possibilities and the fewer the constraints on the sender, the greater the potential for complexity and organization of the system, generated by a set of messages. Communication resulting from a source rich with possibility often gives rise to complex novel forms and unexpected arrangements. But communication resulting from a highly constrained or information-poor source potentiality gives rise to simple impoverished systems. Thus, it may be reasonable after all to see a positive association between disorder and information.

The Process of Communication: An Allegory

A story may bring this discussion down to earth. In 1501, in Florence, Italy, the great artist Michelangelo, chisel and mallet in hand, stands before a massive block of marble considering his many options. By his side, a friend observes the artist at work. Ignorant of the artist's intention, this observer is at a total loss in answering the questions "What will this block become? What will he make of it?" Michelangelo, however, has something specific in mind. He begins his work. Chips of marble pile deeply on the floor. The observer, returning frequently over the next couple of years to watch and learn, detects the emerging outlines of a human form. After three years, the artist completes his great creation, and the observer's patience is finally rewarded with a stunning sight of the magnificent *David,* a defining masterpiece of the Italian Renaissance.

Think of the uncarved block of marble as a set of possible messages, each representing one form or figure that could be shaped from the material. The possibilities, of course, are numberless, and, with reference to the block alone, each one has an equal probability of being realized. The information contained in this set of possibilities is maximal. The artist's friend, observing the block before a single chip had been removed, is completely uncertain about the final result. Ignorant of the intentions of the artist, the friend has nothing to go on and simply must wait expectantly. With Michelangelo's labors, patterns emerge, and the observer's uncertainty is progressively reduced by the introduction of constraint. The appearance of the human body limits the immense set of possibilities to a much smaller set by eliminating those that are not human bodies. Some predictions are now possible, although, even at this point in the emerging form, the number of persons in the world who could be depicted by the artist constitutes a very large remaining subset. Further specifications reveal more—the person is a male, a young male with a classic form and pose, and so on. And again, the range of possibilities grows smaller by a process of elimination. Eventually, the observer's ignorance, reduced chip by chip, vanishes altogether. Finally, only one possibility remains, the one that stands before the observer as *David.*[9]

In skeletal form we have the essential elements of a system of communication. The observer or receiver entering the artist's studio off the street is originally in a state of complete uncertainty. As a homogeneous mass of stone, the block itself is the totality of possible messages, immense and perhaps infinite in number. Michelangelo is the transmitting source, the one who selects from this rich set just those messages that will be sent. The sculpting itself represents the transmission of messages of ever greater specificity with the effects of removing the ignorance and the uncertainty of the observer. Each swing of the mallet could be interpreted as a yes-or-no decision by

---

9. Michelangelo apparently imputed forms to the uncarved block. The job of the artist is simply to unveil them from the stone. He says as much in this popular statement attributed to him: "There are in blocks of marble images that are sumptuous and essential, if only we have sufficient genius to liberate them."

the artist with respect to answering the question "Shall this part remain—yes or no?" and thus contains one bit of information. As great subsets of possible forms are eliminated, constraints are introduced that increase the receiver's confidence in deducing the artist's final intention.

From this instructive allegory—which actually is not an allegory, but a literal example of communication—it is clear that Shannon's theory, originally intended for highly technical applications in electronic networks, has a great range of application in a more intuitive or general and less technical approach. So its relevance to artistic creation is neither unique nor accidental. This example also serves as a preamble to subsequent chapters where our intention will be to employ the theory of communication in a similar way as a complex isomorphism to speak about and further understand theological matters by constructing a metaphysical version.

Constraint

In the Michelangelo story, each application of the chisel results in a further limitation of the limitless field of possibility inherent in the block of marble, making it that much easier for the observer to anticipate with increasing certainty what would come next. Earlier, we referred to this introduction of bias in the altered frequency in a set of messages as constraint or redundancy. Shannon and others, including Samuel Morse in his famous dot-dash code, observed empirically that English is not in a state of maximal informational disorder. In reading and writing, letters are never present in a proportion suggesting equal probability. In fact, anyone who is familiar with the language has great predictive power; it is called spelling. The letters *th* are often followed by the letter *e,* and an attentive reader of this book would likely recognize "Shanno" as "Shannon," even without the concluding *n.* This constraint or limitation of randomness in language, also described as the repeated appearance of some letters more often than others (redundancy), adds to the efficiency of the transmission and storage, even though it reduces the freedom of choice of the source and the sheer amount of potential information. In the precise terms given by Ashby, constraint exists when "the variety that exists under one condition is less than the variety that exists under another," and the "set is smaller than it might be."[10] The constraint can be intrinsic to the message set, as it is with natural language, or it may increase over a period of time

---

10. Ashby, *Introduction to Cybernetics,* 128.

in the development or construction of a complex object, as in the case of Michelangelo's *David*.

The disadvantages of constraint appear at the extremes of its employment. Excessive constraint reduces the power of the information source and results in repeated and trivial messages. We have seen this already in the parable of the prisoner's wives. Too little constraint, however, leads to sheer chaos, a condition of complete unpredictability, fine for the workings of a roulette wheel but not for life. Within any active system there exists a range of possibility between enslaving constraint and disastrous freedom wherein the yin of flexibility and the yang of enduring organization are compatible. The ideal is a "Goldilocks Principle," neither too much constraint nor too little.

A musical piece illustrates this balance. Most music consists of a pattern of notes, the melody, that remains consistent throughout the piece. A listener who has never heard the piece takes only a short while to catch the tune and anticipate notes with accuracy. The music has a structure that gives it identity and integrity. Yet, substantial variety is present as well. A performance of the symphonic work requires playing thousands of notes written specifically for perhaps dozens of instruments. The musicians and the conductor are not slavishly constrained by the notes on the page but may introduce countless subtle interpretations, making each performance of the piece by that orchestra unique.

Variety is built into the repeated series of notes, but the variety is not maximal or there would be no arrangement. On the one hand, total freedom or zero constraint would mean that any note would be as likely to be played as any other. Each musician would be free to choose a note at random in complete independence from the other members of the orchestra. Cacophony or noise would be the obvious consequence of such total autonomy. Consequently, each new note would come as a surprise, and the listener humming along would be out of the question. Some modern music seems like noise to many because the variety present there is greater than the variety found in classical music, and the mode of constraint is weak; there is less arrangement to the arrangement. On the other hand, if the constraint on the performers were great and only a single or at most a few notes were permitted, the piece would be trivial and boring, and for most listeners would also qualify as noise. Aesthetic accomplishment lies between the extremes of pure heterogeneity and pure homogeneity.

In musical composition and performance, constraint may originate in several ways. One of these occurs at the source. The composer creates the original work and subsequent performances must abide by the creator's established limits. The musical passage exhibits constraint determined by the composer and incumbent on anyone who would perform the piece in fidelity to the composer's intentions.

A second form of constraint arises in a posture of spontaneous attention, often found in the performance of jazz known as a "jam session." A gathering of several musicians may begin with a specific theme or a specific piece of music. Each member of the group then contributes unique variations, with the only rule being that any new notes must be consistent in harmony and balance with what has gone before. The musicians play off of one another extemporaneously, but not in complete independence. The constraint builds as precedents develop from the feedback processes of each musician in the dual roles of transmitter and receiver, performer and appreciator. A complex order evolves over time as each note becomes more predictable based on its predecessors. Jazz improvisation is thus a self-organizing system. The final constrained arrangement arises from the communication between the several performers as they respond to one another and settle eventually into a determinate pattern of musical values variously nuanced. Each musician contributes uniquely to the final result, but also must abide by the direction or tendencies established by the others and by the structure of music itself, including its established foundational elements and its inherent possibilities. Successive notes are selected by reference to what has gone before and contribute to what will come, in a kind of communication karma. Even incidental mistakes may be woven into the creative fabric of the performance itself so as to vanish. The emergent complex arrangement of a jam session is the product of this process of negotiation.

The first of these two sources of constraint is ahistorical. The musical score is given, complete, and fixed from the mind of its creator, the composer, by fiat. The second source is a dynamic process of development involving what we shall call later "open systems," coupled with feedback, and is historical in character.

ENTROPY

The Faces of Entropy

As previously discussed, information has a considerable amount to do with disorder. Shannon's theory requires that the amount of information in a set of possible messages reaches a maximum when all the messages are independent. The probability that any one of them will be sent is identical with that of any other. Since the receiver has no means of predicting which message will be sent and which others will follow, uncertainty has reached its maximum as well. Messages are intended to resolve something, to bring about a settled state of affairs from one that consisted only of potential, in other words, to bring order out of disorder. Yet, it appears that the greatest state of disorder is precisely the one that can be employed to originate, elaborate, and sustain order through processes of communication.

Shannon decided on the label *entropy* as the measure of the disorder of a set of messages. Entropy increases as the probability that a particular message will be sent decreases, that is, as the probabilities even out. Simply put, entropy is a measure of what a person receiving a message does not know about it before it arrives.[11] In terms of Shannon's mathematical model, the entropy of information systems closely resembles the entropy of thermodynamic systems. In the interest of developing this model further, some discussion of this thermodynamic version of entropy is helpful.

Increasing entropy in a system can be thought of as the approach of that system to equilibrium, a final state of complete disorder where no further meaningful change can occur. By "meaningful" we mean that the system can do no more work. Systems with increasing entropy run down as they consume and degrade their finite store of available energy and eventually fall apart. The second law of thermodynamics, one of the most fundamental and well-established in all laws of science, dictates that the entropy of an isolated system (one with no outside source of energy) is bound to increase over time.

This increase can be understood in two ways. It can mean that the system consumes complex chemical sources of energy with the production of heat along the way. The heat dissipates, never to be recovered for additional use. Indeed, efforts to recover and reconstruct depleted sources of energy would cost more that any benefits they provide. The irreversible conversion of complex energy sources into heat tends to bring the temperature of the system to a state of equilibrium where any place in the system has on average the same

---

11. Jeremy Campbell, *Grammatical Man: Information, Entropy, Language, and Life* (New York: Simon and Schuster, 1982), 103. *Grammatical Man* is a clear and readable introduction to Shannon's ideas and to the applications of communication theory in science and society.

temperature as any other part. Now, work is possible only when a temperature gradient or difference exists between places in a system so that heat can flow from the hotter place to the colder on doing useful work along the way. But this results in a leveling out of the temperature in both places, eventually reaching equilibrium, where no further work can occur. This is why the mythic perpetual motion machine does not exist. The second law is inviolable.

An alternative way to understand increasing entropy is with reference to the ever decreasing order of the components of a system.[12] A pack of playing cards is a system. The order of the deck is at its maximum when the cards are arranged in terms of the four suits and within each suit in terms of the numbered sequences plus the jack, queen, king, and ace. The constraint in the system is complete. As the deck is dealt, anyone familiar with cards can predict the next card or any subsequent card by simply examining the previous one. Since the information communicated by any single card is predictable and trivial, very few interesting games proceed from a sorted deck. Shuffling destroys the order of the deck by increasing the randomness of the whole system. After a single shuffle, that order is disturbed but not yet completely destroyed; it is still possible to predict with some degree of confidence, perhaps half of the time, the identity of the next card dealt. Further shuffling increases the disorder and the uncertainty of anyone's predictions, until finally the random distribution is so great that further shuffling will make little additional difference. The chances of any one card being dealt are identical to those of any other. In other words, the entropy of the system is maximal because the deck is a homogeneous distribution of microstates (the cards). All conspicuous order has been destroyed. Of course, it is possible to undo the effects of shuffling by consciously sorting the deck card by card until it returns to its original configuration. But this requires information processing, the equivalent of doing work in thermodynamics.

The second law stipulates that all systems tend toward increasing states of entropy over time. This is because we inhabit a universe of constant motion and change, the equivalent of shuffling cards. Indeed, time itself can be understood to proceed in one direction (the so-called arrow of time) because systems subject to processes analogous to shuffling will always move from a state of order to a state

---

12. The originator of this perspective of statistical thermodynamics is Ludwig Botzmann, the nineteenth-century physicist and mathematician. See Campbell, *Grammatical Man*, ch. 2.

of disorder. Of course, it is possible that in the process of shuffling a deck of cards, the infinitesimally small chance could be realized that the deck actually returns to its original ordered state. This state is just as likely, in terms of statistical probabilities, as the appearance of any one of many possible arrangements in the equilibrium. But orderly arrangements of the deck (those arrangements that are capable of being described by an algorithm) are a relatively small number of the set of all possible arrangements. The proportion of this set consisting of disordered states is much, much larger. Thus, it is highly unlikely that time would reverse with the reappearance of the original order of the entire pack.

Other illustrations of entropy and work taken from everyday situations are readily available. A lovely ice statue is striking as it sits atop a buffet table at the beginning of a dinner banquet. As the evening proceeds, the ice melts and the form vanishes, dissolved into water collected in a large puddle at the statue's base. The ice statue represents high order, easily identified and appreciated by the guests. The puddle is its fate after the molecules of water changed from their complex frozen state and merged together as a simple and uniform fluid. The heat in the room is passed on to the molecules of frozen water, increasing their energy and shuffling the system from an ordered state to one of the random distribution. While it seems preposterous to suggest that the water on its own could spontaneously form an ice statue, the statistical account of entropy does not rule out this possibility entirely. But it does claim that the probability that this highly organized state would occur over the countless equally possible states of random distribution of molecules is so low as to be virtually vanishing. Its occurrence would be understood as the miraculous reversal of time's arrow, perhaps the thermodynamic equivalent of turning water into wine.[13]

A final example is taken from our everyday experience of energy consumption. The gasoline in the tank of an automobile is a

---

13. Wesley Salmon offers an interesting account of statistical irreversibility: "There is a small but nonvanishing chance that an ice cube will form spontaneously in a thermos of cool water. Such an occurrence would be the result of a chance clustering of relatively nonenergetic molecules in a particular place in the container. There is a much greater chance that an ice cube will be present in the thermos of cool water to which an ice cube has just been added. Even if we had no independent knowledge about the ice cube having been added, we would confidently infer it from the mere presence of the ice cube. The low entropy state is explained by a previous interaction with the outside world, including a refrigerator that manufactures ice cubes" ("Statistical Relevance," in *The Nature and Function of Scientific Theories,* ed. Robert G. Colodny [Pittsburgh: University of Pittsburgh Press, 1970], 258).

complex chemical mixture of high order molecules. The burning of the fuel in a combustion engine is the explosive breaking down and shuffling of these molecules accompanied by a violent release of energy. Some of this energy, a small portion, actually, does work and propels the vehicle. The resulting products, the exhaust emissions, are the simplified residues of the process. In a world without the second law, these degraded fumes could conceivably be returned to the engine through a hose attached to the exhaust pipe to do further work by somehow reassembling themselves along the way. But that absurd arrangement would be a perpetual motion machine, the equivalent of a card deck recovering its original order through constant shuffling alone, or a puddle of water arising spontaneously to create an ice statue.

The Decline of Order

An intimate connection exists between entropy and information. Donald MacKay associates the two ideas in his definition of entropy as that "which measures the amount of information needed in order to specify precisely how the total energy is distributed throughout the system in question. The higher the entropy, the more 'scrambled' is the distribution of energy, and the more questions remain to be answered."[14] Unanswered questions mean great uncertainty, and uncertainty is removed by information. With this in mind, MacKay describes the second law of thermodynamics as "the amount of information (number of bits) required to specify the precise microstates of an isolated system increases to a maximum as time goes on."[15]

Increasing entropy in a deck of cards through repeated shuffling means that the five of hearts may no longer follow the four and precede the six. To locate this particular card, then, requires dealing the deck, one card upon another, until the five of hearts is come upon. In that puddle, all that remains of a highly ordered ice statue after it melts are the original molecules of water aimlessly distributed. Finally, the complex hydrocarbon molecules of gasoline are broken down into simpler ingredients by combustion. No longer is it possible to claim that the atoms of hydrogen, oxygen, and carbon are located in complex organic molecules. Cards are shuffled, ice melts, gasoline is burned. The microstates of the components involved in these processes become increasingly randomized. Thus,

14. Donald M. MacKay, *Science, Chance and Providence* (Oxford: Oxford University Press, 1978), 36.
    15. Ibid., 37.

the uncertainty of an observer can only grow with each passing moment.

However one describes it, progressive entropic degradation is the fate of all material systems. There is no exception to the universal truth that all things are born and perish. Even the universe itself, if it is a closed system, will eventually run down and dissolve into a uniform equilibrium state. Entropy is a concept of transcendental proportions and appears in the intuitive notions and myths of numerous religions. In Buddhism, entropy is evidence that all things are in the inescapable clutch of *anicca* or "impermanence." Hinduism assigns the task to the god of destruction, Shiva, whose dance thunders through the Himalayas. The bleak Norse epic the *Edda* depicts the gods warring incessantly in the hastening darkness of the world.

But there is another side of the issue. The logic of the second law dictates that some original order must be present if decay into disorder is to occur. New card decks are sorted. Ice statues begin with lovely forms. Prior to combustion, the chemistry of fossil fuel is complex. The order we see in the world is generated and sustained by the input of ordering agencies or the operation of selection mechanisms, as in, for example, evolution. These agencies and mechanisms are communication systems. When coupled by feedback with other systems, they provide the wherewithal for the emergence of organization, for the movement of a system further from equilibrium and toward increasing order. The second law is not violated. It continues to operate through the expenditure of information and energy in the construction of this order and the subsequent degradation and death of all creaturely systems. But the result is a gradient of information, an organization of considerable complexity, that stands out in the field of uniform entropic processes.

SYSTEM

The Systems Approach

The connection between communication or information theory and the notion of *system* is simple: the act of communication often leads to an increase in organization at the receiver's end, or a bunch of independent elements enter into some larger association because of the communication that occurs between them. Constraint is introduced in the patterns of exchange of information and the result is greater arrangement. An organized entity is a system, roughly defined as an enduring whole consisting of its components and the relationships between them. System is thus a synonym of order and an antonym of chaos.

"System" is also an obnoxious term. In popular speech and culture it often represents unilateral authority and control, "the system," and invites hostile declarations of autonomy from those under its alien influence in efforts to "beat the system." Generally, system is associated with the aims of some technocratic elite to engineer and manage society through the development of massive and efficient organization. Despite this reputation, the term is as ambiguous as it is vague in its application. There are state systems, social systems, institutional systems of every description, as well as mechanical systems, weapons systems, weather systems, electronic systems, biological systems, philosophical and theological systems ("systematic theology"), and information systems.

These numerous associations suggest that the concept of system is either trivial and innocuous or universal and profound. Its visionary proponents, preferring the second of these characterizations, claim that the ubiquity of the concept means that systems are everywhere. They prophesy that a concerted attempt to understand the structure and dynamics of systems in general would lead to a breakthrough in our understanding of the world paramount to a paradigm shift in science. By seeking out and investigating the common attributes of all natural and social systems, their isomorphic structures, the once seamless garment of human knowledge, currently fragmented into compartments of disciplinary specialization, could be reknit. The elaboration of the structure and dynamics of systems in general is known as "general systems theory," a field-encompassing field of inquiry, a discipline to embrace all disciplines and an intellectual supersystem in its own right.[16]

Systems theory is an "approach" or "program," a generalized framework of explanation. The "synoptic holism" promoted in systems thought is diametrically opposed to reductionistic approaches

---

16. See Ervin Laszlo, *Introduction to Systems Philosophy* (New York: Gordon and Beach Science Publishers, 1972); idem, *The Systems View of the World: The Natural Philosophy of the New Developments in the Sciences* (New York: George Braziller, 1972); Ludwig von Bertalanffy, *General System Theory: Foundations, Development, Applications* (New York: George Braziller, 1968); Joel de Rosnay, *The Macroscope: A New World Scientific System* (New York: Harper & Row, 1975); Fritjof Capra, *The Web of Life: A New Scientific Understanding of Living Systems* (New York: Anchor Books, 1996). See also James E. Huchingson, "Quo Vadis, Systems Theory?" *Zygon: Journal of Religion and Science* 20, no. 4 (1985): 435–44.

that dominate the special sciences. Reductionist models often universalize an exclusive kind of order or organization—for example, in mechanism—and claim that it is the only true order to which all other kinds of order must conform or be "reduced" for validation. This instance of intellectual imperialism sunders the essential diversity in unity that characterizes the world by refusing to take seriously the vast range of diverse systems in nature and society.

The systems approach looks for the most general features or isomorphies exhibited by any system. Machines are systems. So are organisms. It is not necessary to reduce organisms to machines in order to understand them. Both classes of systems are situated on a spectrum of systems complexity. They share common features ("invariances") that are specified in novel and unique ways depending on the system under investigation. Reduction is fruitful within limits for the same reason that metaphors are fruitful. Each approach discloses underlying similarities of structure and action that characterize the classes of systems being compared. Mechanism errs in claiming that these features count only if they are described with the specificity appropriate for mechanical systems alone.

Ecosystems, for example, are sometimes spoken of in terms of both organic and mechanical metaphors. Each of these, while fruitful and revealing, carries excessive suggestive power. An ecosystem is literally neither a machine nor an organism. Yet, machines and organisms, as well as ecosystems, are literally systems. The isomorphic structures or invariances displayed in common by all three kinds of systems are what permit them to resemble one another in the first place. Proponents of the systems approach advocate the use of a language that reveals and relates these systems through the articulation of inclusive isomorphies as opposed to collapsing unilaterally one specific class of system into another with resulting distortion and equivocation.

Systems theorists are interested in the constitutive wholeness, the inherent integrity of systems. The material stuff of the system is decidedly secondary to the interests of investigators. They do not ask, "What is it made of?" but rather, "How is it arranged?"[17] In simple, even trivial, terms, a system may be defined as a bounded arrangement or whole consisting of parts or components and the relationships between them. Indeed, the "whole" is nothing more than the integration of the parts through their relationships. But

---

17. See Laszlo, *Systems View of the World,* for an excellent discussion of the nature of systems.

this does not mean that the whole is nothing in itself, an illusion or a gestalt perspective originating and existing only in the eye of the beholder.[18] The obligatory cliché, "the whole is greater than the sum of its parts," carries the basic truth that the parts of a system are knit together by the interaction between them and give rise to a being of greater complexity. In the absence of these interactions the "system" becomes a simple swarm, mob, or heap with minimal association between units. In such absolutely primitive systems, the only way to speak of wholeness is through summation or an arithmetic tally of the sheer number of elements or the arbitrary physical forms that emerge when the components are simply heaped together. Piles of sand have little intrinsic unity.

Systems are not necessary physical and static. A language is a system, as is a piece of music. The elements of each, letters or notes, are arranged in specific patterns with assigned frequencies. The patterns emerging within language and music are the wholeness that gives the organized units an overall structure. Linguistic and musical systems are also dynamic. They change and evolve within larger environments and persist actively as patterns of expression.

Complexity

A fundamental characteristic of any system is its complexity. A system's complexity is defined by the variety of elements, their number, and the richness of the connections that bind them together as a system. Take away the complexity, and only the disconnected parts remain. A system is simple or merely complicated if it can be described by merely tallying its constituents and perhaps mapping their location. A system is complex, however, if it can only be understood by including the mutually defining associations between its parts or between the system and the larger environment.[19] A simple system, even with a great number of indistinguishable parts, is little more than a heap. A complex system is a whole. Organization is everything.

---

18. Some simple systems are, in fact, observer dependent. Radio towers miles apart have lights to warn approaching aircraft. One flashes every two seconds, the other every five. Someone who is in a position to observe both towers would notice that the lights flash simultaneously every ten seconds. Otherwise, they are out of sync. This periodic phenomenon is a purely formal relationship having nothing to do with any prior arrangement between engineers when they constructed the towers. Nor is there is any mutually qualifying communication between the two towers that is crucial to complex natural systems. Yet, even this constitutes a system that can be mathematically expressed.

19. Paul Cilliers, *Complexity and Postmodernism: Understanding Complex Systems* (New York: Routledge, 1998), vii.

Complexity, or the degree of internal organization, may be very simple or highly involved. For example, a rain cloud is a simple system. The cloud consists mostly of mist in the form of minute water droplets. Several forces, including wind, temperature, atmospheric conditions, and electrical fields, bind the countless droplets together and give rise to an appreciable level of complexity. But this complexity pales beside that of a living cell, which is an extremely complex system. While the variety of the cell's components far exceeds that of the cloud, the cell's complexity is truly determined by the profound degree of organization or richness of connection between these parts. The totality and the intensity of these arrangements give rise to an emergent quality not to be found in the cloud—the quality of life. Life is a function of complexity, a fact recognized by the theologian and paleontologist Teilhard de Chardin, who said that biology is the physics of immense complexity.[20]

The complexity or level of organization within a system depends substantially on the communication between parts. In the simple system of a rain cloud, the components are very loosely connected. The droplets behave in partial independence of one another, meaning that few mutually conditioning relationships exist between them. Anarchy prevails as the great masses of particles rapidly assume numerous states relative to each other in short periods of time. Conditions are far different within the living cell. The molecules, chemicals, and organelles of the cell behave in mutually restrictive ways that taken together constitute the metabolism of the cell. This level of organization would not be possible without exchanges of information between the various subsystems. These exchanges have the purpose of introducing constraint between parts so that each will be radically limited in the number and type of states it can assume in that environment. The anarchy or range of independent action by the parts in the whole that is so appropriate in a roiling thunderhead would be fatal for a living organism. Organization is a condition of restriction or constraint that gives rise to greater overall integrity and stability, that is, wholeness, in the system.

Self-Organizing Systems

The organization of relatively simple artificial or mechanical systems—for example, an automobile engine—is imposed from the outside by conscious intention as a premeditated act. The con-

---

20. Pierre Teilhard de Chardin, *The Phenomenon of Man*, trans. Bernard Wall (New York: Harper Torchbooks, 1959), 150.

nections between parts are built-in from the beginning in the engineering process. The engineer becomes the communicator with respect to the engine in the same sense that Michelangelo communicated his mental image of David to the block of marble. The final arrangement of mechanical components or subsystems is the settled and uniquely determined product of many decisions. The arrangements between the parts arose from the imposition of an external act of communication. The parts themselves have no say in the matter.

Very complex and dynamic systems, including living systems and the programs of electronic systems such as high-speed computers, are capable of self-organization.[21] Here the system starts as an initial set of possibilities that narrow over time in response to constraints imposed by both internal and external environments. Rich connections grow as components are joined in very specific and highly differentiated or specialized ways. The result is a system of impressive complexity and emergent wholeness. Unlike the automobile engine, the elements of an evolving system, a natural system, do have some say in the matter in the sense that they participate in the mutually conditioning act of reciprocal adjustment. This reciprocity or dialogue of subsystems that gives rise to greater richness of connection is communication, but with feedback. The final result is a number of systems tightly knit through links that collectively define them.

Coupled Systems and Evolution

Self-organizing systems are found throughout nature. An important dynamic process of biological evolution is symbiosis, the coupling of distinct species for their mutual advantage that carries with it profound modifications of the very essence or nature of each partner. One case in point is that for over one hundred million years, bees and blossoms have had a perfectly workable symbiotic relationship of major importance. Given the evolutionary model, we could imagine that once upon a time the ancestor of the bee struck

---

21. Self-organization resembles the classical Greek notion of *physis*. Aristotle drew a sharp distinction between *techne* and *physis*. *Techne* is the act of creating a product or forming it from without. The realm of *physis* is that of natural things having their being by virtue of self-contained energies and urges. The phenomenon of self-organizing systems is currently referred to as *autopoiesis* in cybernetics and systems theory. Do artificial self-organizing systems (e.g., intelligent or learning systems) smear the boundary between *techne* and *physis*? For theological implications of *autopoiesis*, see Niels Henrik Gregersen, "The Idea of Creation and the Theory of Autopoietic Processes," *Zygon: Journal of Religion and Science* 33, no. 3 (1998): 333–67.

up a relationship with the ancestor of the flower, probably quite by accident. The selective advantages provided by this early critical encounter tilted the development of both species in the direction of increasing specialization. Over many generations the bee developed organs (a proboscis, sensitive eyes, a homing instinct, a taste for nectar, and a social structure or hive) so as to exploit the bounty of the blossom. The flowering plant, in turn, accommodated the bee with attractive and colorful displays and nectar, and also created its own organs to take advantage of the bee's attention (sexual organs, disposable genetic material or pollen). One can imagine that this delicate process of coevolution continues today at the exceedingly slow and invisible pace that characterizes such processes in nature.

Clearly, continuous communication is occurring, even in this simple account. In its prototypical form, each party represented a set of possibilities for evolutionary development awaiting some focus or restriction experienced as messages that would limit this set to some smaller subset of possibilities. The mutual engagement provided these transmissions from the insect to the plant and the plant to the insect. The final consequence is two highly differentiated forms that are inextricably interdependent. Each member of the duet has "heard" the other and adjusted accordingly within the additional limiting conditions of environmental circumstance. Evolution displays a direction in part through this self-enhancing dynamic of cooperation that produces progressive differentiation. Growing constraint in mutually evolving species is just another way of saying that evolution builds on its successes.

The bee and the flowering plant constitute a coupled system with feedback from two very different kingdoms of life. The bonds linking the destinies of both species are so powerful and determinative that we may speak, as Ervin Laszlo suggests, not of the separate existence of each partner along with a set of relationships, but of their rich "interexistence" within that set.[22] The relationships are the whole of which the bee and flowering plant are highly integrated contributing components.

Most coupled species systems are not so congenial or obviously beneficial to the participants as the win-win arrangement of the bee and blossom. The prey-predator system is at least as prevalent. Still, the general model of systems in communication mutually conditioning the future evolution of each species explains the lion and the gazelle, fox and rabbit, and hawk and prairie dog as well as

---

22. See Laszlo, *Systems View of the World*, ch. 2, "The Systems View of Nature."

the bee and blossom. Entire ecosystems consist of communities of species that have adapted to conditions that they have imposed on one another. "Ecosystem" is a label identifying some recognizable and bounded whole consisting of this comprehensive integration.

The Edge of Chaos

Immensely complex biological communities exhibit dynamic properties that no pile of sand or simple homogeneous system could ever possess, including spontaneous self-organization and adaptive behavior. By standing back from the particular arrangements in the living world, we are better able to grasp the overall process, the big picture, of evolution itself. Hans Küng calls upon Rupert Riedl, who follows Nobel laureate Manfred Eigen as an expert witness for his contention that freedom and necessity coemerge in evolution on this global scale:

> Only by thinking in systems can we see the strategy of genesis. Gigantic systems of hierarchically organized internal and external causes interact on one other. In all this *genesis* operates with the supremely ambivalent antagonism between necessary contingency and contingent necessity. Through all its strata it preserves what begins as chance, as indetermination, but ends as creativity, as freedom. And there is continually a growth of what emerges as necessity, as determination, but ends as law and order, as a sense of direction, as the meaning of possible evolution.[23]

By following Riedl's policy of "thinking in systems," we can see how complex organization arises in life through the operation of accident and opportunity. No creatures are destined to establish particular links. Those structures arise out of the mutual advantages provided by the give and take of communication established during original accidental encounters. These arrangements, initiated in purely contingent fashion, solidify and bring constraint to the prior set of possibilities. The contingency is necessary in that without it no opportunities would arise. And the necessity—the constraint introduced by the enduring relationships—is contingent in that it is in consequence of that initial spontaneous association. From chance comes opportunity. From opportunity comes structured association.

---

23. Rupert Riedl, *Die Strategie der Genesis: Naturgeschichte der realen Welt* (Munich and Zurich: Piper, 1976); quoted in Hans Küng, *Does God Exist? An Answer for Today*, trans. Edward Quinn (Garden City, N.Y.: Doubleday, 1980), 645.

And from structured association comes ordered complexity and further, heightened potential. Riedl's "strategy of genesis" in evolution is the communicative process by which a range of possible states ("necessary contingency") found in any one moment is reduced to just one state ("contingent necessity") in a subsequent moment through the process of specification or selection.

The narrowing of potential in this evolutionary act of communication should not be seen as impoverishment. Actually, the constraint generates profligate diversity. The initial association between the first bee and the first blossom provided the prototypical potential for what we now have—countless instances of symbiotic interexistence linking insects with flowering plants. One has only to climb to the tree line in the high Rockies in August and walk by a descending stream lined with a riot of flowers of every shape and color—a linear bouquet—or perceive the exquisite specificity with which species of orchids irresistibly attract preferred insects to appreciate the "creativity and freedom" made possible by this single strategy of symbiotic transaction. Nature establishes a theme, as in music, and allows all manner of spontaneous variations to play out in its performance.

There is a price to pay for this beauty and creativity. Complex natural systems reside dangerously on "the edge of chaos," hovering in a surge zone of Riedl's "supremely ambivalent antagonism" between the chaos of contingency and the established order of necessity. On this edge, living systems find the power to employ the chaos as opportunity for beneficial associations resulting in the co-evolution of further complexity. Some of these situations are highly critical in that they rely on unpredictable triggering events that unleash sudden movement either toward catastrophe or further self-organization. Mitchell Waldrop succinctly sums this new vision of complexity: "The edge of chaos is the constantly shifting battle zone between stagnation and anarchy, the one place where a complex system can be spontaneous, adaptive, and alive."[24]

This "edge of chaos" between chaos and order resembles the surge zone or dynamic interface between the turbulent sea and the stable land. It is a place where special requirements are expected for species that share both realms and where rock and shell are ground into sand. Paul Tillich was fond of expressing his special affinity

---

24. Mitchell Waldrop, *Complexity: The Emerging Science at the Edge of Order and Chaos* (New York: Simon and Schuster, 1992), 12. See also Stuart Kaufman, *At Home in the Universe: The Search for Laws of Self-Organization and Complexity* (New York: Oxford University Press, 1995).

for the seashore.[25] There he felt the power and immensity of the ocean as it met the massive substance of the land. The encounter represented for him both power and being, two important concepts in his metaphysical theology. Complexity is the state between order and chaos where power and being combine to give rise to systems that, as Waldrop says, are "spontaneous, adaptive, and alive," and, we should add, as Riedl does, "creative and free."

Feedback

The most interesting systems are responsive systems, that is, those that take action to blunt or amplify changes in their environment. "Cybernetics," the study of such systems, is the term coined by Norbert Wiener for "the science of regulation and control." He derived the term from the Greek *kybernetes,* "steersman," indicating that a responsive system, like a pilot maneuvering a ship through treacherous waters, guides itself through environmental circumstance toward the most favorable outcome. Systems with cybernetic capabilities are teleological. They have a purpose to sustain themselves in a stable way and even to pursue goals. That they do these things is no mystery. No internal or conscious intention need be imputed to a cybernetic system. Its adjustments may be the product of programmed responses to anticipated environmental conditions. This happens with automated rovers on the surface of Mars as well as with a pronghorn antelope grazing in a high meadow. Intention or true purpose enters in with anticipatory consciousness or foresight, a capacity most evident in but not exclusive to *Homo sapiens.* But even in our own species, teleological envisioning of future situations serves the same purpose, to allow humans to take action that will realize the most favorable outcomes.

Cybernetics includes the study of two fundamental kinds of regulation and control: homeostasis, or negative feedback; and heterostasis, or positive feedback. *Homeostasis* is action taken to dampen or cancel a disturbance or a deviation from a preferred or normative state in order to maintain stability. In the language of cybernetics, some part of the output of the system is fed back as input to modify subsequent output in order to maintain a preferred state. The home thermostat is coupled with the furnace to sense the temperature of a room and convey instructions that will either turn the furnace on or off, thereby maintaining room temperature about

25. See Paul Tillich, *My Search for Absolutes* (New York: Simon and Schuster, 1967).

a norm determined by the setting of the thermostat. The thermostat is set, say at seventy-two degrees, for this purpose. The setting
is the norm, and the coupled system maintains the room temperature about the norm. A similar process is found in the human
body, whose internal thermostat is set around 98.6 degrees. If the
body's temperature threatens to drop below this assigned value,
certain instinctive reactions are triggered, including shivering and
the movement of the blood to the inner core for the protection of
vital organs. If the body overheats, perspiration removes some heat
through evaporation. Thirst urges the body to replace fluids lost to
evaporation, and common sense, also a feedback process, leads it
to seek shade. Of course, the mind plays an important role in these
adjustments; we don heavier clothing in cold weather and remove
it in warm weather, close and open windows, and even reset ther-
mostats! Large numbers of regulatory processes sustain the human
body in a continuing state of internal balance referred to as health
or well-being.

Homeostasis often involves a dynamic and continuous process of
adjustment. Balancing a broomstick in the palm of the hand is an
entertaining challenge for children. The hand and eye are coupled
so that any movement of the stick in this delicate system triggers a
movement of the hand in the same direction to dampen or correct
the tilt. Success means that the stick remains more or less vertical
but always in a teeter-totter motion around this normative state.
Gimbaled nozzles of ascending rockets pivot back and forth on the
commands of sensitive gyroscopes redirecting the thrust of the engines to keep the missile on course in exactly the same way. The aim
of negative feedback, then, is toward moderation of the extremes
through a process of compensation to neutralize movement away
from a preferred state of dynamic equilibrium.

Instances of homeostasis frequently involve coupled systems in
communication—for example, the prey-predator relationship. The
population of a predator, a pride of lions, is kept in check by the
population of its prey, a herd of gazelle. The lions, in turn, regulate
the gazelles. Populations of both species vary around optimum numbers. The regulatory device is simple. If the lion population reaches
such numbers that the population of gazelles is diminished below
the numbers needed to support the lions, a die-back in the lion population will occur. This event will allow the gazelles to recover their
lost numbers to a point of flourishing. Once again, the lions respond
to the renewed abundance of food, reproduce in greater numbers,
and consequently raise the mortality rate for gazelles. This process

returns the savanna system, the habitat of both species, to its original balance in preparation for another cycle or boom and bust.[26]

The second form of feedback, *heterostasis,* acts always to amplify, not cancel, deviation, resulting in some variable being accelerated to runaway proportions. If the wires in the thermostat are accidentally crossed, electrical messages sent to the furnace will be reversed. The furnace is turned on and stays on as the thermostat registers increasing temperature in the room; or as the temperature falls, the furnace remains off and the room becomes ever colder. Bad economic news triggers a selling spree in the stock market. Stockholders react and begin to sell in great numbers. The resulting panic feeds upon itself, generating more selling. The market ends up in a state of "free fall."[27] A third example: One nation is alarmed that its neighbor is apparently taking up arms, and begins to arm itself. The second nation takes notice and increases the pace of its own military preparations for defensive purposes. The first nation perceives this as confirming its initial assessment that its neighbor does indeed have aggressive intentions. Both nations mass armies on their common border. The initial perception, right or wrong, has escalated to runaway proportions, to an arms race and the real possibility of war.

Amplifying deviation through a triggering disturbance is the cybernetics of the barroom brawl, and in many instances results in acceleration to destruction or exhaustion. In other cases, however, heterostatic loops, far from being destructive, dramatically increase a system's organization. In research that won him the Nobel Prize, Ilya Prigogine discovered that escalation can move a system to a state far from equilibrium, like the vertical broom teetering in the hand of the child. The system is so delicately balanced that tiny fluctuations can trigger reinforcing changes that spontaneously transport the system to a higher state of complexity.

SYSTEMS, OPEN AND CLOSED

Only open systems display cybernetic behavior. *Open systems* are capable of importing or exporting material and information, of

---

26. De Rosnay, *Macroscope,* 9–12.

27. Stock markets are driven to wildly gyrating highs and lows by the reinforcement of trends in computer selling and buying and through opportunistic traders who monitor stocks closely and respond immediately. The same phenomenon, known as "pilot-induced oscillation," occurs in high-performance aircraft. The pilot will overcorrect the pitching up or down of the nose of the aircraft, amplifying the maneuver, resulting in rapid loss of control.

relating to their environment, or of coupling with other systems as message sources and receivers. *Closed systems,* however, lack such capabilities. They have sealed, impenetrable boundaries. Living things, including lions and gazelles, are open systems of great complexity. Classical machines, like spring-wound clocks, are relatively closed systems with little complexity.

It seems that there can be no totally open or closed systems. A completely open system would be influenced by all environmental forces and disturbances. Being open without reservation, it would have no way to counter or resist these disturbances. A radically open system would lack integrity or "otherness" and would simply melt into its environment and vanish. A completely closed system would be unresponsive to any environmental stimulus. Like the impassive Unmoved Mover of classical theology, nothing would make any difference to it. In a sense, the system would be invincible and perhaps immortal, not subject to the forces of corruption and change, but only at the great cost of sacrificing all vital engagement with the world.

Systems sometimes share a common goal of maintaining their identity despite challenges by relying on protective strategies consistent with their character as open or closed. A fencer defends against an opponent by deftly parrying (literally "foiling") the opponent's repeated thrusts. The medieval mounted knight, encased in armor and mail, accomplishes the same goal through passive shielding without resorting to active interdiction.

Neither negative nor positive feedback is possible outside the process of communication. Feedback is perhaps the most practical of all communication processes since its goal is to reduce uncertainty in order to respond most adequately to internal and external change for the sake of continued or enhanced well-being. Communication with feedback is far more complex than simple transmission in a single direction. In coupled systems, communication occurs in both directions, and often each party undergoes change as a result. The transmitter is itself altered by the rebounding consequences of its own signals in the form of other signals transmitted by a receiver, also in response. This ongoing dialogue alters the probabilities of the message for all engaged parties by modifying constraint—that is, the likelihood that one message will be sent over another. Both the constraint in a set of messages and the selection of any particular message or signal depend upon the specific signals received in response to some previous message or signal. From these exchanges patterns of precedent arise. Uncertainty diminishes (recall the earlier account of improvisation by a jazz ensemble). If all uncertainty were permanently removed from the environment, no further feedback would be necessary. Given the continuous flux of events in all circumstances of life, this final state is hardly imaginable.

Natural systems, then, are born and sustained by communication processes. Their very integrity, wholeness, and wellness both as individuals and as members of greater associative arrangements are orderly and timely responses to their environment. These responses are in consequence of a continuous flow of information that provides the basic stuff and substance for the construction and the maintenance of organization—the essence of life.

CONCLUSION

Information, variety, constraint, entropy, open and closed system, feedback—these are concepts enmeshed in a larger framework of associations that may be applied to a vast range of natural and social phenomena. To this extent, the perspective borders on ontology and, in its absolute generality, on metaphysics. This primer of select important elements of communication and systems theories gives us the perspective and vocabulary for developing theological themes throughout the remainder of this study, beginning in the next chapter with the primordial chaos of the Genesis account.

– 5 –

The Pandemonium Tremendum

◪ Now that the philosophical suppositions have been laid out and the conceptual apparatus presented, it is time to turn to theological construction. The first implications will be about the classical concept of chaos, the turbulent source of confusion and destruction brooding darkly in the pre-dawn of the creation and remaining today insidiously embedded in all mortal conditions. This classical description of chaos as an unholy mess is by no means the whole story. After justifying how chaos can be the object of thoughts and words, we will describe its place in the Genesis account and suggest that it is more central than much of the theological tradition suspects.

CAPTURING THE ELUSIVE CHAOS

Chaos beyond and within Creation

The first premise of philosophical theology is God, the second, being, and the third, chaos. No one would argue our first two choices in this list (although some would reverse the ranking), but the third requires considerable justification, which will be provided in the next several chapters. The initial task is to explore ways of discussing chaos at all. Chaos has an odd hybrid or dialectical character that contributes to its elusiveness. It is more than nothing, less than something, not quite anything. Thus, at the end of his informative article on the subject in the *Encyclopedia of Religion,* N. J. Girardot has every reason to conclude that any attempt to define chaos is involved in an undertaking of exquisite irony.[1] With respect to its nothingness, chaos cannot be subjected to the vaunted purifying approach of the *via negativa,* for this would lead to its elimination entirely. Yet, at the same time, the quest to distinguish

---

1. N. J. Girardot, "Chaos," *The Encyclopedia of Religion,* vol. 3, ed. Mircea Eliade (New York: Simon and Schuster Macmillan, 1995), 213.

the form or essence of chaos by direct examination likewise is misplaced. It has none. Chaos, by its definition as a state of complete disorder and confusion, is undefinable. It is no wonder that theology has, for the most part, skirted the topic, only pausing now and then on its way to a discussion of the nature of deity to condemn chaos as a blind and fulminating adversary of God.

Perhaps an effective strategy for discussing the character of elusive chaos (but not its "nature") is not by negation or affirmation, but by contrast.[2] Here, both the negative and positive aspects are given their due. By emphasizing what chaos is not, the language of contrast is primarily negative. But the conclusions may be positive, suggesting what chaos is. At this point in the discussion, these divisions loosely correspond to the two locations of chaos—its position beyond the creation in an absolute or transcendent sense and its position in the creation in an immanent sense.

First, we will consider chaos beyond the creation. God and chaos are ineffable, but not for the same reason. On the one hand, God is beyond words, and finally beyond ideas, because, being infinite, the divine boundlessness would be compromised by any association with the finite, creaturely world. Human language evolved to respond to the practical needs of life, to communicate about this and that. God is not a this or that. Words and concepts that work well in ordinary conditions fail miserably and even result in falsehood and distortion when applied to the infinite. Analogy is pressed into service to avoid complete theological impotence. Metaphors and symbols are also fruitful. But these conceptual tools, when taken with ontological certainty, compromise infinity as well. On the other hand, the problem with chaos is not about compromising its infinity by attempting to describe it. Rather, it has to do with the very essence of the subject. Chaos has no nature except paradoxically the nature of being absolutely inchoate and indeterminate. Words are labels for the determinate, the finite and informed. Chaos lacks any modes by which it may be named. It is "the name of the nameless, the form of the formless."[3]

Pure chaos is anarchy (an-*arche*, having no form or organizing principle), a continuum of disordered states. These states are acausal; they have no explanation based on some prior directing

2. Another approach to chaos may be found in Stuart Chandler, "When Worlds Fall Apart: Methodology for Employing Chaos and Emptiness as Theological Constructs," *Harvard Theological Review* 85, no. 4 (1992): 467–91.

3. Lao Tsu, *Tao Te Ching*, trans. Gia-fu Feng and Jane English (New York: Random House, 1972), 14.

agency or defining context. They are indeterminate, "not yet," "no more," or "never." Chaos is ungoverned; no organizing principle directs or limits the anarchy. It is not a whole, for wholes possess an order and complex form. Chaos is not one, it is many, and the many are devoid of arrangement. The many cannot, in turn, be characterized either as units or subsidiary wholes in themselves because this would signify intrinsic individual order despite the complete agitation that abides between them. Chaos itself is an everlasting mixing process of infinite proportions. The mixing is complete and results in a total dissipation or indiscriminate jumble. Shakespeare's words apply here. Absolute chaos lacks

> Degree, priority, and place,
> Insisture, course, proportion, season, form,
> Office, and custom, in all line of order.[4]

Chaos is the annihilation or obliteration of order, pattern, and expectable process. It is the dissipation of arrangement and the continuous dissolution of components by further descent, approaching, perhaps asymptotically at infinity, the formless darkened and yawning abyss. There is no wonder that chaos eludes all attempts at analysis and is amenable primarily to the poetic imagination.

Contextual or imminent chaos, chaos within the creation, is more easily accounted for than chaos beyond the creation because it is everywhere in human experience. Chaos may be teased out of the order it infects, not so much as an occupying corruptive force, but as the confused "other" in the midst of order. Chaos commandeers order by employing the power of order against itself. Chaos is present or potentially present in all situations as the identifiable tendency toward corruption, decay, and violence or as indeterminate potential waiting to be shaped and directed.[5] Imminent chaos is elemental in the sense intended by ancient philosophy and more recent alchemy in their enumeration of the primal elements composing all

---

4. William Shakespeare, *The Tragedy of Troilus and Cressida*, act 1, scene 3, lines 83–85.

5. The final paragraph of Albert Camus's *The Plague*, trans. Stuart Gilbert (New York: Random House, 1972), 278, captures this feature of chaos: "As he listened to the cries of joy rising from the town, Rieux remembered that such joy is always imperiled. He knew what those jubilant crowds did not know but could have learned from books: that the plague bacillus never dies or disappears for good; that it can lie dormant for years and years in furniture and linen-chests; that it bides its time in bedrooms, cellars, trunks, and bookshelves; and that perhaps the day would come when, for the bane or enlightenment of men, it would rouse up its rats again and send them forth to die in a happy city."

things. *Fire* is clearly violent and consuming, the very emblem of chaos. *Air* demonstrates its chaotic tendencies in wind and storm. As the raging river, ascending flood, turbulent sea, and mounting storm, *water* has historically been the reigning symbol for chaos. And finally, the chaotic moods of *earth's matter* are expressed in earthquakes and volcanic eruptions. Chaos abides or infects, in the words of the poet Gerard Manley Hopkins,

> All things
> counter,
> original,
> spare,
> strange.[6]

This description, of course, refers accurately to anything at some time in its creaturely career. Indeed, the pervasive presence of chaos in life is what requires the actions of ordering agencies to establish, sustain, and eventually rescue the good order of the cosmos from the devouring chaos. Peter Berger observes in his sociological study of religion, *The Sacred Canopy,* that the function of religion is "the establishment through human activity of . . . a sacred cosmos that will be capable of maintaining itself in the ever present face of chaos."[7]

Chaos is perplexing. It is neither here nor there, this nor that. Being true to the reality (if one can so speak) of chaos means accepting and working within the ambiguity of its extensive state and status. This is accomplished by steering a course between its negative and positive characters, refusing to deny either, or, better yet, embracing both in a broader, dialectical account.

Chaos in Scripture

Chaos would likely not emerge as an important theological concept were it not for the prominent role it plays in the initial verses of the Bible. The first two verses of the first chapter of Genesis serve almost as a banner headline announcing God's original and definitive act of creation and the primordial state of the world that preceded it. An account of the divine creative process must await later discussion; our concerns will be with the nature and role of the primordial chaos, the description of which is found in verse 2:

---

6. Gerard Manley Hopkins, "Pied Beauty," line 7.
7. Peter Berger, *The Sacred Canopy: Elements in a Sociology of Religion* (New York: Anchor Books, 1990), 51

The earth was without form and void [*tohuwabohu*],
and darkness was upon the face of the deep [*tehom*];
and the Spirit [*ruach*] of God was moving over the face of the
    waters.[8]

Tohuwabohu seems to be redundant; "formlessness" and "void"
seem very close in meaning. The redundancy may be one of emphasis reinforced by rhyme. But other interpretations are suggested,
especially for *tohu* as it appears elsewhere in Hebrew scripture.
Tohu is a "howling wilderness waste" (Deut. 32:10), "trackless
waste" (Ps. 107:40) or "pathless waste" (Job 12:24), and a wilderness occupied only by wild creatures (Isa. 34:11). As that which has
been canceled or negated, the remains of destruction, it also signifies
literally nothing: "They shall name it [Edom] No Kingdom There"
(Isa. 34:12); or is that which is worthy only of God's neglect: "All
who make idols are nothing" (Isa. 44:9), and "All the nations are as
nothing before him; they are accounted by him as less than nothing
and emptiness" (Isa. 40:17). Finally, God "hangs the earth upon
nothing" (Job 26:7), a verse that comes close to suggesting the true
nihil or void. *Tohuwabohu* is emptiness and waste bordering on
nothingness and annihilation.

The earth, that is, the world in its totality (including, presumably,
the heavens as well), has no form or presence. Still, there remains an
unspoken anticipation, prepared for by the announcement in verse 1,
that this state of desolation is about to change, that the earth, merely
a gleam in the eye of God, is *as yet* without form and void.

"The face of the deep" should not be seen as a second distinct
state following that of the *tohuwabohu*. The *tehom*, the deep, is
that upon which this vague and vacuous earth sits or by which it is
surrounded. There is continuity between the formless and void and
the darkened abyss, as if the earth is presently to emerge from the
encompassing depths in the liberating act of divine creation and in
response to divine command, being raised not from the dead but
from the deep. The "waters" clearly are the stuff of the deep. Their
black and abysmal depths are not those of nothingness but of the
trembling sea (Ps. 77:16). The appearance of the heaving, stormy
sea, menacing green with white, frothing waves tossed by a howling
wind, must have provoked a frightful fascination in the Hebrews,
as it has in all peoples throughout history. The *tehom* is also the

---

8. The translation is that of the RSV. See Gerhard von Rad, *Genesis* (Philadelphia: Westminster Press, 1972); Claus Westermann, *Genesis 1–11* (Minneapolis:
Augsburg, 1984).

home of sea monsters, including the Leviathan. The matchless description of the crocodilian Leviathan in chapter 41 of the book of Job includes the vision of the monster agitating the deep, making it "boil like a pot" (Job 41:31). The Leviathan is the dreaded power of chaotic destruction that abides within the deep. Its approach to the surface is signaled ominously by the roiling waters.

This howling wind is the *ruach* or "Spirit of God." Most commentators interpret this phrase in just that way. Just as the churning waters of the deep are disturbed from below by the lurking, stalking Leviathan, so they are disturbed from above by immense cyclonic winds, worthy of God and given extreme emphasis by the association. This wind does not merely brood or hover; it stirs mightily as the storm of God, the *ruach elohim*.

The primordial chaos preceding the initial acts of divine creation is complex and replete with fertile suggestion. It exhibits aspects of emptiness, abysmal depth, devouring menace, and violent agitation or confusion. And yet, there are elements of potentiality, of source and power, not only for obliteration but also for birth. The chaos is not static but clearly dynamic in a threatening and productive way. While it hides and resists creation by guarding its dark depths, its very energy is potentially available to drive the creation's ordering processes.

This account seems to deny the traditional doctrine of *creatio ex nihilo* by positing a distinct reality present with God, presumably for eternity. Such a companion is unacceptable to monotheism for many good reasons. It does appear, however, that in the clear documentation of a primordial chaotic presence, the ancient Priestly composer of these initial verses of Genesis thought differently or was not concerned with the risk of ditheism. This same writer continues in verse 3 with God verbally commanding the creation of a cosmic infrastructure. Since one cannot command a void, it seems important to take the writer seriously and try to offer a reasonable theological accounting of this odd state. More than a child's innocent curiosity about a bedside story inspires the questions. What is the source and status of the chaos on the first day of the creation, and where does the chaos go after the sixth?

CHAOS: A SYSTEMS-INFORMATIONAL ACCOUNT

The Antonym of System

These preliminary comments are encouraging. Perhaps it is possible to imagine the unimaginable, to attempt an account of chaos de-

spite the daunting barrier of the lack of order and pattern displayed
by it. But any investigator should steer between two serious pitfalls.
If chaos is all whir and confusion, would not any project designed
to measure it become confused in its success? Or might the opposite happen? In the process of exploring chaos, its state of disarray
may become transformed into an arrayed state of words and ideas
through the Midas touch of metaphysics. Still, it is encouraging to
remember that chaos is not nothing, and that there is ample documentation of its presence as more than mere deficit, that chaos is
power—the source of its peril and promise—and that chaos is the
raw and elemental stuff out of which order is made.

This project of speaking of intrinsic chaos, especially the primordial *tohuwabohu, tehom,* and *ruach elohim* of Genesis, must be
metaphysical. Chaos is as fundamental as God and being are to the
understanding of anything and everything—how things arise, how
they perish, how they persist in between. In addition, this project is
a theological one; it aims to talk about God. For no full accounting
of either chaos or being is possible without reference to God. Finally, to narrow things further, this God-talk draws upon a limited
and strict vocabulary, a lexicon/store of terms conveying concepts
and connections taken from communication and systems theories.

There is probably no better place to begin an account of chaos
than with the observation that "chaos is the antonym of system."[9]
A system is a whole with contributing components whose natures
are determined by their place and role in the whole. The wholeness
of the system as an arrangement, most often a dynamic, functioning arrangement, is the emergent property of the components and
the relationships between them. A system represents the outcome
of information processes, of messages sent and received through
decisions that progressively limit an initial field of possibility out of
which a system arises as a complex, concrete whole. Chaos must,
in contrast, be a state without wholeness, contributing components,
or web of connecting influences. Organization and pattern or anything whatsoever that could be called a defining form, boundary, or
essence are absent.

To carry this strategy of opposing contrast further, if a system
is a tightly knit "one," then a pure field of chaos must be "many,"
a great many—a totally heterogeneous miscellany of particulars, a
jumbled mess. Each particular of the many is uniquely denominated,

---

9. Stafford Beer, "Below the Twilight Arch: A Mythology of Systems," *General
Systems Yearbook* 6 (1961): 9.

thereby defying classification.[10] Given the impossibility of classification and pattern, each element or particular in a field of chaos resides in splendid isolation. It is detached, independent, free from prior constraint and barren in terms of influencing the future—its own or that of other elements. Context arises from clusters of environmental relationships and constitutes a systemic togetherness. Because no togetherness may be allowed in an accounting of chaos, these bare and barren particulars may be said to be completely context independent in their isolation and frenzied motion.

Quantity enters as well. The degree to which a deck of cards may approximate chaos is limited by the number of states that are possible, brought about by the randomizing of shuffling. The number of arrangements in the fifty-two cards is immense but finite. The confusing and capricious character of the chaos increases with the sheer number of swarming particulars. True chaos is chaos by summation, one discrete unit added randomly upon another. Absolute chaos consists of an infinite tally of such particulars.

A final characterization of chaos is provided by insights from philosopher Robert Nozick, who asks us to consider "the structure of all possibilities."[11] Particular possibilities, of which this structure consists, may be said to exist or not exist with respect to their status in the actual world. But what about the structure itself? Does *it* exist or not exist? Are existing and not existing categories that even apply to the totality of things that might or might not exist? Nozick thinks that they do not. Hence, we have a logical notion of a structure that is itself beyond existence and nonexistence, the determinate and indeterminate. The structure of all possibility is not itself a possibility, but something else (if something at all) clearly transcending our ability to conceive. Theologians employ the term "ineffable" to describe the indescribable. Because chaos, like Nozick's structure of all possibility, floats freely beyond existence and nonexistence, it too can be understood but not directly conceived. It is an ineffable reality described in parallel terms by Charles Hartshorne: "[God is] the uncreated creator, presupposition of existence and nonexistence, itself without presuppositions."[12]

---

10. This does not mean that instances of order within the field of chaos are not possible. Indeed, they are necessary. But it does mean that with respect to the field itself, these instances are spontaneous and arbitrary. The chaos deals with them with absolute *indifference*.

11. Robert Nozick, *Philosophical Explanations* (Cambridge: Belknap Press of Harvard University Press, 1981), 96.

12. Charles Hartshorne, *A Natural Theology for Our Time* (LaSalle, Ill.: Open Court Press, 1967), 69.

What seems to be emerging from these strategies of negative contrast is an intuitive understanding of chaos, not its nature, form, or essence, but its character. Chaos is infinite elemental dispersion lacking all composition, overall arrangement, or predictable pattern. It consists of an infinite assortment of discrete elements, mutually exclusive and jointly exhaustive. That is, chaos is an infinite thicket of variety.

Chaos as Variety

The concept of variety may provide the key to understanding chaos. It may also answer a question waiting to be asked: What are the "particulars" or "elements" that come and go in the field of chaos, the stuff of chaos? The consistent answer, given the preparation up to this point, is "variety." Things are "various" or "variegated"; when taken together, distinctions between them are possible. They are different. Furthermore, while a single object may be "variable" or "vary," that is, changing over time, it cannot be said to contain "variety." Variety is a property of collections.[13]

By way of review, "variety" is a technical term in communication theory. Variety is an attribute of a set of potential messages. The uncertainty of the receiver is proportional to the variety of this initial set. The greater the variety, the greater the uncertainty. Uncertainty is relieved with the reception of messages, wherein this variety is reduced. Information generated in the transmission not only reduces variety but also moves the process from possibility to actuality and toward a settled state. Variety is therefore also proportional to entropy, which is greatest when uncertainty is maximal and no constraint exists in the ensemble of possible signals.

Is variety therefore merely potential? It is that, and it is also the power that comes with potential. But variety is not merely the diversity of a set of potentials—the fifty-two different cards in a deck waiting to be played. Variety is not an attribute of the realm of ideas in Plato's philosophy. Nor does it merely characterize the eternal objects of Whitehead's process vision awaiting insertion by God into a becoming moment, an actual occasion. The basic forms of Plato and Whitehead are already complex entities in their own right and hence represent some prior selection process at work. To this extent they are not primordial, that is, original or originating sources of complex concepts or objects. Variety, pure and simple, is

---

13. W. Ross Ashby, *An Introduction to Cybernetics* (New York: John Wiley & Sons, 1961), 124.

the stuff of distinctiveness. Variety is that which is not yet limited
by anything other than its own disconnectedness, detail, grain, and
texture.

The Pandemonium Tremendum

It follows, then, that chaos, in its primordial manifestation, is an
infinite field of variety, of complete indeterminateness filled with
potency, the source of all created things and one aspect of divine abundance.[14] Representatives of this position include Jakob
Böhme's *Ungrund,* later developed by Nicolas Berdyaev as the freedom of *me-on,* or nonbeing; Meister Eckhart's enumeration of the
natures of divinity as the indeterminate ground, giving rise to a
determinate figure; and Rudolf Otto's phenomenological appraisal
of the holy as the *Mysterium Tremendum et Fascinans.* Primordial
chaos as the infinite field of variety would certainly evoke responses
of dread, foreboding, and creaturely insignificance, just what one
would expect in the encounter of a mere mortal with some residual
tehom lurking in the orderly cosmos. Eckhart used the term *Wüste*
to signify the trackless regions of desolation in which the soul wonders in its quest for God. Perhaps, however, Otto's title could be
modified to capture both the mystery of the primordial *Wüste* and
its chaotic nature. *Pandemonium* captures the character of chaos
as an uproarious bedlam. Hence, *Pandemonium Tremendum* best
communicates the dynamic formless character of primordial chaos.

Primordial chaos, the *Pandemonium Tremendum,* is not limited
to a fitful state of affairs that disallows the emergence of any enduring order. Rather, it consists of infinite variety as understood
in communication theory. This would be an infinite assortment
of discrete events, elements, or states distributed with complete
randomness—and equiprobable distribution—shifting and mixing
incessantly in a condition of complete instability. Each element or
potential state is dead-even with respect to its realization in competition with all other states. Essential also to the primordial chaos is
the aspect of turbulent mixing or elemental agitation, the ceaseless
shuffling of possibilities in a roiling, chaotic sea.

As an infinite field of variety, the *Pandemonium Tremendum* is
not yet limited by anything, even its own collectivity. Each element is
"out of place," without locus or position. Such extreme context independence or utter happenstance is in consequence of the fact that

---

14. See Philip Hefner, "God and Chaos: The Demiurge versus the *Ungrund,*"
Zygon: Journal of Religion and Science 19, no. 4 (1984): 469–85.

the radical disconnectedness allows for no mutual influence, not even simple spatial connection. The elements are present to nothing and hence nowhere (although, as we shall see, they are present to God and therefore somewhere, in or with God).

Bits and Pieces: Infinitesimals of Difference

The *Pandemonium Tremendum,* the model of chaos being developed here, is infinite with respect to the limitless variety of its particulars. These cannot be particular things, forms, or events; they do not fall within the understanding of potentials in classical metaphysics. What terms remain to describe them? One candidate is "infinitesimal," referring in its nominative form to the smallest possible division of matter or time. The smallest division or grain or any material, perhaps the most elementary particle, a quark, or a string in space-time—these are the infinitesimals of the empirical world. A nanosecond or Whitehead's "actual occasion" is perhaps the granule of time.

What, then, would an infinitesimal of variety be? Gregory Bateson offers a fascinating account of a possible candidate in his discussion of the "very peculiar and obscure concept of difference."[15] Difference is contrast. In his most concrete example of difference, Bateson attempts to answer the question "What is it in the territory that gets into the map?"

> We know that the territory does not get onto the map. . . . Now, if the territory were uniform, nothing would get on except its boundaries, which are the points at which it ceases to be uniform against some larger matrix. What gets onto the map, in fact, is difference, be it a difference in vegetation, a difference in population structure, difference in surface, of whatever. Differences are things that get onto maps.[16]

Is difference merely an abstract way of talking about the classic forms or potentials for actualization carried in ideas? In a sense, yes. Insofar as differences may be itemized or categorized as differences in size, weight, color, and so on, they correspond to the classic notions of forms or qualities. Each existing quality reflects a form of its own. But, in another sense, differences are not forms; they are the recognition of contrast between forms, contrasts that are

---

15. Gregory Bateson, *Steps to an Ecology of Mind* (New York: Ballantine Books, 1972), 451.
16. Ibid.

necessary if one form is to be differentiated from another. Without differences there is no form, only uniformity.

Variety involves difference. Difference may be located "between" things: we often say, "The difference between X and Y is...." In a comparative sense, difference is often relative: "X is larger than Y." Difference is continuous or discrete: "X is heavier than Y" (weight is a continuous measure), or "X is traveling east, but Y is going west." Even more fundamental is the primitive perception required for consciousness even to recognize that there are two or more entities between which a difference exists. It is not the case that two entities X and Y are given, and subsequently differences are recognized between them. Rather, X and Y are recognized only because they are first seen as different. The primitive perception of difference occurs simultaneously with distinguishing between things.

In the first chapter of his classic *Process and Reality*, Alfred North Whitehead describes the importance of difference in perception, with a touch of humor and hyperbole:

> We habitually observe by the method of difference. Sometimes we see an elephant, and sometimes we do not. The result is that the elephant, when present, is noticed. The faculty of observation depends on the fact that the object observed is important when present, and sometimes is absent.[17]

Thus, difference inheres not only between things simultaneously present, side by side, but is crucial also in the presence or absence of objects through time. One would suspect that Whitehead's account includes the perception of changes in things that are continuously present: the comparison of an object with itself over time.

What, then, is difference itself within a metaphysical account? It is undefinable, or at best, defined only in terms of its presence in the world. Difference is that which abides between.[18] Differences set things apart, one from another. For things to be individual, they must be set apart. But nothing is ever set apart to be studied in complete isolation—not in this world or in any possible world.

---

17. Alfred North Whitehead, *Process and Reality: An Essay in Cosmology*, ed. David Ray Griffin and Donald W. Sherburne, corr. ed. (New York: Free Press, 1978), 4.

18. The *Bhagavad Gita* lists the five fundamental elements of the world. The first four—earth, air, fire, and water—are familiar. But the fifth—the space between things—represents a real breakthrough. This space, between and not around, is the subtlest of the five. It suggests the equally subtle reality of difference, which also is between things.

Form is detected with respect to the perception of difference between individuals. Are differences, themselves, set apart? There is
nothing between infinitesimals of difference, nothing at all. Differences themselves are not adjacent. They have no context, neither of
the sort that arises comparatively, as with primitive human perception of distinguishing (to take notice is to perceive difference), nor
absolutely with respect to a common background out of which they
arise as distinctions. Emptiness abides.

A simple illustration may clarify this discussion. A famous opti-
cal illusion involves a drawing that can be interpreted in two ways.
One way is to see it as a profile of identical faces facing each other;
the other is to see it as a vase or candlestick. In either case, the
mind's eye interprets what is to be the foreground figure from the
background. A shifting of perspective from one interpretation to
the other requires reversing the background and foreground. That
is, the background for the two faces becomes the foreground of the
vase, or vice versa. Since it is possible to perceive only one of the
two figures in any given moment, a radical shifting in mental perspective is necessary to move from one to the other. The illusion
is fascinating in itself, but the deeper question is, What happens to
the mind of the perceiver during the instant when it moves between
interpretations, between the faces and the vase, when it is *not* seeing
a figure? We would suggest that, in this momentary suspension of
interpretation, the mind resides in a state of maximal existential and
communicative uncertainty. In that instant between decisions it perceives pure difference as a distinction to which forms have not yet
been assigned. Something is perceived, something indefinite. What
that shall become remains to be determined in the next moment
with a choice as the mind informs itself. Until then, the indefinite
object of the perception is indifferent difference and perhaps best
described by the previously mentioned phrase taken from mystical
Taoism, "the form of the formless."

The ontology of the *Pandemonium Tremendum* is an ontology of
difference. This approach is the very opposite of traditional ontologies of classification that depended on the groupings of similar traits
or properties. These ontologies rely on standardization of form for
their insights and conclusions. Seeking the simple unit of possibility
leads beyond possibilities themselves to the ontological notion of
difference or variety itself, just as individual existing beings lead
beyond themselves to the ontological notion of being itself. An
ontology of variety explores radical new territory in this respect.

In communication theory, the variety of messages that may be transmitted from a set does not consist of forms but of differences. When extrapolated into the *Pandemonium Tremendum,* this would suggest that the infinite field of variety is the realm of infinitesimal individuality not yet realized in the concrete world. That is, the messages are potential and indeterminate because they have not undergone the decision process required in communication events to reduce variety, to declare priority through selection processes. The primordial chaos is indeterminate in that it consists of differences that, as yet, make no difference, because no act of differentiation has yet called particular elements out and sent them on their way. For the receiver, the field of possible messages is also indeterminate. It consists of what might be rather than what will eventually come to be in the act of communication. Indeterminateness corresponds to uncertainty. The act of determination is the act of communication, of preference and discrimination, that which defines and makes definite, that which renders a decision, a yes or a no with respect to the actualization of particular potentials or differences. Communication relieves uncertainty by making a determining difference.

The *Pandemonium Tremendum* is the state antecedent to the creation, the comprehensive, unconditioned, and indeterminate source or ground of diversity among determinate things. It is the formless and the void of the *tohuwabohu* and the agitated deep of the *tehom* awaiting God's incisive act of making distinctions, of calling this to part from that, to become determinate and distinctive. It is a mist of infinitesimals, a vast field of indifference.

MODELS OF INFINITY: THE IMAGINATION AND THE LOGIC OF LIMITS

The Loss of Innocent Intuition

The notion of pure chaos as the limit and perfect case of all those instances of chaos we experience in life stretches language, even language that is appropriate for those instances of worldly chaos. Ordinary language is simply inadequate to convey faithfully the extraordinary phenomena at the limits of reality, even when we try to use it for that purpose. And yet, the continuity is not broken. The words have meaning. They continue to function, but not without the recognition that in those far places the realities are enigmatic and bizarre.

The logic of limits in metaphysics sometimes leads to paradox-ical conclusions or antinomies, or dialectical propositions wherein the yeas and the nays are both affirmed. Although the conclusions appear absurd, the logic that leads to them is itself affirmed. An accounting of the *Pandemonium Tremendum* reveals numerous extraordinary aspects that defy intuitive reason. But these aspects and the claims about them are not arbitrary, nor are they incoherent if it can be argued that they must be the case, given the basic premises of the inquiry. Admittedly, this investigation of the primordial chaos is an adventure into a strange domain indeed.

Most of us are inherent realists in our everyday orientation toward the empirical world. We continue to insist, as a prerequisite for serious consideration, that any accounting of reality in all its aspects and range be reasonable in much the same sense as an accounting of reality within the segment of that range consisting of the everyday world should be reasonable. It should make sense and correspond to experience, to intuitive standards. In its efforts to explore the character and range of empirical reality, science has discovered that the world is not really like this. The discovery of counterintuitive phenomena in the realm of the vanishingly small, in quantum phenomena, or in dimensions of space-time in relativity theory, is a consequence of the same reason and empirical inquiry that were employed by Newton to describe colliding billiard balls and accelerating objects. But science no longer insists that its accounts be amenable to the limited band of human experience. The lessons of twentieth-century physics disabusing us of our naïve realism may well carry over into the discussion of the character of chaos.

The power of mathematics is indisputable. It provides us with the purest of reasons and takes us as close to Descartes's "indubitability" as logic can go in understanding the deep structure of the world of our senses and intuition. Yet, when the real-world consequences of the mathematical models are developed, the images they suggest are anything but intuitive. The basic mathematics behind Einstein's derivations of relativity is readily understood by any good algebra student. Einstein's insight of genius was to assign a constant velocity to the speed of light and then to go wherever the math took him. But the result is a nonintuitive reality, a space-time continuum, that is unimaginable because it consists of four dimensions, three in space and the other of time. Equally perplexing is the curvature of this continuum. If certain conditions are satisfied in the cosmos—and this can be discovered only by empirical investigation—the tissue of spacetime may be closed in upon itself as a sphere. Or, as research evidence suggests, it may turn out to be flat like a sheet. The concept or image of space-time as a flexible tissue is an attempt in three dimensions to imagine the conclusions of mathematical deductions that, as some have suggested, "spatialize" time, depriving it of flow and giving it a Parmenidean character.

The math makes perfect sense. It is logically complete. But the innocent intuition is perplexed as practical questions remain unaddressed. If space-time possesses geometrical properties of curvature and extension, in what additional dimensions of space are these located? If our universe turns out to be closed and spherical, where, then, is the universe located? What is the background or "hyperspace" out of which it stands in order to be somewhere that allows for spheres to be placed there? Further, in theories that postulate the existence of multiple universes, each in its own space-time, in what common region do they abide together? How, indeed, is it possible to conceive either multiplicity or collectivity of universes in the absence of some contextual domain that they share?

The way out of these practical problems is simply to recognize that the images of the universe of space-time are metaphorical or isomorphic or both. "Space-time is a flat sheet" certainly qualifies as metaphor. But it is more than that. Metaphors work because there are real, if undetected, similarities between different realities. These similarities are the isomorphies, the structural correspondences, they share. Attributes of space-time that result when one does the math are structurally similar to those possessed by a sheet or tissue in three-dimensional space. Furthermore, the most general theories of physics apply universally, and, because the properties of the universe or universes they describe are based on the authority of mathematics, perhaps the purest form of human thought, they seem to border on metaphysics.

Transfigurations at Infinity

Even more aggravating for the innocent layperson than these questions is the notion of infinity, about which Western philosophy has considerable ambivalence. Historically, the concept has been understood in several ways. One understanding, that infinity means having no limits, was not an idea enthusiastically embraced by some schools of Greek philosophy, including Neoplatonism.[19] The Greeks saw the cosmos as a bounded, ordered place, finite in both space and time. Finitude—limited form—is an essential aspect of

19. Armand A. Maurer, *Medieval Philosophy* (New York: Random House, 1962), 314.

that order that is threatened by the prospects of sheer, engulfing limitlessness. A second understanding is that infinity can mean limitlessness with respect to special qualities or attributes. In Western theism, and in Islam as well, God is properly infinite with respect to the attributes of power, goodness, presence, and awareness. As an omnideity, God is ultimate or perfect through possessing these qualities without limits or reservation. Finally, infinity may be defined as that limit forever approached but never achieved, represented, for example, by Zeno's famous paradoxes. It is this third understanding of infinity that relates to the *Pandemonium Tremendum*.

In some instances, the consequences of what it would be like to achieve an infinite limit can be imagined. For example, increase the diameter of a circle and its rate of curvature decreases. At infinity, the curvature becomes zero, the circumference becomes a straight line that is identical to a tangent, and the edges on opposite sides of the circle become parallel lines. These transfigurations occur only when this limit is achieved.

A second example is best presented in the form of a question. Which of the following two descriptions best defines what we know as circle: a continuous and simple closed curve all points of which are equidistant from another point called the center, or, a regular polygon with an infinite number of sides? The geometrical character of a circle is approached as the limit of the process of repeatedly increasing the number of sides of a polygon, beginning with an equilateral triangle and moving to a square, a pentagon, hexagon, and so forth. At the limit of the procedure, each of the infinite number of sides of the final polygon is a mere point, having no length, thereby making possible the claim that a finite closed curve actually has an infinite character.[20]

Limits apply to the real world as well. An accelerating spaceship, behaving in accord with Einstein's special theory of relativity, could never achieve the speed of light, at least not from the vantage point of a nonaccelerating observer. As the vessel approached that

---

20. These were the sort of arguments made famous in the history of doctrine by Nicholas of Cusa (1401–64). See Jasper Hopkins, *A Concise Introduction to the Philosophy of Nicholas of Cusa* (Minneapolis: University of Minnesota Press, 1978). This process was also known to the Greek mathematician Euclid, who, in his famous *Elements,* demonstrated how to "exhaust" the area of a circle by progressively increasing the sides of an inscribed polygon. At the absolute limit, it is easy to see that the areas of both figures would be identical. See David C. Lindberg, *The Beginnings of Western Science: The European Scientific Tradition in Philosophical, Religious, and Institutional Context, 600 B.C. to A.D. 1450* (Chicago: University of Chicago Press, 1992), 88.

velocity, it would gain mass, and time would slow again (with respect to an observer not aboard the craft). Just on the verge of light speed, the mass would be so great that no amount of energy could accelerate the spaceship further. In addition, time would proceed so slowly that events, including further progress toward light speed, would creep imperceptibly forward.[21]

The Abyss as the Limit of the Pandemonium Tremendum

These illustrations are offered in the spirit of both adventure and caution to support the argument that the application of the logic of limits to the *Pandemonium Tremendum* is methodologically similar to its application in mathematics and physics. The extrapolation of this logic into this realm is the application of isomorphism, expressed through metaphor, to metaphysical realities.[22] Just as the circumference of a circle becomes tangential as the radius approaches infinite length, and a polygon becomes circular as its sides approach infinity in number and infinitesimal in length, so the infinitesimals of difference move toward a transforming limit of their own. Any object may be understood to possess an immense number of qualities. Some of these qualities are gross features—size, color, shape, and so forth. As attention descends into the more minute features, the object becomes more various and complex. Deeper still are microfeatures, which are immense in number. Eventually, one would suppose, this adventure into the heart of the object comes to a halt. The result is no longer the perception of a gross object with simple attributes, but is now a vast crowd of particulars, of singular and apparently dissociated qualities that individually give no hint of their role in the composition of an object. The object as a system has vanished in this process, reduced to a collection of numberless differences.

---

21. Relativity comes into play as well in any account of the big-bang origins of the universe. At T = 0, the moment of creation (or at some very early instant following this event), the universe was a singularity; space was a geometrical point containing all the matter of the universe compacted into a state of infinite density and temperature. This too is a state at the limits of science and imagination.

22. The essential difference between general relativity as cosmology and metaphysical cosmology is that the claims of the latter are not readily tested. In fact, if metaphysics describes those conditions or properties that must be present in all possible worlds, then metaphysics is in principle unavailable for empirical confirmation, for necessary conditions are never missing. Since they are necessarily present at all times and in all places, their absence cannot be reasonably imagined and their claims cannot be falsified. The structure of these examples applies to the infinity of the *Pandemonium Tremendum* with identical isomorphic logic.

Similarities with the *Pandemonium Tremendum* may end here. For any material object, the bounds of the reductive descent appear fixed by quantum limits. Yet, this might not be true. The unpacking of matter through the shattering of complex particulars into their constituents in particle accelerators has never reached any absolute ground. The limits of investigation are more practical than theoretical. If only a more powerful collider were constructed, we could discover yet smaller energetic particles that would perhaps be reducible themselves to a deeper level of yet simpler particles. It is conceivable that the limit of the descent into the heart of material matter would never be attained, perhaps not even at the level of string theory (ever shorter strings?). What, finally, is an infinitesimal of matter?

If this is so, then the world disclosed by physics resembles the *Pandemonium Tremendum*. The infinitesimal of difference may lie at that point of transformation in which a limit is reached at infinity through an endless proliferation of particles on a descending scale. Descent into the primordial chaos would move the texture of the infinite field of variety from a coarse grain to an ever finer one. Pure dispersion would be the condition of the unconditioned at the depths of the chaos. The process would approach a mirrored flatness, like the surface of a pond without ripples or any other disturbance on a calm day. This is a seamless discontinuity consisting of vanishing yet ever more numerous singularities, a most delicate gradation or degradation, the perfectly inchoate, the beginning and the end, pure dispersion, the realm where all distinctions break down into absolute singularities and where context and constraint have long vanished. The singularities are indeed singular. They are units in absolute isolation, even beyond, perhaps, the attributes of singularity or plurality. They may be said to be separated, using a metaphysical metaphor, and infinitely so. This characterization of the chaos and its infinitesimals gives an emphasis to its states of dispersion that appropriately identifies chaos as the true antonym of that which is gathered—a system.

The limit or floor of the *Pandemonium Tremendum* is not achievable, not even by thought, except through the logic of limits and the imagination. To sound out the depths of chaos never reaches completion, because these depths are unfathomable; they continually recede. As the macroscopic chaos is reduced, the flurry thickens, moving toward some asymptotic state—a uniform field of pure indifference, indistinguishable from nothing and the *coincidentia oppositorum* of the particular and the continuous.

The *Pandemonium Tremendum* is the limitless source of beings *and* complete emptiness, simultaneously the *pleroma* and the *sunyata*. With respect to this claim, Paul Tillich, the consummate metaphysical theologian, distinguishes between two sorts of nonbeing, the relative and the absolute. Relative nonbeing, *me-on,* is unactualized possibility; absolute nonbeing, *ouk-on,* is the simple void, devoid of potential, containing nothing and nowhere. The terms apply in this discussion of the primordial chaos. Variety, we have argued, is the source and power of creation, for it is the stuff of communication. Creation is an act of communication. The richness, fullness, and "perfection" of creation, its very being, depend on this stuff of communication. This antecedent variety is *me-on,* relative nonbeing. But at its infinite limits, meonic nonbeing is transformed into oukonic nonbeing, the absolute *nihil* in the vanishing and unbounded dispersion of infinitesimals.

Interpreted through the notions of communication theory, chaos is infinite variety, absolute noise, and complete absence of systematic arrangement and integrity. The *Pandemonium Tremendum* consists of infinite variety characterized as "infinitesimals of difference," the limit of which is the abyss of the *ouk-on,* pure nothingness.

CONCLUSION

In this chapter we have ventured into the metaphysical heart of the system, scouting the depths of the primordial chaos. On the one hand, carrying the subject along with claims of infinitesimals of difference, infinities, and extraordinary limits approached asymptotically, seems like some fantastic voyage into a black hole. The *Pandemonium Tremendum* is different from the systems of order and even the shadow of chaos that we experience in life. On the other hand, the logic of black holes, which are genuine nonmetaphysical objects, also represents the extreme extrapolation of ordinary circumstance stretched, literally, to the limit. In the next chapter we return to this strange wilderness to discuss the role of God with respect to the *Pandemonium Tremendum* before returning to more familiar territory.

– 6 –

The Source of Abundance

"[THE DIVINE LIFE] is the ground of all abundance, and it is abundance itself."[1] This insight from Paul Tillich is the concise theological summation of our model based on an ontology of information. The *Pandemonium Tremendum* is this source of abundance without which God could not be God. Yet, positing a reality that seems to stand apart from God, apparently capable of being characterized without any reference to God, suggests that God is not one, that God is at least two, that God draws upon some other reservoir for divine power and influence, or that God is not supremely simple and certainly not sovereign. And the suggestion that this reality, chaos, reigns with God encourages the conclusion that God cannot conquer that contrary power that frustrates the deity's plans for an orderly creation and corrupts that order once it has been established. The present task is to mount an argument on several fronts to answer these and other questions that are stimulated by the polemic appraisal of the primordial chaos in the theological tradition. These fronts include the role of the chaos in the divine life, God's employment and control of the chaos without compromise of its defining fury and spontaneity, and, finally, God's self-causation as self-address.

Given the traditional assumptions about chaos, the most urgent, if not loaded, question concerns the status of the *Pandemonium Tremendum* with respect to God: How does the primordial chaos stand apart from God in defiance, a contrary, recalcitrant force that God must live with?[2]

---

1. Paul Tillich, *Systematic Theology*, 3 vols. in 1 vol. (Chicago: University of Chicago Press, 1967), 1:242.

2. Very few theologians and philosophers have considered this question. One is Christian Ehrenfels in his *Cosmogony*, trans. Mildred Focht (New York: Comet Press, 1948); also excerpted in Charles Hartshorne and William Reese, *Philosophers Speak of God* (Chicago: University of Chicago Press, 1953), 352–57. In this selection, Ehrenfels writes, "The infinite something in which God works, we can think of only negatively, as the opposite of all that characterizes God. We call it Chaos. God

GOD AND THE PANDEMONIUM TREMENDUM

Variety and Vector

It matters little if the *Pandemonium Tremendum* is conceived as apart from or a part of God. On the one hand, insofar as it can be distinguished as a necessary element in the divine life and discussed accordingly, it stands apart as some "other," demanding its own ontological status. On the other hand, God, to be God, must embrace the primordial chaos as integral to God's own being. The inclusion of chaos within God's life is a major reason that God is God. Here is the key: The primordial chaos does not compromise the power and perfection of God. On the contrary, it is a necessary and inseparable ally of the divine life without which Tillich's claims for divine abundance make little sense. The primordial chaos serves God instrumentally in that it is the source of numerous capacities assigned to God, including divine sovereignty, limitlessness, and creativity.

Also, without these elements it is difficult to account for the immense variety and novelty in the creation within a theology of nature. Unless an appeal is made to the classical image of God as *actus purus,* some sense of divine creativity and some sense of divine abundance of God must be associated with the idea of the divine life, that is, of God's dynamic, self-initiated, and productive action. The God of Thomism is a God who does not move because, being all a divinity can be, this God of pure actuality contains no potential and thus has nothing more to achieve. The *Pandemonium Tremendum* gives a power, depth, and richness to the account of God that is missing in such models of divine perfection and immutability.[3]

---

and Chaos constitute the world.... All unity and universality come from God, all manifoldness from Chaos. Without Chaos God would be just as incapable of producing the world, as Chaos without God" (p. 343). While this description fits nicely into our account of God and chaos, reading further discloses a dualism in Ehrenfels that distinguishes his system from our own. His *Chaos* is the antagonist locked in an eternal quarrel with God from which arises the creation. Our *Pandemonium Tremendum* is the very source of the manifoldness of creation.

3. Despite our preference for a process style divinity, the model of God as the unmoved mover of pure act is, surprisingly, compatible with communication theory, at least upon first thought. The set of messages available to a transmitting agent may be settled and determined. Only the waiting receiver is uncertain about which messages to expect. Donald MacKay makes this point nicely: "If I offer to read out to you the sequence of digits down the right-hand column of your local telephone directory, the probability-for-you that the last digit (or any digit) will be 9 may be 1 in 10. But for the people at the exchange, every digit is fully specified, and talk of probability would be pointless.... [The directory] is so highly ordered that not a single misprint could be tolerated" (*Science, Chance and Providence* [Oxford: Oxford University Press, 1978], 38–39).

While the model proposed here speaks audaciously, almost in terms of a flowchart, of God's functioning components, the intelligibility of such a scheme opens up into mystery. The infinite field of variety is unconstrained, but these words are of the *via negativa*. The *Pandemonium Tremendum* itself is simply unimaginable. By definition it descends into the divine "heart of darkness," the *Ungrund* of the divine mystery. Creaturely chaos is really a shadow in that it consists of particular orders that mingle or move in very complex and random ways. True chaos, chaos itself, embraced by God, distinguishes God from the created order and its chaos. The unconditioned is incomparable.

Locating true chaos in God is not to suggest that God is chaotic, that God and the *Pandemonium Tremendum* are identical. The instrumental inclusion of chaos within God is a necessary premise for speaking of God, but it fails to exhaust the divine nature. In communication theory, variety and constraint, though dialectically related much like yin and yang, are equally necessary for any complete account. The same is true in God. God is at once the infinite source of variety and also the unwavering unerring source of constraint.

The *Pandemonium Tremendum* is the source of variety, but the divine will is the source of direction, the agency of determination. Will, divine or creaturely, is not easily defined. It is not identical with the intellect or with intuition or emotion. "Will" is the abstraction representing a class of determinations best described by the somewhat awkward term "willings." A willing is a specific event requiring decision and intention, or at least direction. A willing is similar to the notion of a vector in mathematics. On paper, a vector diagram is simply an arrow of specific length that indicates the magnitude and the direction of the applied the force. A willing is a vector in that it specifically includes these two factors of magnitude and direction. The force is one of urge, resolve, and commitment, as in the declaration "I will do this." The direction is the specific content of the willing, the "this" that one is resolved to achieve. The abstract "will" is the capacity, power, and freedom to generate willings and to move toward their realization.

In terms of process, the will of God lies between the primordial chaos, which is the source of variety, and the creation, which is the vast and ordered array of specific beings. Indeed, the divine will

---

If the numbers in the phone book can be likened to the ensemble of actualized forms that constitute the impassable Thomistic deity as already determined, then the transmission to creatures constitutes the relief of their uncertainty as they progress toward the fullness prepared for them by God.

is necessary for any creation at all. The primordial chaos contains it own power and energy but lacks either the supportive environment or the directive agency required for constraint to arise. The eighteenth-century philosopher David Hume developed an alternative hypothesis to the design argument by using ideas taken from the Greek atomists.[4] Perhaps, Hume suggested, the ordered world is the accidental consequence of the descent of eternal atoms in the void. The atoms swerve, collide, and combine, thereby giving rise to some persistent order. That order is the order of the world that we perceive and erroneously attribute to an omnipotent divine craftsperson. The fall of atoms is the crude equivalent of the primordial chaos. However, the difference is crucial. The primordial chaos is incapable of generating by random processes of collision any enduring collocation of elements and events that constitute the created order. It lacks entirely any favoring environment for an abiding and durable pattern to emerge and prosper. It therefore cannot serve even as an accidental agent for creation.

Storehouse of the Snow

The ground of difference requires agency. God is necessary as the agent of specification and concretion, the one necessary metaphysical individual for Ogden. The *Pandemonium Tremendum* is, at most, a collection. Yet, even this minimal attribute is too strong, for the elements of the primordial chaos have no relations, no locus, no occupation of a common space giving them a togetherness that would appropriately be characterized, even minimally, as a primitive collection. The very extreme diffusion and dispersion of the primordial chaos means that it is unbounded and infinite. Yet, somehow, it is the source for the bounded and finite creation. The movement from chaos to cosmos is through God as willing agent. The primordial chaos serves as the reservoir or the storehouse upon which God draws for variety in the acts of transmission that subsequently result in the creation and operate to sustain it.[5]

Indeed, the image of the storehouse drawn from the Hebrew Bible, the book of Job, provides a metaphor that is especially fitting for this requirement for God. God interrogates Job in order

---

4. David Hume, *Dialogues Concerning Natural Religion* (Indianapolis: Bobbs-Merrill, 1970), 176–82.

5. For further development of this notion of reservoir, see Martin Heidegger, *The Question Concerning Technology and Other Essays* (New York: Harper & Row, 1977).

to reveal his abysmal ignorance about the common and astonishing phenomena of nature. With a slight hint of rhetorical sarcasm, God asks, "Have you entered the storehouses of the snow?" (Job 38:22). Snow consists of delicate hexagonal flakes of ice, each with an intricate and novel geometrical design. As a deluge of countless exquisite flakes, a blizzard is an accurate and revealing symbol for the infinite variety of the *Pandemonium Tremendum*. Snow is sent by God, but what is its origin? A scientifically innocent fantasy would imagine a storehouse for the snow, available to God to send upon the earth. In like manner, but placed in a metaphysical framework, the primordial chaos is the storehouse of variety that God likewise releases upon the earth to create, constitute, and sustain its integrity and order. If this image is accurate, God is necessary as the power that contains the primordial chaos, the one who "stores" it and places it "at hand" as a ready source of nurturing variety.[6]

Robert Neville's notion of determinative context is useful here.[7] Neville maintains that all things require an ontological context to determine or condition them. The ontological context provides the field of relevance for things to be together, that is, to be mutually determinate, if only in some rudimentary way. To have a context is to have another or others about, to be among them, to be located in terms of some reference, to be a member and hence conditioned by other members. To be conditioned is to be determinate, a specified individual, a "this" with respect to a "that." God is no exception. The creation gives the relevance for God's determination. Consequently, it is not an incidental appendage to God's life, a mere excrescence. Rather, in providing necessary context, the creation is a cocreative companion to God.

The vast *Pandemonium Tremendum* is unconditioned, indeterminate, and ungrounded—absolute bedlam. In this stateless state, it is unavailable instrumentally as the material source for creating and creation. Thus, God, in a manner to be explored momentar-

---

6. This account is a version of Alfred North Whitehead's "Ontological Principle." Causally put, that principle requires that everything must be somewhere. For Whitehead, the only place this could be is in an actual occasion. Beyond or between actual occasions lies "nothing, nothing, nothing." Whitehead's presiding and everlasting actual occasion is God, in whom are located the eternal objects—potential forms for all transitory actual occasions that make up the world (*Process and Reality: An Essay in Cosmology*, ed. David Ray Griffin and Donald W. Sherburne, corr. ed. [New York: Free Press, 1978], 19).

7. See Robert Cummings Neville, *Eternity and Time's Flow* (Albany: State University of New York Press, 1993).

ily, must provide a context for the primordial chaos such that it is made available. But this context cannot be understood as constraint placed on the infinite field of variety. For constraint would deprive the primordial chaos of its inherent potential and compromise its radical indeterminateness. The "wilderness" (*Wüste*) would be a domesticated field. Internally and intrinsically, the elements of the chaos are completely out of place, that is, nowhere, present literally to nothing. There is texture but no contexture. But without context there can be no source standing at hand for the continuous stream of variety generating and sustaining the created order.

The only way to avoid this dilemma is to grant that God confers a minimal context upon the *Pandemonium Tremendum*. This context must be sufficient to render the stuff of variety available to God as the raw material for decision and transmission. But it must not constrain the chaos and limit its inexhaustible power. God gives the primordial chaos a collective aspect, a togetherness such that it is determined to be alongside or adjacent to God. In this sense the chaos is a *complete* chaos, a totality. We might even claim that the very notion of the primordial chaos would be unintelligible (for it could never be properly characterized as "chaos" in relevant contrast to "nonchaos" and so determined in this primitive way) without this minimal determination. As the measureless context of the infinite and unbounded primordial chaos, the divine embrace raises it to the level of availability. That is, God may now take the nowhere of the chaos and employ it somewhere, anywhere God wills.

Spatial images of God's relationship with the *Pandemonium Tremendum* are inadequate and even misleading. It is true that in some sense the chaos must be "alongside" God for there to be the requisite context allowing both God and the chaos to be distinguished and indeterminate. But making too much of God's enclosure of the chaos is problematic, because it is in a state of infinite dispersion and any containment would compromise this necessary feature.

Witnessing Chaos

The way to resolve this dilemma is to specify the divine context of the *Pandemonium Tremendum* in terms of God's function as witness. The divine context is not one of spatial locality but of noninvasive watchfulness and attention.

As an act, knowing may be noninvasive and unintrusive while still remaining intimate, that is, complete in all details. This kind of divine knowing is similar to that found in Hebrew scripture where knowing is deep, complete, and intimate. Ironically, a necessary condition placed on divine knowledge of the *Pandemonium Tre-mendum* is that it impose no order, arrangement, or organization on the primordial chaos. This, of course, would compromise its func-tion, reduce its power, and, consequently, reflect back upon God to proportionally limit divine sovereignty. God entertains the chaos by attending to its every particular and every move but without altering the perfect havoc within. That is, God does not police the chaos in any way to direct the swarm of infinitesimals by enforcing external constraints. Rather, God stands back and witnesses. Without this omniscient attention, God would be unable subsequently to utilize the chaos as a storehouse and source of messages. So, we may say that God *assays* (witnesses) the chaos as a preliminary stage, and eventually God *essays* (evaluates and composes) the chaos by em-ploying its variety to compose the creation. God comprehends but does not apprehend the chaos. The chaos is thereby given the neces-sary context but without the sacrifice of its absolute unconditioned character.

It seems odd to argue for conditions placed upon God for the purpose of defending the character of absolute bedlam, reputed to be God's supreme adversary. Nonetheless, the argument is pursued for the purpose, ultimately, of redefining the divine attributes, mov-ing away from essential to operational definitions. Any interference into the fundamental unstructured quality of the *Pandemonium Tre-mendum* would deny God the power and freedom to be God, since to limit the primordial chaos would be to limit the infinite source of variety from which God composes creation.

God's appreciation of the *Pandemonium Tremendum* that is un-adulterated by order or arrangement includes a restriction on the divine foresight. In keeping with traditional accounts of chaos and evidence taken from instances of chaos in human experience, the primordial chaos contains motion. The chaos is not only various in its limitless manifold states, but also is variable, that is, capable of being characterized as process. The chaos is in spontaneous flux where multifarious particulars appear, vanish, and perhaps reap-pear unpredictably. The flux is continually shifting and wavering; the mutability of the chaos is complete and capricious. Process is necessary because the chaos is power, not only potential power that passively awaits realization by an external manipulative agent, but also power in its own right, capable of exploding and spilling over into the cosmos. Further, the chaos is appropriately processive because variability requires it. Each possibility represented in the infinite field transforms incessantly with each passing manifestation counted as a contribution to the ever growing sum of the variety itself.

Chaos is rarely depicted as a quiescent state. From the stormy waters of Genesis to the fiery impermanence of *anicca* in Buddhism, literature, mythology, and metaphysics universally describe chaos in dramatic and violent terms. Chaos is a state of maximum excitation or, as information theorists would say, total noise. The infinite assortment of discrete states shifts incessantly with complete instability. This aspect of turbulent mixing, of elemental agitation, in the ceaseless shuffling of possibilities in a roiling chaotic broth means that God cannot predict any immediate subsequent state of the chaos, at least none based on the extrapolation of previous patterns or trends. The history of microstates offers no clues as to the future. All states are anomalous with respect to past trajectories. But here, even anomalies make no sense, for anomalies are data that fail to conform to a pattern. No pattern, no anomaly. If there were a pattern, no matter how weak, then of course, the chaos would be counterfeit. Given this reality, God's knowing of the chaos is active and continuous. God cannot blink. God must "look again" to renew knowledge of the chaos, which is, by definition, always discrete and momentary. One may say that while God has no knowledge of the chaos, God knows it as the "eternal now" of God's witness.

In yet another sense, God may be spoken of as "knowing" the *Pandemonium Tremendum*. W. Ross Ashby provides an insight for this point:

> A set's variety is not an intrinsic property of the set: the observer and his powers of discrimination may have to be specified if the variety is to be well defined.[8]

The sweep of God's knowing is particular and yet cumulative. The survey is something of a continuing inventory of the possibilities of the primordial chaos. Without this survey, God's employment of the chaos as the material for creation would be impeded. Ironically, for God to use the chaos fully and avoid the predicament of Plato's Demiurge—to struggle with a resistant or inert matter—the sheer dynamic confusion of the chaos must be respected and preserved.

For God to be all-knowing, divine knowledge must extend far beyond the actual events and objects in the particular concrete world,

---

8. W. Ross Ashby, *An Introduction to Cybernetics* (New York: John Wiley & Sons, 1961), 125.

a world that represents perhaps a tiny segment in the vast spectrum of possible worlds. Divine omnipotence must include these unactualized worlds. A God who is in partial ignorance of the potential set of messages that might be sent in order to bring about an orderly world is not very articulate. The world that comes from the messages transmitted by such a narrow-minded and inexpressive deity will be missing much of the richness and detail it could have had. Classical theology has God as the beginning and the end, the Alpha and Omega of history. In the sense discussed here, God is also the Sigma, the sum of all possibilities as the source of the divine abundance.

Ashby's dictum further suggests that chaos is the equivalent of confusion in a mortal observer who is in no position to define the variety present in a complex situation. But God is not confused. God is certain about every particular of the infinite field of variety. Hence, although there is no system, there is knowledge. In the world, chaos is disorder with respect to a particular order or class of order. The *Pandemonium Tremendum,* however, is disorder with respect to any possible order or class of order. This is true except for God, whose knowledge is complete though changing, and for whom the chaos is not confusing. God's sweeping and penetrating survey of the primordial chaos is congruent with the infinite range of the field itself, and in perfect resolution of detail, even to those depths approaching the void. This combination of breadth and depth is a kind of ordering of the chaos. For order, in one of its definitions, is a state of complete knowing. If the position of every element in a random distribution is known to an observer, then that state is not chaotic for that observer. Rather, it displays a unique order, unique in the sense that its particular arrangement is not an instance of some more inclusive pattern, nor is it generated by an algorithm.

The Professor's Office

A good analogy of this rendering of omniscience along the lines suggested by Ashby's insight is a professor's disheveled office in which piles of books and papers are strewn everywhere. A student entering the office will, to paraphrase Mark Twain, have to take soundings in order to navigate through the clutter. In the absence of any rhyme or reason to serve as a guide, the student will be in a state of complete uncertainty with respect to the location of any particular item. However, the professor, far from being absentminded, can locate any item without hesitation. Unlike the ignorant student, the professor's certainty resides in the knowledge of the whole territory in absolute detail—in all its microstates. For the professor in his office, no pattern exists, but certainty does.

God may be said to possess knowledge of the *Pandemonium Tremendum* in the same way the professor possesses total knowledge of the office. God's inventory is complete for any combination of microstates that the system of variety assumes in its constant shuffling. Each state is preserved with respect to its "leastness," understood as absolute context independence, simplicity, and irreducibility. God's perception of the chaos is not derived inductively from existing patterns, but individually. Each infinitesimal microstate is an object of divine attention in its pure context-independent status. Knowledge of particulars rather than of collections is perhaps the only way the chaos can be known without compromising its fundamental autonomy. A field of infinite difference requires unlimited discrimination or resolution. God's survey of the chaos is inclusive yet discrete. Divine discretion is just this absolute and undivided attention paid to "the least of these," even to the depths of the chaos. God's perfect distinguishing of the infinitely subtle states of the chaos can be identified partially with the divine omniscience. God's powers of discrimination are unlimited (an understanding of omniscience), and God's powers to communicate and create are also unlimited (an understanding of omnipotence).

With respect to God, the delicate task of envisioning the *Pandemonium Tremendum* is to know its content without containing, constraining, or otherwise introducing bias into the complete bedlam. Since, as we shall see, creaturely perception requires some sort of prior selection process before something definite is known, the divine perception of primordial chaos cannot be modeled after the perception of creatures. Even the Whiteheadian deity grades and ranks the eternal ideas in order of relevance among themselves and in terms of their compatibility with the order of the real world. For the God who keeps the storehouse of the chaos, this process of grading cannot be the case, for it would be utterly destructive of the potential of the chaos for creation and constitute a limit on the power of God overall. Thus, God's perception of the microstates of the chaos must be completely indifferent, at this point, with respect to their instrumental or intrinsic value in any divine scheme or plans.

Sigma and Sovereignty

Divine sovereignty, a combination of power and the freedom to exercise it unconditionally, is in turn based in the divine omnipotence. God's complete survey of the *Pandemonium Tremendum*, from Alpha to Omega through the process of Sigma, or summation, renders the elusive and freestanding microstates of the chaos available to God in the process of self-constitution and eventually for creation as well. God's functions as witness (this unbiased inventory) and agent (the implementation or shaping of the material of chaos in communication) are inextricably connected, as they are in the human creature and, indeed, in all intentional beings. God's actions, though they may be analyzed into antecedent and subsequent phases, are nonetheless accomplished in one continuous sweep. It is in this seamless process that one may speak of deity as "simple" or claim that all of God's necessary attributes are necessarily unified in such a fashion that to speak of one is to speak of all.

God surveys the *Pandemonium Tremendum* with impartiality, for partiality would mean a movement away from the equiprobability of any microstate. This bias or preference would predispose the chaos away from its unconditioned state to one with built-in bias. Without this bias, the elements of the chaos are properly neither here nor there, and that is exactly where they must be. The entire field of variety is circumviewed by God, who takes inventory of its microstates through summation or tally, yet holds each distinctly in sight. In this sense of summation, God contains the primordial chaos without restriction. The mathematical process of summation or simple counting serves better than the metaphorical image of spatial containment of the infinitely dispersed field of variety. God "counts" the microstates and, subsequently, "counts on" this variety.

That God counts on the *Pandemonium Tremendum* as the source of divine abundance renders the doctrine of *creatio ex nihilo* inconsistent with the system we are proposing. The doctrine receives extensive support from most theologians. Philip Clayton gives voice to this support when he says, "The theological significance of a creation out of nothing cannot be overestimated."[9] The main reason for such enthusiastic endorsement is that some sort of eternal material alongside God would be coercive, limit the divine freedom, and compromise God as the single source of all reality. But acknowledging the idea is no easy thing, for its acceptance includes the obligation to explain how the only alternative, pantheism—the

---

9. Philip Clayton, *God and Contemporary Science* (Grand Rapids: Eerdmans, 1997), 21.

creation of the world out of God's own being—is avoided. Most responses include appeals initially to omnipotence and eventually to mystery. It seems that the idea was embraced by early Christian theologians, not because it was persuasive but because it was protective. To some extent, *creatio ex nihilo* is a defensive doctrine intended to refute charges of a compromised and weakened deity if some coeternal material were allowed.

The assumption that a coeternal reality to God would fatally compromise divine sovereignty is not the case for the *Pandemonium Tremendum*. In actuality, the primordial chaos serves as the source of divine power and freedom, and is the storehouse for the abundance that originates and nourishes the creation. Recognizing its copresence with God simply acknowledges these contributions. Moreover, the primordial chaos is no antagonist to God. It represents the grounds of all possibility and is available to God on call as the vocabulary of the divine speaking out.

SHIELDING THE CREATION FROM CHAOS

On the Leeward Side of God

The problem presented by the primordial chaos is not for God, but for the creation. As its name suggests, the *Pandemonium Tremendum* is not a passive, bounded region of moderate activity. It is nothing but trouble. The fundamental feature of absolute dissipation compounds the inherent fury of the chaos by expelling its power radiantly. If this profound volatility alone were the case, then the cosmos would never arise, for any region of order would be devoured immediately upon its birth. Chaos may be the necessary material cause of the world, but an appeal to it for the complete explanation for the world is insufficient because it cannot behave itself.

For there to be a creation, God must fulfill several responsibilities. One is to channel requisite variety into the cosmic regions, where it builds order. God nurtures the world by releasing impounded variety provisionally, or, to use a stronger image, God pumps a rationed and rational (in the sense of proportion) quantity of variety as the material for the construction of orders in creation and creaturely systems. A second major responsibility of deity is to contain the chaos as it strikes out insanely against any attempt to contain its dissipative ferocity. God shields the cosmos against this surge. Resting on the leeward side of God, the order of the cosmos is divinely protected from being swept away.[10]

In between chaos and cosmos lies the entire range of regulated flow. The degree of this regulation is the result of God exercising powers of separation and decision. Divine agency is exclusively the agency of communication. God's power to transmit is itself without limits; otherwise, God would be unable to baffle the *Pandemonium Tremendum* entirely. The margins of the containment would leak daunting variety. This consequence of spillage onto the creation is what one would expect of a lesser god or demiurge.[11]

God halts the dissipation of the *Pandemonium Tremendum* by containing it in an envelope of constant decision. These decisions gather variety into differentiated regions, the regions of yes and no. They are the first order of business for God—the primordial determination that provides material for the creation itself. Differentiation is the origination of all order. It is as primitive as waves separating from the smooth featureless surface of the sea. But it is enough to baffle the expanding squall of chaos. It proceeds no further.

The baffling of the *Pandemonium Tremendum* is nothing like constructing a firewall or partition. It more closely resembles a chess match in which one player knows all the possible moves on the board and uses this exhaustive knowledge to counter the opponent at every turn. This, of course, was the intention of Deep Blue, the IBM computer that challenged reigning world chess champion Gary Kasparov.[12] God's interdiction ("to speak between") of the primordial chaos is similarly the divine countermove for the random excursions of every infinitesimal.

Does divine interdiction contradict the earlier insistence that God must not violate the *Pandemonium Tremendum* if it is to perform as the unlimited source of God's abundance? Perhaps, but we should emphasize that the power of God to interdict is the consequence of

10. In Christianity, the calming of the storm and the stilling of the sea by Jesus in the Gospel of Mark (Mark 4:35–41) is a story indicating that Jesus possessed God's power to command chaos to obey his will for the protection of the endangered.

11. In fact, this option is one of several available to theodicy, the theological attempt to justify God, given the presence of evil in the world. By questioning God's omnipotence (defined here in part as the baffling of the primordial chaos), the greater attribute, God's omnibenevolence, can be salvaged. God wants to shield the creation, but can't.

12. Of course, the analogy can be carried only so far. In its first match with Kasparov in 1996, the computer was defeated. A rematch one year later had different results. After receiving additional information from its handler programmers about contextual situations, the machine was victorious.

God's own variety—it takes variety to counter variety—and the sole source of God's variety is the primordial chaos. Hence, the chaos can be baffled only through the preservation of its own infinite and chaotic character. God fights fire with fire.

This metaphysical description of divine interdiction of primordial chaos has a profound theological message as well. In a mythic and metaphysical interpretation, John Haught makes the important point that the divine *kenosis* (the self-emptying or self-limiting of God), usually reserved for discussions of Christology, may be imaginatively applied to the creation, especially when combined with insights from kabbalistic Judaism. Haught's reference to Michael Wyschogrod's interpretation makes the connection nicely:

> [The kabbalists] invoked the notion of *tsimtsum,* by which they meant that the absolute God, whose being fills all being, withdraws from a certain region, which is thus left with the being thinned out in it, and in this thinned out region man [the cosmos] exists.[13]

With respect to our scheme, what is "thinned out" is the *Pandemonium Tremendum,* whose omnipresence would frustrate the nascent creation. The divine kenotic act is to baffle the primordial chaos, protecting the creation from its overwhelming power.

THEOGONY

The Cosmological Question

In a broader and more inclusive sense, the subject of creation is not limited to a discussion of the first chapters of Genesis. Creation does not begin with "In the beginning...," because God was already present in that beginning. The audacious mind will push the inquiry further into the metaphysical past, asking, "What is the beginning of God?" Classical theism has always considered this question of ultimate priority to be nonsense, or at least to rest on a complete misunderstanding of the nature of God as no more than a very great being whose attributes, equally great, are nonetheless similar to the characteristics of any existing being. In the language of ontology, God's essence is existence. God cannot be conceived

---

13. Michael Wyschogrod, *The Body of Faith* (New York: Harper & Row, 1983), 9–10; quoted in John Haught, "Evolution, Tragedy, and Hope," in *Science and Theology: The New Consonance,* ed. Ted Peters (Boulder, Colo.: Westview Press, 1998), 242.

as not existing, any more than a triangle can be conceived without three angles. Triangularity is as necessary for the concept of triangle as existence is for the concept of God. Since no creature enjoys necessary existence, each creature is contingent, and questions about its cause are legitimate. But God is not contingent, and the question of a cause for God is nonsensical.

Furthermore, to qualify as God, a being must possess several additional unique attributes, including eternality and omnipotence. In practical terms, that which is eternal by definition has no beginning. The question of birth cannot be put to it. With respect to omnipotence, a being of infinite power has no peer or rival, no other being who could be the cause of its arising. With respect to both attributes, God is everlasting.

The deity of classical theism is itself the unconditioned power of being. Consequently, it endures none of the predicaments of finite, creaturely beings, including the necessity of being caused to be and the fate of ceasing to be. In any event, if the true nature of divinity is rightly grasped, the question of its cause simply vanishes.

However, for certain models of divinity, the question of divine origin is valid. In process theism, inspired by Whitehead, God is an individual, ubiquitous and everlasting, a very special individual, to be sure, but nonetheless, one whose explanation is not clearly contained in its existence. God and creation share a common status. It is just that God is the maximal individual, while creation consists of countless other individuals who collectively depend on God to shepherd them. This total system of God and world has no obvious explanation. It simply is, and, according to Whitehead, always has been. This is a universe similar to the one described by Bertrand Russell as the one brute fact, by which he meant that although the universe is contingent, it has no first cause; it always was and will be. Perhaps, as some have argued, the vaunted principle of sufficient reason applies to particular things in the universe, but not to the universe itself, in which case the adventure of reason ends finally in absurdity: the existence of a total contingent system without an originating cause. This inexplicable givenness of the cosmos, seemingly by magic out of nowhere, is hardly satisfying.

The model we are proposing transparently resembles Whitehead's system, albeit with several very real differences. It therefore is subject to the same problem, the so-called cosmological question.[14] The cosmological question is valid because the system of

---

14. H. P. Owen, *Concepts of Deity* (New York: Herder and Herder, 1971), 52.

God and world seems to have no grounding beyond its own structure. It sits upon nothing. Whitehead conceded as much when he
wrote, "God is the ultimate limitation, and his existence is the ultimate irrationality."[15] Classical theism, in contrast, has a powerful
grounding, the infinite ground of being, being itself, for which the
question of sufficient reason (why does the God of being exist?) fails
to apply.

A response to the problem involves both mythic and metaphysical elements, a kind of *Urgeschichte*, or primordial history, about
the timeless "once" that logically precedes the "once upon a time."
The mythic narrative about a series of connected occurrences is
about realities that are beyond time. What sufficient grounding can
we identify for the chaos-God-creation system proposed here?

Plenteous Emptiness: The Void-Plenum

We submit that the chaos, or *Pandemonium Tremendum*, is the
proper source of that grounding. As described earlier, chaos me-
diates between radical nonbeing (*ouk-on*) and relative nonbeing
(*me-on*). The chaos is transformed by continuous degree as its
microstates descend into ever greater regions of multiplicity and
dispersion. The image is one of a deepening maelstrom of pure
indeterminateness populated with riotous particulars in complete
context independence. The limit of this descent is the void. The
primordial chaos consists of microstates that approach *ouk-on*
asymptotically.

The *Pandemonium Tremendum* is theoretically without context,
too, unbounded and unconditioned. But, effectively, God, in the
divine surveillance of the chaos, provides a type of context, not
so much for the whole, the collective, as for each microstate with
respect to God, but not with respect to one another. God is the great
determiner, on the one hand, but also the unobtrusive witness, on
the other. The void, residing at the depths of the primordial chaos,
is plumbed by God, yet remains itself without context.

The meonic reality of the *Pandemonium Tremendum* (its noise),
its potency, fades with the manyness of its microstates or infinitesimals into a radical emptiness (its silence). It would be tempting to
characterize this emptiness as the void or abyss, but that would be
misleading. While it is literally nothing, it is what remains when
nothing is left, or more appropriately, when all is present. The

15. A. N. Whitehead, *Science and the Modern World* (New York: Macmillan,
1925), 221–22.

primordial chaos in its dispersion and its infinity may equally be characterized as a plenum, an infinite multiplicity. The chaos is the *Ungrund*, the fundament and basin of the divine life, the ground and groundlessness of God, eternal and uncaused, at once the answer to the cosmological question and the most profound mystery.

The conclusion of this story is that, if the *Pandemonium Tremendum* contains radical nonbeing, then the cosmological question has a possible answer. Nonbeing is accounted for within the framework of fundamental things. The primordial chaos is grounded in absolutely nothing. All creation takes place from the power of the chaos through the will of God. In an absolute sense, it is *creatio ex nihilo*.

God's Self-creative In-speaking

The task remaining in this proposal as a solution to the cosmological question is to account for God as will and intention, as the agent who shapes the stuff of chaos into creation.

Perhaps a word of caution is prudent here. The following speculative account of how God achieves determinateness by arising from the *Pandemonium Tremendum* may seem excessively primordial and metaphysical—some distant preface to Gen. 1:1. The intention is to continue the story of the primordial chaos, God, and creation progressively and coherently. The landscape upon which this scene is played out is the far country encountered by any attempt to push the margins of the imagination and stretch ordinary language to describe extraordinary situations. To this extent, the scene differs little in character from descriptions of the quantum field out of which the initial singularity spontaneously appeared as the seed of the big bang and eventually our sprawling universe. Also, this account, though possibly strange to monotheists, may well resonate comfortably with Hindus, Taoists, and Buddhists, whose traditions deal with limit situations all the time.

God represents the power of decision. For anything to be requires decision, the yea or nay regarding a set of possible messages, signals, or states. But this God is also the result of such an act. Theogony, the birth of God,[16] is really the arising of a conditioned particular reality (God as will, witness, and intention) from the primordial ground of the unconditioned. God is born out of an act of self-address, an aboriginal posit, spontaneous and unattended, from which God

---

16. Hesiod, "Theogony."

derives God's own context, thereby giving God determination to be the great determiner.

The idea here is that God is constituted, actually self-constituted, by an internal act of communication, wherein variety taken from the *Pandemonium Tremendum* is configured to give content to the divine will. The question is thus, How does God arise *causa sui* as a determinate reality, given the account of the primordial chaos? One response lies in the concept of context. Context dependence and thus determinateness means to have an *other*. Absolute simplicity, that state attributed to divinity in refined yet uncompromising fashion by medieval theology, actually results in no God at all because the requisite other is missing. To be is to speak and be spoken to. "When we are silent we are one, when we speak we are two."[17] The appearance of God is the primordial posit, the aboriginal taking place, the divine self-creation of God as out-spoken in the creation of the other as context. The originating seed of divinity is the primordial bit, the yes or no that is reduced to zero bits by a great decision to be rather than not. God separates from the primordial chaos through this spontaneous declaration and takes a stand in it. Henceforth, both God and creation become possible as mutual others, partners in a common context.

Meister Eckhart (d. 1327), the great German mystic, envisioned divinity in a radical and yet similar way. On the one hand, Eckhart speaks of the Godhead, an ultimate state beyond existence and nonexistence. On the other hand, God comes forth from the Godhead into being and engages the creation. Indeed, creatures have significant say in the becoming of this God: "God 'becomes' God," writes Eckhart, "when all creatures speak God forth: there 'God' is born."[18] This "God," while possessing all the attributes appropriate to a singular deity, including eminent being, is nonetheless apart from the Godhead. Eckhart speaks of God residing in the *parvis,* or outer sanctuary of the temple, rather than within the heart of the Godhead.[19]

Eckhart's vision of deity resembles the communication model in several respects. His Godhead corresponds to the *Pandemonium*

17. Pieter Arie Hendrik de Boer, *Fatherhood and Motherhood in Israelite and Judean Piety* (Leiden: E. J. Brill, 1974); quoted in A. R. Peacocke, *Creation and the World of Science* (Oxford: Clarendon Press, 1979), 138.

18. Meister Eckhart, *"Nolite timere eos,"* in Oliver Davies, ed., *Meister Eckhart: Selected Writings* (London: Penguin Press, 1994), 234.

19. Meister Eckhart, *"Renovamini spiritu,"* cited in Ian Almond, "How Not to Deconstruct a Dominican: Derrida on God and Hypertruth," *Journal of the American Academy of Religion* 68, no. 2 (2000): 331.

Tremendum where absolute noise and silence coincide in a state beyond being. His God is the engaging conversational deity who emerges from the primordial chaos and self-completes by breaking this noise-silence in out-speaking the creation as other. "All creatures" subsequently talk back, and God (who resembles Janus, the Roman god of the threshold, in facing both chaos and creation) becomes determinative through this cocreative context.

The notion of some preexisting divine telos or generative Platonic form of God is not part of the process of divine self-arising.[20] Where would this form come from? It could not be part and parcel of the primordial chaos; that option is denied by the teleologically indifferent nature of the chaos as the formless and noisy abyss.[21] If God is will that draws upon the chaos as the material source of its content, there can be no eternal principle, no *arche* or *logos,* that God actualizes. The content of the divine will is therefore not due to the realization of some divine essence. It must be completely spontaneous.

Indeed, an etiological myth about the very beginnings even of God's self-communication could include a primordial utterance, an original spontaneous sound (resembling, perhaps, the "Om" sung out by Brahma, the Hindu god of creation, as the vibratory essence of the creation). Then, as one might reasonably continue in verse two of this genesis of God, the divine will constructs or integrates its own certainty around the nucleus of this aboriginal utterance before turning to the task of creating the world. God constitutes God through the act of surveying variety, selecting from its richness, and self-sending a message. Uncertainly is relieved, even in God in this sense. God then constructs a new synthesis from this material by taking bearings and constructing the divine life.

The oddness of an internal conversation in God is not so strange if we relate it to what commonly goes on inside our heads. Thinking requires language. But how does the mind assemble the words to have a thought? The perplexing quandary is that in order to express a thought one must have "something to say" that directs the selection of proper words or phrases to build a statement that conveys the thought. Indeed, sometimes we know what we want to say but

---

20. For an excellent argument against eternal guiding principles in the Godhead, see David L. Hall, "Process and Anarchy—A Taoist Version of Creativity," *Philosophy East and West* 28, no. 3 (1978): 271–85.

21. The model under discussion here is governed by the ideal of parsimony or elegance. Proliferating or multiplying modes in the divine life unnecessarily violates this principle.

we can't find the right words. In what way or mode is that initial thought present in the mind briefly before it is rendered into language? Prior to any articulation, the thought resides in the shadows of the subconscious as intuition and intention. Finding the words is a selection process in which one draws upon a vocabulary and then conveys the words as messages to one's self. The will or pregnant intention, the latent thought, may then be expressed in no uncertain terms. The creative act of divine self-communication is the simple unbroken movement from willing to a definite result.

Through communicating, or in-speaking, God becomes more than simple will. Divine willings become possible as definite distinguishable elements. A *logos* arises concurrently with the primal act of self-definition. The *logos,* as Tillich says, opens up the divine ground and its darkness, and makes its fullness distinguishable and definite.[22] This *logos* is the continuous process of discrimination out of which God constitutes the divine being with certainty. The *logos* is this certainty that itself becomes the consequent principle for the selection of further variety and the communication of ever more complex messages in an everlasting process of raveling and constructive reflection. God speaks God's word, initially internally in the act of self-composition, and then externally in the out-spoken act of creation. Through this process God becomes a unified center of decision.

We are mistaken if we understand information only in a narrow technical sense as a quantitative measure of the raw material of communication that passes through a channel on its way from output to input, from speaker to listener. Information is power, if by "power" we mean to select and evoke, to shape and build with high resolve. Speech is the most obvious mode of communication. It is a medium of information and, like information, it is the exercise of power, and in this case, the very process out of which God self-constructs.

Divine Sovereignty and the Pandemonium Tremendum

Divine sovereignty is often interpreted as the absence of any restraint or conditions upon God's being and actions. Power and freedom are connected. Clearly, in the theological scheme of things we are describing, divine power resides in God's willings as they draw upon the primordial chaos as their material expression. This

---

22. Paul Tillich, *Systematic Theology,* 3 vols. in 1 vol. (Chicago: University of Chicago Press, 1967), 1:251.

infinite potency exists as a necessary attribute of deity. The prevailing assumption is that the chaos is over against God and that God overcomes its terrible confusion through the exercise of divine power, the source of which is certainly not that freestanding chaos. Far from being frustrated by the chaos or required to overcome it, God's freedom and power are enabled by chaos. Absolute sovereignty in God requires a limitless source of potency that can only be the infinite field of variety, the *Pandemonium Tremendum.*

God is God, first of all, as the original lord, the author of the primordial creative posit, the original decision, based on nothing, that provided the single event from which all subsequent events take their bearings. This first act is the only act of pure spontaneity since it is based on no prior settled context and no preexisting principle of *arche.* It is the parent seed for contingency and contributes to an explanation for the radical contingency of the creation. For, if the cosmos were based on a structure derived from an eternal principle, the cosmos would itself share both in its eternality and necessity. The constitutive creative event is the one true act of anarchy, and its product, the creation, contingent. This is one understanding of what theology means when it speaks both of the sovereignty of God and the *creatio ex nihilo.* God is constrained by nothing and the birth of the creation is triggered by no previous impulse. The initial act is radically free and spontaneous.

The divine primordial posit becomes the context or bearing for further development. God provides the original bounds as well as the original orientation. This, indeed, is what it means to be a creature—to take one's bearings from God.

This is a strong sense of divine sovereignty in that there is no compelling reason why God would do this rather than that, or even do anything at all. Divine sovereignty means no less than complete spontaneity, at least insofar as it is experienced from our side through the limited vision of finite creatures. Far from being capricious and arbitrary, God, of course, has reasons beyond our know. Karl Barth is one theologian who insisted on this view. It provided him with the basis for a theology founded on the absolute transcendence of deity. Barthian categories of lofty majesty, holiness, and glory are based in the supreme self-determination of God, and they are certainly compatible with our model. But here Barth diverges from our program. He insisted that God remains in essence unknowable except insofar as God is voluntarily self-disclosing. Divine aseity is the key to divine sovereignty. It seems that this communication model does not suffer from this fault. God's utter sovereignty is protected and assured in the model. The *Pandemonium Tremendum* is a way of making divine independence plausible. God is liberated from all constraint (negative freedom), and God is the source of absolute abundance or potential (positive freedom). Together, these give us a God who is capable of steadfastness and novelty. The storehouse of the snow is inexhaustible.

At this point we are patrolling the border between the provinces of negative and positive theology, between metaphysical accounts of the divine life and the *Mysterium* itself. Barth's view inspires a radical claim that is by no means rare in Christian theology: "In the first act of creation, God appears as the creator of the world.... Out of the divine nothing, the *Gottheit,* or the *Ungrund* ... God the creator is born."[23] Theology has consistently testified to a certain duplexity in the divine nature. The Greek fathers denominate the deity into the "unoriginate," or *Agennetos,* the uncontained or invisible, and the living, expressive, redeeming, engaging, and responsive Yahweh of biblical testimony. For Meister Eckhart, these were the *Gottheit* and *Gott* respectively.[24] Hindu speculation categorizes them as Nirguna and Saguna Brahman. The Tao Te Ching speaks of the "Nameless" and "Named" Tao, and Tillich has his "God beyond God." In this model, we have the *Pandemonium Tremendum* and God.

CONCLUSION

We have attempted to refurbish the reputation of the primordial chaos by recognizing its contributions, first to the divine life and second to the creation, in terms taken from communication theory. Far from being a mythological fiery dragon or storm god dispatched by a prevailing warrior divinity, the *Pandemonium Tremendum* is the reason for God's absolute sovereignty and the limitless source of variety for the creation. God manages the primordial chaos through the witness of a complete internal survey and the embrace of external acts of decision. Included within this embrace are the grounding of the chaos in *ouk-on*—absolute nonbeing—and the in-speaking of God in the act of self-creation. Together, these accounts provide one

23. Nicolas Berdyaev, *The Destiny of Man,* trans. Natalie Duddington (New York: Harper, 1960), 87. See also Philip Hefner, "God and Chaos: The Demiurge versus the *Ungrund,*" *Zygon: Journal of Religion and Science* 19, no. 4 (1984): 469–85,
24. Rudolf Otto, *Mysticism East and West,* trans. B. L. Bracy and R. C. Payne (New York: Collier, 1960), 30.

answer to the cosmological problem and reinforce the irreducible theological declaration of divine sovereignty. In subsequent chapters we will return to home territory with accounts of the creation in the light of the communication model. Happily, the shape of that discussion will be, for the most part, along more traditional and familiar lines.

– 7 –

An Outspoken God

THE MOST FUNDAMENTAL QUESTION of being, "Why is there something rather than nothing?" has several competing answers, one of which is God. As the conclusion of one of the more viable arguments for God's existence, the answer is attractive both to reason and intuition. In classical theism, the creator God is a being of perfect wisdom, goodness, and power, one whose essence is the divine existence and the power of being itself. Such an imposing reality certainly appears adequate for the task of creating the universe. Yet, the simple assertion that such a being is responsible for the world is incomplete unless it is accompanied by some account of how the task was accomplished. In the absence of such an account, God's creative actions remain in the realm of myths of origin, or magic, or claims of divine fiat based on the intimidating description of God as a being of majestic and peerless power who creates any way God pleases. But words like "majesty" and "power" are not explanations. They cry out for accounts of economy, of the application of power that effectively brings about, sustains, and directs the creation. Otherwise, the ordered creation is best described as "God's immaculate machine."[1] This issue will be taken up here with an analysis of divine power, the means by which God acts to originate and sustain the creation.

DIVINE POWER AND THE GOD BEYOND GOD

Power

If the question of creation, the how of creation, is indeed a question of power, what is its source? How is it exercised? How does God employ power to order, sustain, and guide the creation? How is it that this world of specific and unique features (we can imagine alternative worlds with radically different features) arises?

---

1. Phrase taken from the lyrics of Paul Simon's "One-Trick Pony."

The project that is encouraged by these questions is not exactly an exercise in natural theology, nor is it exclusively an exercise in formulating a theology of nature. Elements of both approaches are involved. Any model of divinity based on conclusions the premises of which are descriptions of the creation is a form of argument and inherently an expression of natural theology. But, if the intention is to clarify the ideas of God and God's relation to the creation, then contributions to a theology of nature may be expected.

In either case, inquiry begins with an examination of divine power. "Power" is a heady but vague term. Power is the capacity to influence, even control, and in extreme forms, to dictate. When linked with teleology, power is the capacity for effective action toward the realization of a purpose. Of course, hurricanes are powerful and they do not will anything. But God is likened more frequently to a person with intentions than to a hurricane. So the model of power as intentional is appropriate when speaking of deity.

In addition, divine power fits nicely into the traditional account of divine causality as being primary rather than secondary. God is the cause of all causes but not to be numbered among them. God undergirds and sustains creation and permits its laws to work freely. This dual category of primary and secondary causes has both strengths and weaknesses. But a major point to be taken from it is that a being of infinite power acts in such a gentle yet efficient manner that the two forms of causality slip smoothly into one another, because divine causality, though working ubiquitously in both a universal and uniform fashion and in particular cases, is never noticed. Indeed, it is not noticeable.

The model or metaphor for the creation as an act of God is important in any specification of the question of divine power and the world. The model being developed here is the creation as the consequence of God's messages or conversation. Creation is the divine composition. The term "composition" is found in discussions of creativity in the visual arts and music as well as literature. The image of the dramatic performance and the symphony are equally appropriate given the underlying isomorphic framework that makes such comparisons possible and accurate in the first place. All composition is the result of communication. In the creation God speaks out, composes. If the world, in fact, resembles the product of speaking, of composing, then to that extent this model of a communicating divinity is reasonable.[2]

2. How God creates and sustains through the act of speaking and the fount of

When seen in the framework of communication theory, the question of the modes of divine power with respect to the creation takes on a somewhat different character from classical accounts. The emphasis of this model is on diversity as a fundamental trait of the creation. Thus the question becomes, How does a God of perfect power and wisdom produce a world consisting of countless specific and unique events? Or, in terms presented by Tillich's ontology, How does Being itself generate beings? God creates and sustains through a perfect, entirely realized and ever active fluency. Even in classical theism with its emphasis on God as *actus purus*, self-communication plays an important role. Everything in act communicates itself as far as possible. The divine nature is supremely in act; hence, God communicates the divine being with perfect fullness. Far from being a passive entity wrapped within itself, God reaches out, speaks out, and the result is the creation.[3]

If God is infinite, and infinity is defined negatively as freedom from all limits and constraints, then chaos, which is just that state, must be present in or to God. Chaos is the infinite reservoir of elemental potentiality. But God is more than this since God is willing, directive, and intentional. These features of personhood require selection and limitation and hence must involve agency—the power to act toward the satisfaction of a goal. Still, potentiality and agency in a God who stands alone are insufficient to explain themselves in a functional or operational way. Creation is required in this scheme as the object of God's intention, or else intentions mean nothing, and the divine agency of decision is without function or purpose—it is superfluous.

The God beyond God?

Paul Tillich's radical idea of "the God beyond the God of theism"[4] offers an insightful parallel to the *Pandemonium Tremendum* and God. God is the ground or power of Being itself. Since Being

---

variety is, in some ways, no less of a mystery than classical metaphysics and its claims that God is the infinite power of being sustaining particular beings. But variety makes more sense in the contemporary world because of the recognition of the plurality in unity in ecosystems and societies. So a language describing God's creative affiliation with the world that expropriates language and ideas from sciences of variety should provide a fertile source for modeling divinity.

3. Armand A. Maurer, *Medieval Philosophy* (New York: Random House, 1962), 172.

4. See Paul Tillich, *The Courage to Be* (New Haven: Yale University Press, 1952), 181–90.

itself is absolutely unconditioned—without attributes or limiting determinateness, the undetermined that determines—no features or properties can be attributed to it except in the sense of symbols. Being itself has no particular agency, capacity to act. It is eternally present as the sustaining power in which all existing beings are rooted and without which all creation would fall into the abyss of nonbeing.

God as Being itself is beyond the God of theism for a number of reasons. The most important is that the God of theism is an individual, a specific conditioned being, and hence less than ultimate. The God of theism, with its ascribed features, differs from other creatures standing out of the ground of being only in that it is bigger or biggest. For Tillich, such a deity is problematic. He rejects it as an inadequate understanding of the Ultimate. Tillich's God of being, the true Ultimate, is personal, willing, and intentional, but only insofar as these features are applied as symbols. Ascribing them directly to Being itself would be a contradiction; they would be conditions imposed on the unconditioned. As an act of God, primordial creation is no different. It symbolizes the power of being as the answer to the question "Why is there something rather than nothing?" God is in the beginning, not in a temporal or strictly causal sense, but as the eternal and ever present source of all things.

The analogue to Tillich's Being itself is the *Pandemonium Tremendum*. But, unlike the power of being, the power of chaos is in a dynamic state of broiling dissolution that precedes even essences. It cannot act on its own to give rise to and sustain a specific or concrete creation. When it does spill over into the world without restraint, the massive flow wreaks havoc. In the communication model, the primordial chaos resembles the ground of being, and God is the self-conditioning, primordial derivative of that chaos. Unlike the ground of being, however, the power of the chaos does not erupt directly into the creation. Rather, it is channeled through God, who gives rise to the creation in the continuous out-speaking or transmission of messages, whose source is the chaos. Thus, God, the required mediating and constraining agency, is Tillich's penultimate deity, the God of theism, an individual agent with attributes, or, more accurately, operational features, giving the deity the look of a personal individual.

Tillich is right: Being itself must be unconditioned. But the question is, how does the absolutely unconditioned give rise to the conditioned, the limited and finite? In sum, the ground of being has no impetus to become the ground of anything in particular. A distinctive operational agent is required. This is the God who is not beyond God.

God as the Principle of Concretion

Actually, the face of this God of theism turns both ways. God faces the *Pandemonium Tremendum* as its impartial witness. God also faces the creation as its partisan agent. God is that necessary reality standing between the unconditioned chaos and the highly conditioned world, or between the purely indeterminate without context and the determinate in context.

Creation emerges when constraint is imposed upon chaos in acts of divine decision. It represents the unique determination derived from a set of possible arrangements that might have occurred, but did not because of God's decisive willing. The chaos is absolute dispersion or infinite multiplicity. It is perfectly neutral with respect to any tendency or preference. To be, that is, to be a finite entity, involves restriction over a range or field of potential. The richness and texture of actual connections in complex creaturely systems suggest that severe constraint exists, for the actual system represents a highly improbable state of arrangement. In the absence of some predisposing factor or principle of limitation, complex systems are unlikely, indeed impossible, if the primordial chaos is assumed. The act of creation is the act of biasing the chaos toward certain persistent arrangements. This act is the act of communication, of decision and transmission.[5]

HOW GOD ACTS

The Question of Miracle

Creation, therefore, requires an agent, a power, principle, or person acting to bring about a novel outcome. Agents act causally; they cause the outcome. For human acts of creation, the kind of causality employed is readily identifiable, especially if the result is a material creation. Humans use instruments of all kinds, including those of their own bodies (e.g., voice, hand) to enter into complex acts of creation. The process of creation is a deft combination of inspiration, imagination, implementation, and appreciation. The implementation phase of the creative act is where the question of cause is normally focused. How is the imaginative concept carried out, brought to fruition, realized, or materialized? To be sure, the

---

5. Whitehead refers to this process as concrescence.

question of creation is far more involved than this. But, with respect to divine creation, the initial question is the same: How does God implement the divine will? Through what powers or processes does the divine act to realize or materialize the world? And to generalize even further, How does God act to bring about any divine willing whatsoever?

Some theologians simply dismiss the question of divine causality by arguing that no single mode of creation is adequate to account for the creative acts of an omnipotent and eternal being. This rejection of the question reduces the options to either mystery or miracle. While mystery may well turn out to be the end of all speculation concerning divine causality, miracle is hardly satisfying. It seems to be a form of causality, but one that makes no sense in that it is a label given in place of an explanation, just as "soporific" was once used to explain why we sleep. "Miraculous" is a characterization not an explanation, and it refers to a surprising and inexplicable event. The claim of miracle is actually a thinly disguised form of ignorance, a non-explanation. To say that an omnipotent being does what it pleases is both inadequate and circular. How does God exercise this unlimited power?

Seeking the Causal Joint

One of the most difficult problems has to do with the so-called causal joint between God and the creation. Any understanding of providence or the implementation of the divine will should include some account of how God causes things to happen. Unless God is somehow likened to the world or unless the world is likened to God in the sense of shared conditions or attributes, a reasonable accounting of a causal joint seems impossible.

Deism provides an easy way out. The cosmos is an autonomous and freestanding system. God does not act (or no longer acts) upon it. There is no causal joint. Pantheism is another way out. God acts continuously, uniformly affecting all things, even to the vibrations of individual atoms. With pantheism, the autonomy of nature is an illusion since there is no moment that, despite appearances, the world goes on its own. The laws of nature are nothing less than the observed patterns of divine, steadfast influence continuously at work. If "the properties commonly ascribed any object are, in the last analysis, names for its behavior,"[6] and if behavior is but the

---

6. A. R. Herrick quoted in W. Ross Ashby, *Design for a Brain: The Origin of Adaptive Behaviour* (London: Chapman and Hall, 1960), v.

patterned expression of divine action, then the distinction between objects and divine action vanishes. Things are God at work, or, to shorten the equation, things are God. Once again there is no causal joint; a single unified reality does not require one. Theism is a difficult way out because this position requires both a real, freestanding creation and the sustaining, directive influence of God. Given such a world and given such a God, the question of how the interactions occur becomes central.

Because of this quandary, the problem of the connection of God and creation has been addressed by a number of theologians. Two important hypotheses have emerged: the "top-down" and "bottom-up" forms of divine causation. Biochemist and theologian Arthur Peacocke represents the first position. God, rather than directly altering some specific chain of events in the world to realize the divine will—as proposed by interventionist models and denied by mechanism—influences the system of the creation as a whole and at its highest levels of integration. This influence has subsequent natural effects on the subsystems of the world as it filters downward through the various levels of nature to provide an environment containing conditions that bring about the specific events God intends.

In Peacocke's words,

> The macroscopic state and character of the [complex] system as whole is a constraint, effectively like a cause, upon what happens to the units of which it is constructed. These latter then behave in ways other than they would have done were they not a part of that system.[7]

In this version of whole-part causality, God remains respectful of the integrity of the created world, none of whose laws are violated.

The second, or bottom-up, position is ably represented by physicist and theologian Robert J. Russell, who locates the causal joint of divine interaction at the other end of the spectrum of being, in the realm of quantum events. Russell takes advantage of the statistical nature of the quantum world, its inherent or ontological indeterminacy, to allow God to influence the appearance of particles undetected and without violating natural laws. These events, once

---

7. Arthur Peacocke, "A Map of Scientific Knowledge: Genetics, Evolution, and Theology," in *Science and Theology: The New Consonance,* ed. Ted Peters (Boulder Colo.: Westview Press, 1998), 199.

amplified to affect higher levels of organization, bring about God's desired changes in the world of everyday objects and creatures.[8]

Each of these accounts has its strengths and advantages. Each preserves the integrity of the creation by allowing God to engage the world indirectly without insulting its integrity through miraculous violations of its order, an order originally ordained by God. Nonetheless, the quest for a full explanation is not satisfied. Certainly, God's disruptive influence on creation is minimized by these hypotheses. In each case, the effects of the initial divine contact are propagated throughout the creation to bring about the desired results without violating any laws of nature. The world becomes an instrument for providence.

The God side of the causal joint is seldom discussed for several reasons, including reverence for and deep appreciation of God's radical otherness, recognition of the inherent boundaries of finite human inquiry concerning the nature of God, and a healthy suspicion of any metaphysical account of transcendental objects. Also, Peacocke and Russell are concerned primarily with developing theories of divine action that avoid disruption of the laws of nature. Consequently, there is little interest in reconstructing the standard theistic model of deity. God is personal (conscious and willing), good (loving and trustworthy), and powerful (omnipotent and omniscient). Still, God's personhood and goodness do not by themselves answer the question of how God exercises divine power. How God exercises power to bring about God's intentions in the creation remains a significant issue.

METAPHORS OF DIVINE CAUSALITY

Two Metaphors

Theologians have suggested numerous modes for divine causality. These include metaphorical and analogical speculation of great imaginative range. One has God taking a "hand" to the creation as a craftsperson molding some preexisting material. Another sees God as divine monarch commanding the world to become as royal subject; A third is the world as the indispensable body of God to

---

8. Expressions of Russell's position can be found in several places. One recent and accessible essay is "Does the 'God Who Acts' Really Act in Nature?" in Peters, ed., *Science and Theology,* 77–102. See also Russell's articles at *www.CTNS.org* and *www.Counterbalance.org.* For several assessments of the bottom-up approach of Russell and others, see the section "Quantum Physics and Understanding God," in *Zygon: Journal of Religion and Science* 35, no. 3 (2000): 489–560.

be moved as any organism moves. And finally, there is the image of God in the likeness of the sun whose rays emanate from the divine reality to become the creation.

The final two metaphors for divine action in this short list are revealing in connection with the communication model. Each of these, the world as the body of God and the world as the consequence of divine emanation, is isomorphic in that it shares certain deep structural similarities with the elements of communication theory.

One richly suggestive metaphor for God's causal relation with the creation is *the world as God's body.*[9] Derived primarily from process thought, this image depicts God as dipolar—as absolute and relative.[10] God is absolute or unsurpassable, the agent of maximum power and influence. But this influence is not exercised over the distance that separates the transcendent divinity from the creation, the common understanding of the monotheistic traditions. Rather, God is continuously in touch with the creation most intimately because the world itself is an organic extension of the divine being. This continuity is the divine relativity, the other pole.

God acts in the world in a manner similar to a person acting through his or her body. By taking thought, the body moves in orderly, intentional ways. The lines of influence are the nerves and the electrical impulses conducted through them. While there is no parallel system of influence for God, the central point is that God operates by instructing the divine body of creation instrumentally to accomplish desired ends. These instructions are not sent by some disembodied mind across the vacuum or void separating the transcendent deity from the world below. God's body is "all inclusive of the creaturely bodies, which are to God as cells to a supercellular organism."[11] God is both beyond and in the world, a position falling between theism and pantheism that process theology refers to as panentheism. Divine influence is present continuously throughout the creation just as my influence is present continuously throughout my body. Indeed, the two can be separated only by abstraction. My

9. See Grace Jantzen, *God's World, God's Body* (Philadelphia: Westminster Press, 1984); Sallie McFague, *The Body of God: An Ecological Theology* (Minneapolis: Fortress Press, 1983). See also James E. Huchingson, "The World as God's Body: A Systems View," *Journal of the American Academy of Religion* 47, no. 3 (1980): 335–44.

10. See, for example, Charles Hartshorne, *The Logic of Perfection* (LaSalle, Ill.: Open Court Publishing, 1962).

11. Charles Hartshorne, *Omnipotence and Other Theological Mistakes* (Rochester: State University of New York Press, 1966), 49.

body and "I" are a unified totality. The "I" that pilots the corporal body is not a separate entity residing in that body. God's "I" is that part of the world that embraces the remainder as its consciousness and unifier. The integrity of the world would be lost without this agent of harmony and arrangement, and the agent would be lost without the world as the instrumentality of experience and growth.

Communication theory is compatible with the image of the world as God's body. The body is a tightly knit or highly integrated and incredibly complex system. This comprehensive complexity is what distinguishes an organic system from other kinds of systems, such as ecosystems and societies, more accurately addressed as communities. That is, a living system is formally no different from any other system. It is different only in the degree of its complexity, which may exceed that of nonliving systems by a millionfold. Any system is the consequence of a process of generation that reduces the number of possible systems to just the one that arises, usually over a period of time and with many steps or phases of development. Each step is a node where decisions are rendered concerning these possibilities. The result is a system that is bounded by its own constitution. Internally, each component or subsystem is determined by the context of relationships with others around it in a network of mutual influence of self-adjustment and growth. The flow of variety in processes of communication is the explanation for the creation, development, and dynamic stability that is a "body" or living thing as a system of bounded complex variety in context.

The panentheistic emphasis of the communication model is that the world is an organic whole, a singular individual of immense complexity. Its complexity, as well as its stability, depends on the dominant subsystem of that cosmic totality, whom we know as God. God is the conduit for a continuously refreshing and nurturing stream of variety without which the world could neither sustain nor renew itself. And God is the source of the context for the world, without which it would remain indeterminate. God is the self-determining determiner. By communicating variety, God partially determines the particulars of the world system, and these particulars, in a great act of mutual integration, constitute the very body of the divine agent who determines them.

God sets the stage for the divine body in two ways.[12] The first is through intimate internal communication. This is similar to the way we maintain our own bodies by several levels of control with

---

12. See Huchingson, "World as God's Body," 340.

some being conscious and others not, as reflected in the subtle and pervasive operations of the sympathetic and voluntary nervous systems. The second way is by attending directly to parts of the body requiring attention. When I stub my toe, first aid is necessary. I first examine it for damage and then take actions to promote healing. God may influence the world in similar ways.

The first approach resembles God's influence as effected through the world and emphasizes immanence. The second resembles God's influence on the world and emphasizes transcendence. The first is God and body as a unified subject. The second is God and body as mutual others and objects. In both ways, the means of divine influence is the fluency of effective communication understood as the production of certainty, the introduction of constraint into a situation of immense uncertainty. Through this process the word (God's selective input of saving variety) is made flesh (the corporeal world arises and is sustained).

The second metaphor for divine action that is isomorphic with communication theory is *emanation*. This metaphor is attractive for our purposes. In traditional accounts, God's outgoing influence on the creation is likened to the light of the sun radiating continuously. Sunlight is not secondary or accidental; it belongs to the very nature of the sun to radiate. But sunlight is created. It is not the essence or stuff of the star. In like manner, God emanates or sends out the divine influence that issues forth as creation. These emanations are not God proper, but the first productions of God that result in the world.

In the communication model, God's will is the source of the initial decisions introducing constraint through the transmission of messages. These messages, or "willings," of God are the divine emanations. The extent of this divine constraint on the flow of variety may itself vary. The emanations from God can range from single highly specified messages (the quanta of variety) that, when received, result in complete certainty, to the free flow of primal variety with little or no constraint as the raw material of creation itself. Highly specified messages are intended to evoke events that steer the world in precise ways. General flows nurture the world with variety sufficient for sustaining creatures or enabling them to make their own decisions. How this occurs will be discussed in detail below. The point to be made here is that the outflow of limited or unlimited variety from the willing or decisive God corresponds favorably with the metaphor of the sun shedding its light upon the earth.

Maxwell's Demon, Maxwell's Deity

The metaphors of divine embodiment and emanation, however suggestive, are limited in explanatory power—a feature of all metaphorical speech. A model of greater formality is needed to explicate the particular relationships and modes of action that constitute a clear understanding of divine influence on the world. We may begin with yet another metaphor—here more like a parable—drawn from scientific thermodynamics and hence more likely perhaps to reveal skeletal isomorphic identities with the theory of divine action than either embodiment or emanation.

This instructive image is the classic account of "Maxwell's demon."[13] James Clerk Maxwell, a brilliant nineteenth-century scientist whose contributions include the initial synthesis of electromagnetic theory, conjured an imaginative being, a demon, as a thought experiment to question the absolute limits imposed upon the physical world by the inexorable operation of the second law of thermodynamics.

By way of reintroducing this principle from our earlier discussion, the second law says that all energy processes tend irreversibly toward a final state of thermodynamic equilibrium where energy dissipates as heat and is permanently unavailable to do further work. This final state of entropy is also represented by the collapse of all enduring order. Through constant shuffling, molecules of matter in a closed system tend to lose their arrangement and become randomly distributed. That is, the differential states of energy they carry mix and meld into a state of uniform temperature and distribution. Again, no work is possible in such a system. Without spending energy there is no way to separate this merge of molecules into regions of faster or slower ones, thereby regenerating arrangement and reversing entropic inevitability.

Maxwell proposed that a tiny demon could accomplish the task by using a frictionless door between compartments. He would open the door as fast molecules passed, capturing them in one chamber of the vessel, but would then deny access to slower molecules by slamming the door as they approached. Eventually, all the faster molecules would be isolated in one compartment and the slower ones in the other. The effect of this sorting process would be to reestablish a state of disequilibrium in the gradient between warmer (fast molecules) and cooler (slow molecules). In such a case, the

---

13. See Jeremy Campbell, *Grammatical Man: Information, Entropy, Language, and Life* (New York: Simon and Schuster, 1982), 48–49.

effects of entropy are reversed; order is reestablished in the system, and work becomes possible.

Maxwell's enigmatic scenario posed problems for his contemporaries who subscribed to the laws of thermodynamics as inviolable. But it was not until the twentieth century that brilliant and ingenious analysis of the demon's actions returned the second law to firm footing. As it turns out, the demon could not identify fast and slow molecules, nor act to separate them, without expending energy. Calculations demonstrated that the demon, in identifying, capturing, and sorting molecules, was contributing to the entropy of the total system to such an extent that the demon more than cancelled out the advantages of the final assortment. Once these expenditures of energy were factored into the process, the second law was vindicated.

An instructive parallel can be drawn between Maxwell's demon and the communication model of God. The demon is to the chambers of molecules in thermodynamic equilibrium as God is to the *Pandemonium Tremendum* and the creation. God surveys and regulates the primordial chaos through a process of decision and selection. These decisions issue forth in the form of specific certainties in the world, as realized possibilities and concrete determinations. The microstates ingredient in the chaos are, of course, not molecular, but the sorting process is the same, for God is the source of messages given over to the creation in the act of determination. God manipulates the uncertainty of the variety within the divine purview by disposing it in certain directions away from randomness and isolation and toward pattern, organization, and relation. The result is an orderly system that is neither the chaos nor God. This system is the creation. As the functioning entity standing between chaos and creation, God is the waist of the hourglass through which primordial variety is released in proper proportions.

The Cosmological Argument

Thus far three essential elements have been identified in the open-ended totality of things that accounts for its existence and its order. These are the *Pandemonium Tremendum*, God, and creation. God is the go-between, that reality who is required in any account about how the orderly and finite world arises from the pure chaos of the *Pandemonium Tremendum*. Despite its infinite potential and dynamic fury, the primordial chaos is incapable of generating and sustaining orderly process and structure. An agent of communication is indispensable for that task. The chaos is the infinite fund of variety and the source of difference in all possible worlds. God manages the incessant eruption of the chaos as the primary agent of constraint, selection, decision, and specificity. As we shall see in chapter 8, creatures perform this function in their own lives as well, but they must rely upon the provisions of variety that sustain the very environments that they inhabit and exploit through decisions of their own. God is both the source of all being, the witness of the primordial chaos, and the sorter, the dominant determiner of arrangement in creation and the power of difference.

One would not be wrong to see a version of the traditional cosmological argument in this discussion. We have argued that the primordial event of creation, indeed, of all events of creation, are events of communication, where an infinite field of variety is subjected to the force of constraint by a witnessing, determining agent, who is God. Out of this continuous decisioning or willing of God, the creation arises. God is the source of originating and sustaining variety as well as the agent of decision and transmission required to bring about the world as its cause.

In its logical structure, this position closely resembles the traditional arguments for God that move from the fact of contingency in all things collectively to the necessity for an external cause to account for them. The existence of the world is derived from a necessary being who is the answer to the cosmological question "Why is there something rather than nothing?" Contingency means depending on something else as the cause and explanation for one's existence. The cosmological question arises logically from the fact of the universe accompanied by the apparent groundlessness of that fact. The world seems spontaneous, uncaused, underived. Yet, given the principle of sufficient reason—the idea that everything that comes into existence must have a reason, explanation, or cause—some prior source of its being must be supposed. That source, monotheism has always claimed, is God.

This is not the place to review or critique the vast literature on the cosmological argument. The traditional argument was conceived in an ontological framework where "existence" and "being" were focal concepts. God is the source or power of being that accounts for the existence of the concrete but contingent world. Within an alternative framework, that of communication theory, the argument, including the precipitating cosmological question, may be rephrased. We have attempted to show that multiplicity, diversity, and abundant particularity are as important as "being" in describing that collective reality we call the world or cosmos. The cosmos is a complex system, not a homogeneous mass. If it were missing either unity or plurality, the world would be something else entirely or, more likely, nothing at all.

Contingency may describe an event arising from chance or happenstance, unexpected or unforeseen. In this sense, contingency is some apparently arbitrary limitation of total independence of a set of states to some smaller set issuing from it in the form of complex, concrete systems. Where we should expect only irreducible chaotic behavior, we find instead an immense collection of definite objects exhibiting orderly arrangement. Why? The cosmos is composed of the stuff of chaos. Yet, the *Pandemonium Tremendum*, the source of cosmic variety, is an infinite field in which all states are equipotential; no particular state or collection of states is favored. Still, somehow, this entirely capricious situation is resolved into a cosmos. First, there is the voracious primordial chaos, and then there is the concrete world. An agency is required for the one to give rise to the other. Or, put in a slightly different version, the creation is a set of messages. The sufficient reason or primary cause in this context means the required message source and transmission agent. If the world could not have arisen as the source of its own messages, then an antecedent message source or transmission agency must exist, and that source is God.

EXERCISING THE POWER OF CREATION

Creation in Three Movements

In the *Summa Theologica*, Thomas Aquinas speaks of three stages of creation. The first is the creation itself. The second consists of the divine work of separation, or *opus distinctionis*. The third is the work of embellishment and elaboration, *opus ornatus*.[14] Aquinas's stages are revealing and insightful. They correspond to the process of creation suggested by the model of the *Pandemonium Tremendum*, God, and the world.

Creation. The initial act of creation, prior to the construction of any concrete reality, is the decision of God to decide. If the process of creation consists of sequential decisions, one naturally looks for the originating decision. God's first willing must be accompanied by an intention, the aim of the urge. In some pretemporal and mythological account, God decided to decide, and creation is the

---

14. Thomas Aquinas, *Summa Theologica*, pt. 1, q. 65 ante art. 1.

eventual consequence. God decides to become God, fully as an active directive force. But a decision is needed even for that context to become. The context that enables God to arise as the divine Other who calls forth the creation out of chaos must first bring forth itself. Perhaps what makes God distinctive is the primordial act, the act preceding all acts, the act of self-creation through the creation of the other. With the generation of context, God becomes God, the willing agent. Karl Rahner captures the irreducible mystery of this primal paradox with this claim: "When God wants to be what is not God, the world comes to be."[15] Unlike creatures, the very desire of God is sufficient to initiate the other as context, as the object and recipient of all subsequent acts of willing.

Separation. The primordial posit resulting in an other or context for subsequent divine action is quite literally the separation of heaven and earth. Following this initial act, the mythic events of the "Creation Week" of Genesis begin. The manner or mode of divine creation is the key to the question of divine causality. An important clue is found in the Hebrew verb *bara* used to describe God's labor. Employed in scripture exclusively for divine creation, *bara* means "to cleave or split,"[16] referring perhaps to carpentry. By itself, this might suggest the craftsperson image. But in the context of the Genesis account, this seems not to be the case. Carpenters do not command or call upon their building materials to self-assemble and form a dwelling. In a more general sense, to cleave or split suggests an act of separation or division that goes beyond construction. Thus, the focus should not be on the orders issued by God, but rather on the intention of the commands—to "separate." The initial act of creation is an act of separation: the separation of the light from the darkness, and the waters under the firmament from the waters above. Separating is deciding and differentiating. God calls this apart from that, and in doing so, communicates. God draws from the infinite resource of the *Pandemonium Tremendum* by progressive division, through speaking yes and no. The indefinite and undetermined becomes defined and distinctive. Commands are messages. Indeed, all speaking out or transmitting of variety is imperative; communication takes place when the variety of a set of possible messages is reduced, as if by command, to a more restricted set or to a single instance. Decision as separation, the separation of

---

15. Karl Rahner, *Foundations of Christian Faith: An Introduction to the Idea of Christianity* (New York: Seabury Press, 1978), 225.

16. Gerhard von Rad, *Genesis: A Commentary,* trans. John H. Marks (Philadelphia: Westminster Press, 1972), 49.

what is to be from what might be and what never will be, is summed up beautifully by Karl Barth: "That which is not is that which God did not elect or will, that which as creator he passed over, that which according to the account in Genesis 1:2 he set behind him as chaos, not giving it existence or being."[17]

Elaboration. God continues to speak out and the creation is further specified. The *opus distinctionis* of Aquinas fades into his *opus ornatus.* The merely possible becomes the probable (some constraint is introduced), and the probable becomes the certain as unique settled instances—multitudes of creatures. The Genesis narrative parallels the allegory of Michelangelo's labors to create David. Rather than using mallet and chisel, God works with commands or messages. But the process is identical in both cases. Consecutive decisions result in a further specification of creation, first in its larger and more general contours, and then in its details. Uncertainty is reduced as work progresses. Eventually, the world teems with living things, and God stands back from day's labors to express pleasure, as if even God experiences the removal of uncertainty as satisfaction.

The *bara* of God, cleaving and splitting of infinite variety through the act of communicating in which cosmos is commanded out of chaos through the progressive detailing of creation, is not yet the complete understanding of the narrative. Not only does God separate and elaborate through a continuous flow of messages, but God also gathers. Gathering is constraint introduced by decision and transmission. The infinite and radically dispersed multiplicity of the *Pandemonium Tremendum* is gathered by God in the act of composing the creation. Gathering is the act of assembling, not only of individuals in a common place, but also for a common reason: to become a community or inclusive whole with systematic integrity. Gathering is for the purpose of relating.

As the creation matures, as its basic elements are introduced one by one into the harmony of the whole emerging system, a new world arises that stands apart from God as an active agent in its own right. By delegating power, God first assigns the earth the task of bringing forth multitudes of diverse living things, and then assigns these creatures relevant tasks as cocreators. They are urged to multiply and fill their respective contexts or habitats. This delegation signi-

---

17. Karl Barth, *Church Dogmatics,* vol. 3, *The Doctrine of Creation,* trans. G. T. Thomson, ed. G. W. Bromiley and T. F. Torrance (Edinburgh: T. & T. Clark, 1960), pt. 3, 73.

fies that power is given not only to the primal couple, Adam and Eve, but also to all living things to self-articulate, to communicate and create on their own. At this point, God has certainly succeeded in creating a context for the divine life.

Sustaining the Creation

Mechanism, determined to protect the autonomy of nature at all costs, is notorious for its emphasis on God as the source of law and order but not of novelty and development. Selective reading of scripture offers clues for the presence of the *Deus*. Yahweh gives the law at Sinai, and the Israelites celebrate and testify to this great act of God that constitutes their birth as a community, as a nation. The image of lawgiver carries over to the early Scientific Revolution. Just as God gave the law to Moses as the source of Israel, so this same God gave the corresponding law to the physical cosmos as the source of its order, an order decrypted by scientific inquiry and laid out in elegant mathematical equations. This concept of a formalized order as a gracious gift of God in the creation of a community and a cosmos is the basis for Abraham Heschel's assertion "All that exists obeys."

Contemporary perspectives on the cosmos have moved far away from this vision of a remote and silent deity whose creation consists of inert, everlasting, and omnipotent matter persisting in its blind momentum, heavy and often foreboding in its insentience, and guided by inexorable laws imposed originally and eternally in effect.[18] A model of divinity corresponding to the dynamic, processing character of a cosmos filled with vital and vibrant activity must include the notion of a God who sustains not just by offering something to stand upon but also by active nurture.

A divine sustainer is a provider of sustenance. Traditional icons include angelic messengers who deliver the life-giving spirit in various ways and thereby partially satisfy the logistical question of how a transcendent God delivers this sustaining nurture. Islamic angelology includes angels whose assigned responsibility is to supply the creation. God's "sheer providingness"[19] is both a distinguishing and conceivably a definitive feature of divine actions toward the world.

18. Bertrand Russell's essay "A Free Man's Worship" is the definitive, if not concluding, statement of this position of the tragic hero destined to be crushed by "omnipotent matter."

19. Quoted in Nancy Frankenberry, review of *Nature's Self: Our Journey from Origin to Spirit,* by Robert S. Corrington, *Journal of the American Academy of Religion* 66, no. 1 (1998): 173.

God sustains the world in the same sense that a homemaker actively sustains a dwelling. Without constant attention, the input of variety, the house would fall into disrepair and eventually go completely to pieces. Neglect is the absence of communicative input that would maintain the house in the face of decay, in the face of entropic degradation. The unattended house does not merely fall apart. It is taken apart by any number of forces, visible and invisible, in its environment. Because houses are not responsive systems, they are vulnerable to these eroding influences. The homemaker, with hammer and nails, paint and brush, and an intelligent eye for what needs fixing, is actually a part of the total system of the dwelling. This person is the source of variety or information that is required to sustain the order of the entire system in the face of constant threats of corruption. With his or her active vigilance, the house may weather, but it will not collapse. Basic order requires constant replenishment of variety to establish a constant state of dynamic equilibrium. The homemaker is the *logos* of the house, its active source of wisdom and order. The homemaker may be seen as transcendent of the house as its manager, or as the immanent, indwelling subsystem of reflection, detection, and maintenance.

The parable of the house is a relatively simple illustration of divine sustenance of creation. A more complex illustration would be a gardener and a garden. Here the garden is not passive, inert, and static, as the physical wood and brick house is. Rather, it consists of active, self-elaborating, self-sustaining living systems, the plants, and a transcending or superreflective system, the gardener, who actively channels the forces of growth and organization inherent in the living community in ways that would fund its development and prevent the garden from reverting to a patch of weeds.

In accord with either analogy, God actively sustains by providing ceaselessly an essential ingredient to creatures. God spoke or commanded the world to be originally, and the speaking continues as flow as a divine monologue that is far from being prolix. If God were to cease this unbroken utterance and become silent, the world would wither, become undone, or revert to the primal chaos. To put it bluntly, if God shuts up, the creation shuts down. God's constant speaking out is like the wind sustaining a kite in flight or a breath sustaining the whirling paper windmill in the hand of a child. God's celebrated steadfastness lies not only in the dependable daily rounds of seedtime and harvest that marked the cycles of agrarian societies, but also in the divine supply of novelty that nurtures and animates the creation. The contingency of creation lies in its utter dependence upon the perpetual flow of this "supply" of sustaining variety provided by God, who, as the prophet Isaiah wrote, neither sleeps nor slumbers.

CONCLUSION

The subject of this chapter, the exercise of divine power directed toward the creation, is based on the premise that fruitful analysis is possible through the reference of communication theory. By building upon the discussion of previous chapters, our description of how God acts upon the world contributes at least to a productive alternative rendering of traditional doctrines. God moves from uncertainty, as understood in communication theory, to certainty through a process of decision and realization. The divine will is selective intentionality. In the act of creating the world and acting upon it, God decides incisively, cutting through the material of the *Pandemonium Tremendum* in a continuing act of binary inquiry. God says yes and equally no in originating, elaborating, and sustaining the creation.

– 8 –

The Mighty Throng of Creatures

HAVING EXAMINED THE BASIC PRINCIPLES of the communication model of divine action in the previous chapter, it is time to focus further on the broad features of God's actions toward the vast multitude of beings that constitute the creation. The notions of variety and its release or transmission that have served us well in earlier chapters are extended here to construct a picture of how God relates to the responsive inhabitants of the creation.

CONSTRAINT AND UNCERTAINTY IN PROPER PROPORTION

Constraining Order and Liberating Variety

At the risk of asserting too much, it is nonetheless probably accurate to say that most persons experience their lives as some combination of limiting constraint and liberating flexibility. At one extreme, fatalists emphasize inevitability, while at the other, existentialists emphasize freedom. Still, the testimony of most human beings, we suspect, would include experience of both limits and freedom. Any account of the world context involves both constraint and choice. Where there is order there is also chaos; where there is simplicity there is also complexity; and where there is constancy there is also change. These paired elements are not necessarily in the tension of opposites. Actually, they are complementary and mutually engaging. The worldly context is unpredictable, rich with variety and texture, and perpetually in process (liberating). And yet this overall character gives rise to organized, relatively uncomplicated, and repetitive states (restraining). Indeed, the order could be reversed; we could as easily claim that overall constancy of things provides faithful support for change within and among them. It is all a matter of conceptual presumption rather than logical derivation. Still, to discuss a worldly context that includes both features in some proportional balance, one must begin somewhere; we arbitrarily begin with order.

The creation may be described as a whole or singular totality whose unity varies from tight to loose but is always present. Creation, separation, elaboration, the phases of creation discussed earlier, have resulted in a world teeming with creatures whose supportive environment is fundamentally reliable and trustworthy. The world has an order discerned by science with admirable success. While opinions on the presence or absence of disorder in nature vary among observers, one may argue that with the possible exception of the unpredictability of quantum events, true disorder or randomness is rare. And even when we recognize what seems to be disorder, there is always the possibility that the indeterminate behavior is only apparent, perhaps the manifestation of some deeper, governing "hidden variables" or laws. Order reigns in the laws of nature and echoes in the logic of mathematics that accounts of them. Even chaos theory is not about chaos, but rather about unpredictability.[1]

All living systems readily recognize and exploit patterns of order in their environment. The human brain, the premier instrument of order, is so adept at this skill that it will go so far as to invent order where none is present. Humans see faces in clouds and cold fusion in test tubes even though these phenomena do not objectively exist. Despite the risks, all exploration and all learning are in consequence of there being something to discover and learn, some constant pattern of events or forms in space, tones, colors: syntax in language, rules in sports. In terms of communication theory, learning involves removing uncertainty about a state of affairs and perceiving constraint communicated by a set of messages given from natural, social, and cultural environments. Without constraint, no learning is possible.

Since the transmission of messages occurs as a process, temporality—the passage of time as a succession of events—is perhaps the most important source of order. In the experience of sentient crea-

---

1. Even when disorder is intentionally desired, it must be labored for or intentionally calculated. Randomness is a very useful tool for avoiding bias in the analysis of statistical samples. Ironically, disorder, as an artifact, must be intentionally calculated. It must be manufactured through artificial processes. Computers that have been programmed for the task generate synthetic randomness. These programs consist of a strict set of "orders" dictating the strategy of avoiding ubiquitous order or bias in the frequencies of certain numbers to produce unpredictability. The result is a string of random numbers of arbitrary length that satisfies these conditions. It appears that even disorder has its rules.

tures, time is experienced not so much as simple duration, but as an incessant or uninterrupted flow of constrained variety, of messages or signals. These patterns resemble a musical melody consisting of a series of repeated notes, related partially according to deeper laws of harmony.

Experience leads a listener to a musical piece to expect certain repeated patterns based on past transmissions. The listener's certainty grows until he or she can hum along with confidence. Speaking more generally, future states or collections of notes are probabilistically predictable by reference to similar states from the past. An ever growing constant past provides long-range clues to the future. Ignorance of the past means that each new event will come as a complete surprise. The receiver's uncertainty is partially relieved by accumulated experience of a constant environment. With expectations based on growing trust in the redundancy of messages, the receiver faces the future with confidence.[2]

Despite our understandable need for a reliable world, major risks follow from unquestioned dedication to order alone. Decay and death are assured in a cosmos from which all novelty is banished for the sake of absolute regularity. This closed system inevitably reverts not so much to a state of chaos as to a profound state of equilibrium, of complete stability in the dead-even sameness of entropic degradation. Under such conditions, all microstates of the system occupy a monotonous milieu of randomness. The this and the that are no different. Significant change is no longer possible. Complexity vanishes, leaving the stability of endless uniform duration. In a situation where all distinctions vanish or where constraint is total, the novelty in future messages is zero. Certainty is complete, but there is no longer any need to pay attention to the repeated transmission of trivial messages with little information content. Dante's account of the lowest circle of hell in *The Inferno* is not of a roaring conflagration, but of a frozen sea into which the souls of the most evil of men are eternally locked.

Fortunately, both theologically and ontologically, the creation is not a closed system with a sealed fate of either seizure or rigor. It is

---

2. Traditional myths of origin and of end celebrate the victory of order over disorder, of God over chaos, and express the primary concern of early societies for a dependable world, one in which the future is faithful to the past in eternally returning cycles and over which they might have some reliable control. Marduk conquers Tiamat, the queen of the dark, surging sea of chaos. The Leviathan, who lives in the vast depths of the *tehom,* is to become the divine plaything and the eventual entrée of the great banquet at the end of history.

open to the input of the stream of variety from its creator. God gives possibility and freedom as well as order. Possibility and freedom are to be found in the infinite texture of life. This texture, consisting of variety in complexity, is in consequence of a process where God first elaborates the world and then encourages the world to elaborate itself. Elaboration is the realization of variety, constrained for the sake of order, but immense for the sake of freedom. In the place of chaos, God offers a trustworthy and reliable world full of resources for creaturely employment and construction and sustains the world with a constant replenishment of nourishing variety.

Rules and Frequencies

Another approach to degrees of order and freedom considers the relationship between rules and frequencies. Constraint in a system, including biological systems, language systems, even systems of games such as chess, may be imposed on two levels. Rules are a form of constraint since they limit the range of possible outcomes from a total set to some smaller set. Constraint also appears as different frequencies in the elements of a set. Certain letters of the alphabet, groups of letters, and even words are more probable; they have a greater likelihood of occurring in a text. In either case, rules or frequencies, the resulting patterns of redundancy provide a foundation of order or orders that make for a predictable and dependable world.

The laws of nature constitute a set of rules. The laws of physics and chemistry simply have no exceptions; they apply to the behavior of all matter and energy universally and uniformly. The enterprise of science assumes the rule-bearing character of the cosmos in order to discover its laws and to explain the patterns of nature that emerge on the basis of their reign.

Still, not all phenomena are as straightforwardly predictable as the temperature at which a flask of water will boil at sea level or the gravitational attraction between two planets of known mass and separation. Building on nature's inexorable laws are natural systems whose behavior is complex and varied. Certainly, their behavior is constant, but it is not without novelty and surprise. Any complete description of the actions of even relatively simple living systems— insects, for example—would include probabilities. Living systems tend to behave in very constant ways, especially in large numbers, but even here any account of this behavior would be based in the language of frequency and probability. The laws of nature represent severe constraint, while the laws of life and evolution and the laws of the human social and cultural environments represent moderate constraint detected as frequency distributions within a set of possibilities.

Numerous commentators have noticed this feature of our world without which it simply would not be a livable place. A world that is tightly unified by severe constraint in all its orders is trivial, while a world that is loosely ordered to the extreme is discordant and havoc ridden. A tightly determined universe, argues John Polkinghorne, leaves no room for freedom and responsibility.[3] It is in "the iron grip of Calvinistic predestination." A loose structure, however, "dissolves significance." In such a world, "meaning can drown in the rising waters of chaos." The world that we do in fact find is in "equilibrium between these rigidifying and dissolving tendencies." In promoting his "Irenean theodicy," philosopher John Hick makes a similar observation. Free beings, he says, can grow only in a world that "operates according to general and dependable laws," but that also "presents real dangers...trials and perils."[4] Finally, Spanish philosopher of history José Ortega y Gasset writes that "man finds that the world surrounds him as an intricate net woven of both facilities and difficulties." In the absence of the facilities provided by a gracious world, we would not exist, but without the difficulties, we would not be challenged to grow and create.[5]

Within the framework of our discussion, this fortunate accommodation between too much and too little order in the creation is a matter of constraint imposed on the incessant stream of variety that forms and feeds the world. The world is regular and reliable; we can depend upon it and employ its resources instrumentally for our advantage. Some significant constraint is present that suggests that a selection process is at work biasing the equiprobable in definite directions. But the world is also uncertain and new in every succeeding moment. The bias is only partially compelling. True freedom exists as the ability of creatures to make decisions for themselves from a substantial range of possibilities. The redundancy present in the world and in all human activities is a loose balance between total

---

3. John Polkinghorne, "Creation and the Structure of the Physical World," *Theology Today* 44, no. 1 (1987): 57.

4. John Hick, *Philosophy of Religion*, 3rd ed. (Englewood Cliffs, N.J.: Prentice Hall, 1983), 48.

5. José Ortega y Gasset, "Man the Technician," in *History as a System* (New York: W. W. Norton, 1961); reprinted as "Thoughts on Technology," in *Philosophy and Technology: Readings in the Philosophical Problems of Technology,* ed. Carl Mitcham and Robert Mackey (New York: Free Press, 1972), 297.

constraint (fate) and total uncertainty (accident). Hence, our experience, as well as that of other sentient creatures is, as one writer puts it, "not too dull, not too exciting."[6] This situation is consistent with the image of God as communicator, as one who constrains the creation and necessarily so if it is to have any order at all, and yet who builds into the world considerable freedom or free play.

THE DIVERSITY OF BEINGS

Divinity Is in the Details

Robert Pirsig, in his twentieth-century classic *Zen and the Art of Motorcycle Maintenance,* describes a scene in which the central character is teaching composition. He assigns his classes the task of describing small things. The more the students search for detail, the more they discover:

> In one class he had everyone write all hour about the back of his thumb. Everyone gave him funny looks at the beginning of the hour, but everyone did it, and there wasn't a single complaint about "nothing to say."
>
> In another class he changed the subject from the thumb to the coin, and got a full hour's writing from every student. In other classes it was the same. Some asked, "Do you have to write about both sides?"[7]

The lesson they learn is that if one does "some original and direct seeing," it will become abundantly clear that life is infinitely textured. Its boundless assortment of variations cannot be exhausted by human accounts. In this sense the English mystical poet William Blake is right: infinity can be held in the palm of the hand, the infinity of distinctiveness, of variety.

In the present moment, the ever increasing power of high-speed computers is enhancing this "original and direct seeing." The ability of computer graphics, for example, to capture detail and replicate complex movements with precision is in direct proportion to the sheer quantity of information that can be rapidly processed into forms and images. The richness in texture, individuation, and potential for dynamic action in computer simulation reveals and confirms

---

6. Title of chapter 5 of Jeremy Campbell, *Grammatical Man: Information, Entropy, Language, and Life* (New York: Simon and Schuster, 1982).

7. Robert Pirsig, *Zen and the Art of Motorcycle Maintenance: An Inquiry into Values* (New York: Bantam Books, 1974), 186.

the boundless variety of the world and provides a model for the role of information in the generation of this variety.

The truth is, heaven and earth are populated with a mighty throng of creatures—millions of species representing numberless individuals. These may be classified in accordance with a taxonomic system of labeling with regard to common characteristics and evolutionary heritage, but the fact is that each label may cover a vast population of particular individuals. Furthermore, each of these individuals, though it represents a standard form identified by its genus and species, is unique in its many variations from the representative Platonic ideal for its class, and consists of details and details within details the enumeration of which would fill entire libraries.[8]

One would be hard-pressed to satisfy the task of identifying any two individuals that are exactly alike. Snowflakes are precisely defined. But here, variability is recognized in the old adage that no two snowflakes are alike. This claim, though untestable (who can examine every snowflake that falls?), is based on the fact that each snowflake consists of one hundred million, million water molecules. Each arrangement is bound to be unique. Even though it is trivial and may be neglected in favor of the similarities between snowflakes, individuality remains a pervasive feature of nature, and a suggestive one at that.

This concrete novelty includes the most elementary particles, the ultimate simples of the material world. Electrons are treated as if they emerged from the same production line following the big bang. Each carries an electrical charge, also in the same quantitative value. Electron charges are treated on the assumption that they do not vary any more than inches or centimeters vary. And yet this cannot be the case. Every electron must differ—for example, in charge—in some exceedingly minute degree from all others, even though this difference, on the order, perhaps, of one part in a trillion, may be

---

8. A wonderful expression of this claim is the painting, a triptych, by Dutch painter Hieronymus Bosch (1450–1516) entitled *The Garden of Earthly Delights* (*El Jardin de las Delicias*), which hangs in Madrid's Museo del Prado. The central panel depicts a virtual riot of activity with detail upon detail. The painting provides the inspiration for Terry Tempest Williams's book *Leap* (New York: Pantheon Press, 2000). On a visit to the Prado, Williams is stunned by the painting, and returns daily to scope out (literally, with a pair of binoculars) the immense detail of the panel. She counts thirty-five species of birds alone, deftly rendered by Bosch. Williams uses the experience to call for the preservation of diversity in nature with the same spiritual passion that great art is valued and preserved.

treated for all practical purposes of experiment and calculation as no difference at all.

Science, Standardization, and Design

Theologian and philosopher of science Bernard Lonergan recognized that the neglect of individuality in physical constituents is a necessary position for science in its goal of achieving a unified perspective on the world:

> When chemists have mastered all the elements, their isotopes and compounds, they may forget to be grateful that they do not have to discover different explanations for *each* of the hydrogen atoms which, it seems, make up about fifty-five percent of the matter of our universe.... Every chemical element and every compound differs from every other kind of element of compound and all the differences have to be explained. Every hydrogen atom differs from every other hydrogen atom and no explanation is needed.[9]

But the assumption that all electrons and hydrogen atoms are identical gives rise to beliefs about the nature of reality, that it is regular to the extreme and standardized through and through.

The propensity and passion of the Western mind for ideal generalized order and the inherited Greek notion of the singular wholeness of the cosmos make this habit of thought and method inevitable (and, as Pirsig's teacher discovered, also make problems for essay assignments in composition classes). The Greeks had two characterizations of the cosmos. They felt comfortable with the description *to pan,* "the whole," because it expresses the unity of the world. They felt less comfortable with the alternative, *ta panta,* "all things," because it did not.[10] The scientific quest for universal lawfulness in nature requires a strategy of neglecting differences in instances of a class of phenomena in order to emphasize similarities, for only in likenesses are universal patterns to be recognized. Unity trumped plurality then and does so now.

It is no surprise that because of this assumption undergirding all scientific inquiry, the intuition of a supreme mind or cosmic designer frequently arises. The emphasis on standardizing members of

---

9. Bernard Lonergan, *Insight* (New York: Philosophical Library, 1958), 28; quoted in Patrick H. Byrne, "God and the Statistical Universe," *Zygon: Journal of Religion and Science* 16, no. 4 (1981): 347.

10. Paulos Mar Gregorios, *The Human Presence: Ecological Spirituality and the Age of the Spirit* (Amity, N.Y.: Amity House, 1980), 21.

a class effectively discounts idiosyncratic differences as anomalous and trivial and makes certain theological speculations inevitable. The specific model of God suggested by this approach is inevitable as well; God is the conclusion of a syllogism whose premises are claims about the cosmos as a reflection of rational ideals. In their absolute conformation to regular form and behavior, particular instances confirm these ideas. This divinity is a *Deus* of sorts, a cosmic mind whose initial function in creation was to implement some ideal blueprint into material reality. The subsequent and tacit task of science is to disregard the imperfections, the differences in detail between members of a class of phenomena, and reconstruct the blueprint. One should not be shocked that the success of this project is suggestive of a divinity in whose mind these elegant concepts and equations originate.

The Irregular Universe

The model of God implied by a universe that is profoundly irregular and consists of creaturely inhabitants who are (to risk an oxymoron) uniformly irregular as well is far different from the rational mathematical divinity who creates an elegant universe.[11] Common experience reveals the world of life to be "an astonishing cataract" and "immoderate deluge"[12] of specific individuals. Reality is a nearly impenetrable thicket of plurality, a brawling commonwealth of being. Being is informed as beings, with eachness, otherness, and suchness as primary ontological features. These features are the gifts of extravagant difference, of radical individuation. The primal source of the particular forms inhabiting the creation is God. One may even say that this diversity represents the immanence of the *Pandemonium Tremendum* as it is incarnated in the corporal world. This God, unlike the intelligent designer, revels in the fulfillment of creatures through their individuality and not their uniformity. The deep texture, richness, and diversity of the creation are far more suggestive of a God who lives with the vital chaos than one who configures the creation in accord with static forms.

If described in the light of variety rather than being, the traditional hierarchy of all beings, the "great chain of being," provides insight. The Augustinian version is that this hierarchy, with its extremes of the abyss at the bottom and God at the apex, represents a

---

11. Brian Greene, *The Elegant Universe: Superstrings, Hidden Dimensions, and the Quest for the Ultimate Theory* (New York: W. W. Norton, 1999).

12. C. S. Lewis, *Miracles: A Preliminary Study* (New York: Macmillan, 1968), 167.

stratification of grades of being and nonbeing. All creatures, slotted appropriately somewhere along the spectrum, are composed of both being and nonbeing. This accounts for their common mortality as well as for the presence of evil in the world as privation, as fault due to lack of being. If being and nonbeing are replaced by system and chaos respectively, then creatures are, likewise, combinations of both. However, unlike Augustine's version, this amalgamation of order and variety is not a kind of privation. Creatures are not deprived of fulfillment because they are complex. Rather, this combination is the only possible one for a world of maximum quality. Unlike being and nonbeing, diversity and order in complex beings do not constitute a dualism of opposition.

As Charles Hartshorne observes, this bias results from our failure to appreciate the spectrum of possibilities that exist between two extremes:

> One often condemns things or persons as defective because their complexity is inadequately integrated into "unity" or simplicity; but then equally, one often condemns them because their unity integrates inadequate variety or complexity. The good as we know it is unity-in-variety or variety-in-unity; if the variety overbalances we have chaos or discord; if the unity, we have monotony or triviality. The one defect is in principle as serious as the other, for infinite triviality would be as bad as infinite chaos, since neither would have any value whatsoever.[13]

Reality presents itself to us not as simple continuous being, the stuff or substance of classical ontology, but as a vast multitude of beings. Encountering the countless leads us to make two observations. The first is that the world exhibits constraint; the number and kinds of things that exist is a small proportion of the number and kinds of things that might exist. Absolute variety has been limited by some transmitting and governing agency. Of all possible worlds, only one is known to be actual. The second observation is that the actual world also exhibits a profligate fecundity. At any given time it is populated by an immense multitude of diverse beings whose numbers are beyond tally. This constraint and this fecundity are clues guiding ontological and theological inquiry along the lines of

---

13. Charles Hartshorne and William Reese, *Philosophers Speak of God* (Chicago: University of Chicago Press, 1953), 3.

communication theory and reveal a deity whose emphases are some-what different from those celebrated in the classical models based on the Greek notion of forms.

THE STREAM OF VARIETY

Divine agency has numerous modes. All have to do with the release of variety into the world in the act of communication. One of the most important modes is to establish a context in which creatures can "have their being" as well as "live and move." God's intention is not to order the world—to design it and then implement that design as fiat—but rather, to provide context for the world to design itself in response. Through the creation God establishes the conditions for possibilities of development in complex living things, including humans. These conditions shape complex systems and confer upon them their own capacity to create. The mundane or worldly context consists at all levels as an embracing field of variety, incarnate va-riety. The gifts of divine articulation mentioned earlier—eachness, otherness, and suchness—are conferred not by divine fiat as fixed, settled, and full blown, but as the emergent consequences of an im-mensely diverse context. Interaction with a rich context gives rise to creatures as centered yet open systems with powers of decision, of communication, that resemble isomorphically those of the creator.

As one who sets contexts, God would appear to act as the *Deus* who configures the world, first by implanting the propensity to evolve and then moving away to allow that evolution to occur. But this appearance is mistaken. The *Deus* is a retired and silent divinity. In contrast, the God of communication is always abroad in the form of a continuous font of variety that nourishes and per-turbs the world as nurture and noise when injected into the creation. "Earth is crammed with Heaven," wrote poet Elizabeth Browning in *Aurora Leigh*. God is a catalytic agent. God disturbs situations of equilibrium by introducing noise into systems, driving them to higher orders of complexity and stability. Natural systems, sensitive and alert, thrive on the infusion of unorganized variety. This infu-sion is accompanied by an uncertainty that impels natural systems toward new and novel forms.

As we have said repeatedly, constraint signifies that communica-tion and decision processes are at work reducing the primal field of variety, the *Pandemonium Tremendum,* to discrete and settled instances. The appropriate image is that of a great cascade of un-differentiated informational variety descending from the elemental ocean of chaos into the creation. Constraint is imposed on the cascade at every point, beginning with the actions of God and moving downward in a hierarchy of decision systems of greater to lesser compass. This stream branches into numerous smaller streams and these again into successively smaller ones, ending finally in an immense number of capillaries feeding individual beings and their subsystems. The nodal points where the streams branch and multiply are the places where decisions are made, where constraint is imposed on the inexhaustible parent stream through decision events in a process that is then repeated in descending fashion and with ever greater limitation until the individuals of the existing world at any given moment are rendered definite and concrete.

Stafford Beer, a pioneering systems theorist, studied what he calls "the flow of specifying information" and offers an example from product manufacturing that clarifies our concept of the incessant stream of variety:

> An order for a product that is still in the mails has infinite variety: It may be a request for anything, even something that the company does not make. When the order is booked...some variety has now been lost. At the planning stage, more of this variety is shorn away; and the production proceeds more and more into decisions taken. When the product is ready to leave the factory, there is just one bit of information left in it: the answer to the question whether it will be dispatched or not.[14]

In like manner, a world filled with natural systems, especially living systems, is continuously engaged in the assimilation or reduction of variety from the "raw" state to an organized state. Creation is a system for absorbing or destroying variety in the construction of particular ordered creatures whose complexity represents low entropy or high order. Life operates in a medium of carbon chemistry, but it also operates in a medium of variety. Indeed, carbon atoms, with their vast potential for bonding in complex ways with other elements, consume tremendous variety on their way to producing the protoplasmic stuff of life.

Immense variety in the world suggests the unleashed *Tohuwabohu, Xaos,* the *Ungrund,* or the *Tao.* The world at any moment is

---

14. Stafford Beer, "Below the Twilight Arch: A Mythology of Systems," *General Systems Yearbook* 6 (1961): 16–17.

the product of a series of decision processes in which immense variety is reduced to zero in the concrete being. The original stream, albeit the quantity of its flow diminished at each node through decision, persists to the end point of selection in terms of the resolution of single bits where the last *t* is crossed and the last *i* dotted, and certainty is finalized. What should not be lost in this account is the grand notion of God's limitless fecundity. "God," says John Haught, "is the infinitely generous ground of new possibilities for world-becoming" and "an infinitely liberating source of new possibilities and new life."[15] The virtue of a communication model is that it offers an account, similar to Beer's flow of specifying information, to help make clear how "the infinitely generous ground" and "liberating source" of new possibilities becomes effective in the creation.

KYBERNETES

Two Modes of World Management

Natural systems manage environmental variety not by defeating it, by imposing preexisting structures of perfection that result in a static, stultifying, and even life-denying equilibrium. Rather, they behave like grand opportunists, choosing this or that possibility in the world in accord with the tactical need of the moment. In a second fruitful concept, Stafford Beer refers to the former mode as "management by aesthetics" and the latter as "management by cy-

---

15. John Haught, "Evolution, Tragedy, and Hope," in *Science and Theology: The New Consonance*, ed. Ted Peters (Boulder, Colo.: Westview Press, 1998), 241. Also, this raises an issue about the generative powers of the world. Is this world of bewildering diversity and complexity the source of its own variety? Certainly, no one would deny that creatures are sources for some or even a considerable amount of the variety we find in the world, if by "source" we mean that they generate variety by making decisions that distinguish this from that or that they communicate. However, in one sense, the creation cannot be the exclusive source of its own variety. The capability of creatures to generate variety is dependent, in turn, on the existence of creatures with that capability. In some real sense, creatures are the sufficient causes of one another, but only if their mutual context is already given. "In the beginning" there was no context, no relational causal mechanisms, no environmental playing field on which these information-generating events, this self-elaboration of the creation as a world teeming with life, could occur. The source of this context is some original and originating posit or decision from which all other decisions take their bearings. Also, the communication model is a variation on the process paradigm. In process thought, all things are essentially events requiring a constant source of reinvigoration to maintain the ongoingness of the world from one moment to the next, in the same sense as images on a computer screen seem to endure, although in reality they are maintained by a constant flow of electrons.

bernetics."[16] In Beer's account, aesthetics signifies conformation to transcendent ideals, to the "Beautiful," for example. In contrast, cybernetics means harmonious, relevant adjustment that contributes to the complexity of the creaturely system, to its self-regulation, growth, and actualization, and to its integration into the total realm of creaturely systems that, when taken all together, constitute much of its environment.

A parable may help in rendering these abstract models in more concrete terms. The principal of Pythagoras High School has a management style of the aesthetic sort and insists that all teachers adhere strictly to an ideal grading system: 90 to 100 percent is the A range, 80 to 89 is the B range, and so on. This principal permits no adjustments to be made, no curving of grades based upon varying classroom conditions, student capabilities, or subject difficulty, not to mention idiosyncrasies of teachers in their grading procedures. The principal of Pythagoras High is obviously Neoplatonic in adhering to absolute standards rigidly applied. The principal of a second school, Norbert Wiener High School, has a cybernetic style. This principal permits flexibility of judgment by individual teachers. They may adjust their expectations according to the varying conditions of class and subject difficulty, as well as to errors in their own performances. As a result, student grades are not calibrated to some ideal scale; rather, they reflect individual performance relative to the immediate competition, to other students within the real-world classroom context.

Management by aesthetics tends toward gnosticism. In its efforts to impose unilateral standards from an eternal and transcendent realm upon an unpredictable world, it generates a state of enmity and prodigal alienation between creature and creation. For the gnostic manager, the apparent resistance of matter to the act of being informed as well as its apparent tendency to revert to chaos seems to betray an incompetent, if not evil, source of all things. Management by cybernetics, however, is transactional, synergetic, pluralistic, and liberating. Its approach confirms the world in all its commotion and riotous vigor—the "chaos" that threatens the Neoplatonist.[17]

The goal of management by cybernetics is not to conquer chaos

---

16. Beer, "Below the Twilight Arch," 14–15.

17. In his book *The Human Use of Human Beings: Cybernetics and Society* (Garden City, N.Y.: Doubleday, 1954), Norbert Wiener discusses several interpretations of evil, including Manichaeanism, or absolute and intrinsic evil, and contrasts it with simple disorder or relative and, presumably, correctable evil.

in the midst of life, or to drive it from the walled city of order, but to draw upon it, to optimize rather than to perfect, and to maximize potential with respect to the range of compatible order existing in the commonwealth of creaturely systems that comprise any single being's life province.

Kybernetai in a Relevantial Universe

Creaturely decision systems may be simple and automatic, such as the formation of waves on a body of water. The interaction of the water and the wind is determined by a few laws of hydrodynamics, although their manifestation is infinitely varied—no two waves are exactly alike. The initial conditions of the sea and the governance of these laws compel the results. More complex systems, especially living and sentient systems, carry out these processes in very different ways, most of which are responsive in character rather than dictated by prevailing laws applied uniformly. We will refer to any responsive system as *kybernetes* (plural, *kybernetai*), or "steersman," noted earlier as the Greek term from which "cybernetics" is derived.[18]

An account of the *kybernetes* as an open decision system embedded in a dynamic world context implies Shannon's theory of communication. Any single organism represents a history or biography of decisions the consequences of which are traced in the enduring patterns of its organization. The individual forages on the immense variety of its environment provided as energy, materials, nutrients, and sensory media such as light and sound, carefully selecting what is advantageous and relevant as a portion of all available resources. It then responds with behavior triggered by the tiny impulses of energy within its nervous system, often amplified millions of times, projecting them constructively into the vicinity of the world. Life is a constant communication project whose overall aim is to build a world in which to find a place to flourish.

This goal, the instinctive obsession of every *kybernetes,* revolves about a singular focus on relevantial information. Recalling our discussion of Maruyama's three universes of information from chapter 1, the relevantial universe consists of information that addresses the existential or urgent concerns of the individual. In more classical language, one might say that a creature that seeks to meet its urgent needs is striving to realize its proper telos or nature as the most relevant goal for its life.

---

18. A neologism credited to Norbert Wiener. See Campbell, *Grammatical Man,* 276.

The relevantial and relational universes of information are inseparable. Their connection represents the truth of the model of management by cybernetics and leads to a fundamental dialectic or ontological pairing of the individual and its context or community that Paul Tillich identified as "individualization and participation."[19] Individuals can be neither subdivided internally nor absorbed into some larger reality externally without the destruction of the quality of individuality. Yet, individuals must accommodate both the fact that they are composite, that is, composed of components subsystems, and the fact that they are contributing members of some larger whole of which they are components or subsystems.

Complex, composite, and context-dependent creatures are centered; they are overall expressions of the harmonious integration of their parts working in unison to fulfill and sustain the telos or nature of the particular individual. This centeredness allows the individual to sustain its own unity while actively engaging its larger context. Living individuals are thus open systems of impressive complexity that explore their world, ingest relevant information, and organize themselves in response to inner needs and outer circumstances. As centered open systems, they grasp and shape their world just as they are, in turn, grasped and shaped by it. By engaging in a definitive act of specifying themselves, living systems contribute to the totality of relationships constituting the system of creation—the inevitable consequence of the process of individuation and participation.

The Community of Open Systems

Note that we speak of "individuals"—in the plural—in recognition of the tension between the unique creature itself and the plurality of creatures. Individuals must participate in some larger transactional context of give and take, of mutual adjustment and ever increasing association. Out of this interplay emerges an overall systems structure that is compatible with the particular forms of its various individual participants. Henry Nelson Wieman defines this process of communal or ecosystemic solidarity, which we have called "interexistence," with eloquent precision when he speaks of the increase in connections between individuals that results in

> systems of meaning having intrinsic value, previously disconnected so that the qualities of the one could not get across

---

19. Paul Tillich, *Systematic Theology*, 3 vols. in 1 vol. (Chicago: University of Chicago Press, 1967), 1:174–78.

to the other one, so unified that each is enriched by qualities derived from the other. Meaningfully connected events, once instrumental, now become component parts of a total meaning having intrinsic value.[20]

Somehow, countless individuals engaged in their concrete pursuits with no unifying purpose mutually construct a contextual community based in enduring relationships. This congruency of the relevantial and relational universes in terms of meaning and value is the axiological dimension of the ontology of interexistence. The mystery and the beauty of a community of *kybernetai* are that both the community and the centered open systems composing it co-arise. Neither takes historical or ontological priority; they come together.

Matter and Matrix

The intention of God in this process of providing abundant nurture for creaturely systems is, according to the theologian Jürgen Moltmann, to open closed systems. Creation itself is an open system, but the tendency of creatures is sometimes toward becoming closed. God's response is to "indwell" with the creation. "The indwelling of the limitless fullness of God's potentialities therefore means the openness of all systems of life, *par excellence,* and hence that they will be eternally living systems and not fossilized ones."[21] Within the framework of our discussion, this means that God provides the variety that enables the openness of creaturely *kybernetai* to increase and flourish.

Creatures are open systems that not only function to manage and regulate the overwhelming variety to which they are continually exposed, but also to absorb this variety to expand the range of their vital influence. Creaturely systems must input this variety from the very environment that imperils their internal stability with its tidal chaos.

The incessant stream of variety is perceived by open systems as noise, but not necessarily in any frustrating or destructive sense. Such systems preside (although not always consciously) over their own development as individuals, and summatively as species. They use some of the power of elemental variety as the *materia prima* of

20. Henry Nelson Wieman, *The Source of Human Good* (Chicago: University of Chicago Press, 1946), 60.
21. Jürgen Moltmann, *The Future of Creation* (Philadelphia; Fortress Press, 1978), 126.

evolutionary advance. Noise is always interpreted initially as disturbance. But disturbance triggers action to contain and exploit it. The disturbance is employed to create and amplify patterns. Noise is transformed into signal through decision processes that reduce uncertainty and bring about consequences advantageous to the living system.

Order is itself a creature, the consequence of the natural disposition of things to self-arrange through creative association over long periods of time. Even matter, mortified by modern chemistry and physics, which reduced it to mere material, inanimate and passive, has made a comeback through a reassessment of its fundamental constituents and its role in the dynamic order of nature. The idea of matter as fixed in character, inert, and unresponsive is replaced with emphasis on its restlessness, propensity to organize, and insurgent character. Matter is the generative matrix, the fertile stuff of life. The rocks, Alan Watts liked to say, peopled the earth; they were "peopling rocks."[22]

Indeed, within the rubric of communication and system theory, "matter" is replaced by the "matrix" of organization and relationship, consisting of the dynamic forces of wind, water, and the earth and sentient beings, whose purpose is to establish their own lives by looking after their own relevant interests. This constant striving on the part of innumerable multitudes of *kybernetai* does not result in a disordered world. Rather, it gives rise to broad associations—for example, the bee and blossom or predator and prey relationships discussed earlier. These creatures seek to impose constraint upon the immense potentially destructive chaos or noise represented in the environment. They seek their individual good by engaging in a transactional flow of mutual creation, adjustment, and common affiliation. Biological evolution, with its mechanism of natural selection giving rise to the web of relationships that constitute a stable system, is this same transactional flow. The world is thus composed of sentient beings in an interdetermined network of mutually qualifying causes and effects. It consists of complex webs of events so intricate, so imbued with chaotic elements, so unrepeatable in encompassing such a multitude of unique and uniquely interacting beings that standard linear models of causality do not apply. This wondrous global phenomenon of interexistence is as close to a miracle as one is likely to see in the world.

---

22. Alan Watts, *The Book: On the Taboo against Knowing Who You Are* (New York: Random House, 1966), 89.

CONCLUSION

In this chapter we have introduced several concepts that relate to God's action toward a creation teeming with vital creatures. The rationed release of variety into the world is intended to establish a stable balance between novelty and constraint that allows for creatures to optimize their own fulfillment. Creatures live in the everlasting stream of variety and utilize for their own actualization through decisive responses and concerted action as *kybernetai*. The joyful noise of God's funding of variety is the raw material with which creatures compose their own existence singularly and together to return this noise to its originator as a great symphony. That they accomplish this in numbers beyond tally and with limitless diversity testifies to the success of God's loving actions and is evidence that recommends the communication model of the divine economy.

– 9 –

In the Image of God and the World

WE ARE OUR OWN GREATEST MYSTERY, one that has to do primarily with our status as creatures—or more. The premise of this chapter is that the communication model of creatures developed in the previous chapter carries over to inform our self-understanding as persons. It also suggests extensions of that identity into novel features that make us self-elaborating and historical creatures. All this is described within the rubric of the image of God in theological tradition. So, persons, as we will try to show, are in continuity both with the world and with God.

Of Beasts and Divinities

According to the book of Psalms, we are a little lower than God but a bit above the beasts of the field (Psalm 8). Our self-assessment gyrates wildly between these divine and beastly connections. The volatility of opinions regarding our self-assessment is likely to continue since each side is capable of offering a consistent version of its own claims to an audience, the rest of us, that is irreducibly conflicted. Still, the communication models we are advocating may, in some small measure, contribute to the clarification of our ambivalence if not also to its resolution. The human animal is in continuity with both the angels and the beasts in its position halfway between the world of nature and the world of spirit and ideas. Indeed, our culture is the embodiment of this duplex identity. Human society consists of fantastic artifacts in engineering, art, and science that transcend anything found in nature. And yet, those very things are generated through processes that employ the laws of nature and the raw materials it provides. We need those beasts of the field if we are to resemble deity.

This predicament of duplexity has great consequences for our image. On the one hand, we reflect the *imago Dei*, the image of God;

on the other hand, we share with all other creatures, including the beasts, an *imago mundi,* an image from the world. What we must do is interpret these two images according to the communication model and argue for a continuity between God, world, and humankind. Obviously, there are very significant, even definitive, differences, but, because the model applies common categories to all three, there are important similarities as well.

THE IMAGO MUNDI

The Soul of the Human Kybernetes

First, the *imago mundi.* The human species is in continuity with all of sentient and even insentient beings. We are open systems and members of the total system of creation. Granted, affixing the vague label of "open system" will not go very far toward solving anybody's identity crisis. This is a problem of all abstraction, and Kierkegaard knew it: abstractions dissolve and deny the unique subject. All we can say in consolation is that at least the systems model celebrates diversity and embraces the unique individual. Ludwig von Bertalanffy, the acknowledged father of modern systems theory but a poor neologist, refers to the application of broad categories of the system model to human behavior as "progressive de-anthropomorphization."[1] He finds this tendency to be "progressive" because it promotes insight and principles of interpretation for unifying complex phenomena that otherwise seemed so different. Bertalanffy understands human behaviors to be specific instances of patterns found generally in very high order, complex, open systems. His intention, shared by almost all systems theorists, is to unify the personal, sociocultural, and natural worlds under a single idiom that would also respect the differences between them. But achieving this goal requires surrendering cherished ideas about the uniqueness of persons. Our task is to include the idea of God in this idiom, and, in doing so, to show that the *imago mundi* and the *imago Dei* are in continuity.

As mortal offspring of the earth, persons are *kybernetai.* They absorb tremendous variety from rich natural and social environments and utilize it as the fundamental stuff of self-organization and the generation of complex experience. The brain, the organ primarily

---

1. Ludwig von Bertalanffy, *General System Theory: Foundations, Development, Applications* (New York: George Braziller, 1968), 242.

but not exclusively involved in this process, takes sensory input, assesses its significance, and responds appropriately, first through the body and then through tools. Simply sitting in my chair and composing these thoughts on a computer requires literally trillions of specific neural firings to accomplish. Photons of light from sentences I have just composed on the screen strike the retina of my eye, where they trigger electrical signals that are transferred to my brain's visual cortex through the optic nerve. This information, translated into images, is shared with other areas of the brain, where judgments of all sorts occur to produce a coordinated response amplified millions of times through the nervous system to activate specific muscle groups in my hands and fingers for the purpose of typing further sentences. The loop is completed when, once again, my brain registers the new letters and words on the computer screen with either approval or disapproval. I have created my own environment in this process with aspects that are available for my judgment and alteration.

Modify the situation to include another person with whom I have a conversation about the words and thoughts on the computer screen, and the situation becomes incredibly complex. In this case, two open systems exchange highly selected information that triggers untold responses at all levels of the conversationalists, including the mental, emotion, and physical dimensions. In such transactional contexts, loops upon loops of feedback responses occur in very subtle and overt ways and yet knit smoothly into a total response.

All experience, the registration of variety by an open system, is disturbance. The system is "disturbed," that is, impacted and altered at least temporarily by events. Disturbances are not necessarily destructive. Open systems must be disturbed to live and thrive. Disturbance is actually opportunity as well as crisis, depending on the circumstances. Complex open systems, primarily organisms, interdict the flood of variety bombarding them through subtle decision processes by which the variety is blocked or absorbed.[2] The mind, whose seat is the brain, constructs itself and manages complexity by foraging on the limitless possibilities open to it that are generated internally by its imagination and externally by its environment. As an organ of openness and decision, the mind-brain fulfills a

---

2. In his penetrating analysis of information, W. Ross Ashby discovered "the law of requisite variety," which says that "only variety can destroy variety." Open systems must be complex in order to store variety sufficient to counter or interdict the disturbing variety, the noise, of their environment (*An Introduction to Cybernetics* [New York: John Wiley & Sons, 1961], 206).

dual requirement. Its function is both to control the great surges of information washing over it constantly from the environment as disturbing noise and to absorb a portion of this variety as the source and stuff for the construction of an inner range of possibilities employed to counter that assault. In the absence of these abilities, self-directed individuals as reflective centers of action and response would never arise.

Both mind and person arise as phenomena most sharply at the growing edge, the ever widening circumference of the human organism as it grapples with the world. Even the concept of "soul," as defined by Novalis, is welcome here: "The seat of the soul is where the inner and outer worlds meet, where they overlap; it is in every point of the overlap."[3] The highest order loops are in the process of formation along the limbus or boundary of experience, where the accumulated and organized knowledge of the person system is combined with the ever changing search to solve new problems and assess new experience. The soul is the complex center of control, decision, and response living precariously along the surge zone between order and chaos.

The function of the seat of this soul, the brain, to absorb and process variety, suggests parallels in evolution. The wing is a major adaptation made possible by the presence of air, just as fins and flippers emerged to take advantage of water. Imagine that in the distant future, following some cataclysmic event that scoured the earth of all life, an extraterrestrial paleontologist happened upon the shriveled cinder of planet earth. After discovering fossil remains of wings and fins, that logical creature could easily infer that the planet possessed both an atmosphere and hydrosphere at some time in its distant past. By analogy, the brain is an evolutionary response to an invisible circumambient element, the incessant stream of variety, in the same way that wing and fin are responses to their respective media of air and water.

The marvelous and intricate complexity of the human organism that allows for this sensitivity to the world and the refinement of its response to it is thus a product of the same processes of interaction and adaptation found universally in evolution.

Bertalanffy tells the evolutionary story succinctly:

Life spirals laboriously upward to higher and higher levels, paying for each step.... It passes to levels of higher differentia-

---

3. Quoted in Linda L. Moyer, "Personal Perspective," *Christianity and Crisis* 46, no. 3 (1986): 54.

tion and centralization and pays for this by loss of regulability after disturbance. It invents a highly developed nervous system and therewith pain. It adds to the primeval parts of the nervous system a brain which allows consciousness that by means of a world of symbols grants foresight and control of the future.[4]

The human body, including the brain, is a stratified historical record of the negotiated arrangements made over billions of years by the multitude of *kybernetai* inhabiting the earth. In this sense, we are the microcosm of evolution. The structure and capability of the human organism is given a priori to individuals and referred to as our "nature." But for the human species it is a posteriori. That is, those characteristics that mark us biologically as members of our species were worked out through trial and error combined with the retention of favorable adjustments and opportunistic affiliations to construct the mind and body, the same mind and body that make us human. Each human phenotype is a version of this continuing narrative of evolution interpreted here through the categories of communication theory. We are the verbatim transcript of the incessant buzzing and booming conversation between numberless *kybernetai* building a state of interexistence, the biosphere, over vast extents of time.

The Personal Kybernetes

At this point we may properly reintroduce the notion of person. Paul Tillich, whose rich ideas have done much to inform our communication model, defines "personality" as "that being which has power over itself."[5] A person, therefore, is a being "who alone among all beings has the potentiality of self-determinism and, consequently, of personality."[6] It follows that mind and person are closely associated in Tillich's anthropology, for mind is the seat of reason, and the function of reason is to grasp and shape. Personality is the consequence of the mind grasping and shaping the self. As every psychologist knows, there is no possibility of having power over one's self without some consciousness of that self. A person is a self-directing agent, that is, one who makes conscious decisions

4. From Ludwig von Bertalanffy, *Problems of Life;* quoted in Charles Hampton Turner, *Maps of the Mind: Charts and Concepts of the Mind and Its Labyrinths* (New York: Macmillan, 1981), 180.
5. Paul Tillich, *Systematic Theology,* 3 vols. in 1 vol. (Chicago: University of Chicago Press, 1967), 2:115.
6. Ibid.

from a field of contingencies that includes the decider too. There can be no overestimating the importance of this component, which is, for the most part, unique to the human species. Self-reflection, the literal envisaging of one's own self imaginatively in numerous possible situations, is an act of constructive self-witnessing. Any person can become an object to himself or herself, an object about which judgments are made. Would pride, guilt, and a host of additional attitudes be possible without self-objectification? Indeed, psychological counseling consists of two such persons reflecting evaluatively upon one of them, the client, as a third party or subject projected between them.[7]

The mode through which personal power is effectively utilized is, in true cybernetic fashion, through self-reflective feedback. The witnessing self constitutes one terminus of a loop the other terminus of which is the object image of that self in various situations. The witness may recall instances from past memories and assess them. Or that person may project himself or herself into possible futures, also assessing them, often in comparison with those past images. On the basis of this considered and hopefully rational, as well as affective, critical witness, the person makes choices that reduce the contingencies of the future to specific goals for action and pursues them accordingly. These goals are always altered, at least with respect to details, as further experience is acquired in working toward them. The preferred image itself may be altered as well. But, in all cases, the feedback process continues as the person shapes the self with incremental increases in maturity, power, and autonomy. And in the end, if indeed there ever is an absolute completion, the self ideally becomes more and different, transformed positively according to its own emerging design.[8]

Speaking in terms of teleology, building a life is similar to creating a work of art. Earlier we described Michelangelo's creation of *David* as a series of messages transmitted by the sculptor through

---

7. This capacity for self-reflection is often a psychological and ontological nightmare for persons. Because of this dual location of being the observer and the observed, we entangle ourselves in paradoxes and dilemmas from which there is no exit. The classic study of this predicament in the context of systems and communication theory applied to human interaction is Paul Watzlawick, Janet Helmick Beavin, and Don D. Jackson, *Pragmatics of Human Communication: A Study of Interactional Patterns, Pathologies, and Paradoxes* (New York: W. W. Norton, 1967).

8. Charles Hampton Turner, in his book *Radical Man* (New York: Doubleday, 1970), develops a refined map of the cybernetics of the self that influences our discussion.

the uncarved block of marble. The finished statue represents both the frozen narrative history of the project and its desired goal. The only difference is that the human person achieves fulfillment of a desired end through constant negotiation with others who constitute the various situations through which he or she must work. Michelangelo, left to his own dreams and devices and in the privacy of his studio, pursued his project unilaterally with feedback coming primarily from his own aesthetic judgment applied to the emerging details of David's figure.[9] In general, however, the processes are identical when interpreted within the framework of the communication model. In each case, an artist is at work choosing from a vast range of possibilities in a progressive sequence of determinations that lead ultimately to the actualization of a unique individual.

The ability to choose is, of course, the essence of freedom. Yet that very freedom is founded on the existence of a most complex entity—the brain—capable of assimilating vast amounts of variety and molding it into meaningful concrete images from which real-world choices are made. Creaturely *kybernetai* enjoy finite freedom, and often the normative principles by which choices are made are themselves bounded by circumstance and heritage.[10] That is, the inner and outer limits experienced by even the most complex of centered open systems carry a degree of determination in freedom. Still, as long as the individual is truly open with respect to possible futures and employs standards of choice (even if dictated) that enhance fulfillment and well-being in deciding between these futures, freedom is present.

THE IMAGO DEI

The Humanity of God

Our attempt to construct the notion of person from below as an exemplar of the general model of the centered open system, the agency

---

9. For the sake of historical accuracy, this is not strictly true. Michelangelo sculpted the hands and feet of the statue disproportionately large because he knew that it would be displayed out of doors, where such distortions in scale were necessary for balance and perspective.

10. James Gustafson makes an interesting point about the partial dependence of ethics on the biological situation of our species: "No doubt the near equality between male and female births provides the biological prerequisite for monogamy as a normative form of marriage. If the ratio of male to female births in our species were 1:4 we can be sure that polygamy would be both statistically normal and morally normative" (*Ethics from a Theocentric Perspective: Theology and Ethics* [Chicago: University of Chicago Press, 1981], 240–41).

of selection acting upon its world and responding to it, results in an *imago mundi*. The *imago* is no visual image but rather a system of isomorphic correspondences shared by a tremendous variety of open systems inhabiting the earth at all levels of the terrestrial hierarchy of complexity. Any attempt to introduce God into the discussion would seem to be theologically arbitrary since the general structures shared by all creatures would find no corresponding isomorphic features in God upon which to base any concept of the *imago Dei*. Theologies of utter transcendence that refuse to postulate any similarities between creator and creature, must be equally agnostic with respect to the *imago Dei* unless they are comfortable with an absolute dualism in human nature.[11]

The doctrine of the *imago Dei* is a grand opportunity rather than a problem whose answers are threatened by logical incoherence. A constructive comparison of God, detailed in chapter 6 and the personal *kybernetes* described above, reveal isomorphic correspondences that, when taken together, qualify as an *imago Dei*. Granted, the success of such a comparison is guaranteed by the fact that our accounts of both God and person have been consciously constructed from the beginning according to the same communication model. It should be no wonder, then, that at the end we should discover that many features are held in common. The inquiry moves in the other direction as well. Any Godlike feature possessed by humans can be understood equally as a humanlike feature possessed by God. Our model thus allows for reversible speculation in ways that traditional theology would likely find unacceptable. Despite this circularity, the exercise to detect some of these isomorphies is useful not only to emphasize similarities but also to specify dissimilarities between God, ourselves, and other creatures.[12]

---

11. This dualism consists of two fundamental qualities, one natural and one supernatural, absolutely distinct and yet residing side by side in the same creature. Paradoxes generated by such theologies, especially regarding anthropology and Christology, litter the ontological pronouncements of the early church councils. They also leave the very notion of the human creature in the image of the divine to be a theologically suspect or, at best, perennially unresolved question.

12. Contrary to Western anthropocentric tradition, the *imago Dei* is not restricted to the Adamic creature, *Homo sapiens*. It is to be found in lesser degrees in all living things and in many nonliving systems as the power to specify through the process of selection. Humans are merely the chief exemplar of a propensity found in all natural systems. This capacity is exercised in nonsentient systems through the operations of strictly determined forms of systems behavior, or it may even result from "tychism," or the operation of pure chance. Evolution from the inanimate to the animate is continuous but not without what Teilhard De Chardin refers to as "threshold leaps." At some point in evolution very primitive systems achieve a complexity enabling them to engage in selection based on internal or centered structures and modes of

Monotheistic faiths require personhood (or at least personal features) as an indispensable attribute of God. That is, the *imago
Dei* can be understood to mean that we share the personal qualities with God. A person is an agent who manages variety through
self-conscious decision processes. A person is one whose powers of
discrimination arise over time through the consolidation of experience and learning. If personhood is a proper attribute for deity,
then these dynamic features must apply to God as well, but in ways
that are appropriate for the divine life. God manages variety, too,
but that variety is in the infinite field of variety, the *Pandemonium
Tremendum.* God also discriminates and "learns" by drawing upon
the primordial chaos progressively to constitute God's self through
decisions and then sharing these decisions with the beloved creation
in its role as the cocreating context.

The Divine Kybernetes

Because a person is inherently social, the primordial God is not
yet a true person. Only the engaging God qualifies, and this God
becomes possible only when there are others to engage. Inherently
and instrumentally, the world satisfies that condition.[13]

At this point, even the sovereign spirit of God in the divine
functions of creator, sustainer, and director is conditioned by the
emerging complex system of the world. As is true of any artist,
God is subsequently forced to adjust all later decisions to the conditions established as consequences of earlier ones. The supreme
context independence that God enjoyed at the moment of the
original posit is replaced by the requirement that God reckon or
negotiate with the emerging cosmic community to assure its well-
being and further its evolution. God, therefore, becomes, to some
extent, context dependent. God makes a contribution and so do
creatures.[14]

---

behavior that are not determined completely by either the chance or the necessity of
the environmental envelope.

13. This point is made by A. N. Whitehead as the primordial and consequent
natures of God (*Process and Reality: An Essay in Cosmology,* ed. David Ray Griffin
and Donald W. Sherburne, corr. ed. [New York: Free Press, 1978], 342–51).

14. The prior question is, Does God surrender the divine context independence
voluntarily, or is the coupled system arrangement with creation a logical and ontological result of God creating at all? The answer may reside in the love of God for the
creation. That love requires engagement. God becomes an other to the creation for
the sake of the creation as other. The state of interexistence that develops between
God and creation, entangling God, so to speak, in the joys and woes of the world,
is the necessary consequence of a voluntary association.

Subtly yet surely, a mutual negotiated partnership, a coupling, emerges between God and the creation. Communication becomes conversation, and God becomes involved in the world. God is the One, but the one among the many who are themselves singular in more than a numerical sense. God plays along, so to speak, in the dynamic interexistence of things among themselves. Being involved *in medias res,* "in the midst of things," means that even God must adjust accordingly.

Theologically, the voluntary act of an infinite God to self-limit for the sake of the beloved other is *kenosis,* divine renunciation or self-emptying.[15] The idea first arose in the claim of the apostle Paul that God self-emptied in Christ, and has been interpreted in a number of ways, including the radical understanding of the short-lived Death of God movement. We use the idea in the sense of self-limitation. God is self-determining. But to be determinate one must be specified or individualized. This can be achieved only where there is an other over against whom one can stand. The creation provides that place for God. Complex creatures are *kybernetai* in that they act and respond, and persons are *kybernetai* at the highest level of engagement. For the *imago Dei* to apply, and for other good theological reasons as well, God must be a responsive agent, a career that makes no sense without others. The costs to God are the limits imposed upon divine action by the true otherness of the creation. God cannot draw upon the *Pandemonium Tremendum* to bring about just any state of affairs since the vast number of such possibilities would be destructively incompatible with the specific order of the actualized creation. Love for the world and concern for its integrity requires that God give way and tailor divine action in a responsive way by considering consequences—capabilities found only in a *kybernetes.* Besides, the profound scriptural claim that God loves the world makes no sense without the beloved—the object of that love. It seems that if love is an essential ingredient in the divine life, creation is necessary.

Numerous passages from scripture could be cited in support of this profile of God's interaction with the creation. A most suggestive one is found in Isaiah 55, emphasizing the creative, sustaining feedback property of the divine word, the Hebrew *dabar:*

---

15. For a fuller discussion of *kenosis* as renunciation, see Nancey Murphy and George F. R. Ellis, *On the Moral Nature of the Universe: Theology, Cosmology, and Ethics* (Minneapolis; Fortress Press, 1996).

For as the rain and snow come down from heaven,
and do not return there until they have watered the earth,
    making it bring forth and sprout,
    giving seed to the sower and bread to the eater,
so shall my word be that goes out from my mouth;
    it shall not return to me empty,
    but it shall accomplish that which I purpose,
and succeed in the thing for which I sent it. (Isa. 55:10–11)

The Word of God, the dynamic fructifying stream of variety of
the divine, echoes in its return to its transmitter as confirmation
that the divine intention has been satisfied. This is an exact metaphor for the process of cybernetic regulation. Furthermore, *dabar,*
like the rain, nourishes and vitalizes, or, again in terms of the communication model, resembles the elemental variety required for the
preservation and flourishing of all particular beings.

Cocreators: The Act of Naming

Finally, the communication model sheds light on a claim frequently
voiced by theologians that the *imago* signifies that humankind is a
cocreator with God, a partner in guiding and nurturing the creation.[16] The Genesis accounts suggest this vocation clearly. The
primal couple is called to "till the garden and keep it" (Gen. 2:15).
Unlike jungles or deserts, gardens consist of plants selected and arranged by intelligent custodians. Also, Adam is assigned the task
of naming the animals as they parade in view species by species.
The intention of this scene is clearly to promote the proper status of humankind as that creature who completes the essences of
all other creatures by assigning them names. In the ancient world,
names were more than simple taxonomic labels. They were keys to
the souls of individuals. To name individuals is to complete their
nature, their creation, and hence to control them.[17]

Ontologically, names distinguish and define, in some final sense,
that which, while in silence, is only partially real because it is yet

---

16. Philip Hefner, *The Human Factor: Evolution, Culture, and Religion* (Minneapolis: Fortress Press, 1987).

17. This concept should not be alien to postmoderns. Alphanumeric strings (series
of letters and numbers that identify one's bank account, credit card, or social security
status) have replaced names. We are warned regularly to guard these things jealously
lest they be used by the unscrupulous to steal our possessions, our money, and even
our identity.

to be fully determinative. As we have seen repeatedly, communication is the decisive act of separation, of selection, of determining this from that. Names call forth the singular from the multitude just as messages of all sorts eliminate uncertainty by reducing a set of possibilities to a single actuality. Since all creatures do this in their management of the incessant stream of variety, they too qualify as cocreators who, in every act, define and delimit their world in exactly the same way that God originally called the creation to be through commands of separation. The great difference between humans and other creatures is that humans not only name others but also name themselves. The act of self-naming is the most profound indicator of the power we have to objectify ourselves, reflect upon that object in imagined future contexts, and move forward decisively (even though frequently with ambivalence and less than complete resolve) to actualize one of these futures by eliminating all the others. Thus, we design ourselves by anticipation, arrange our own lives, assign our own names.

In exercising the power of naming, Adam was conferring upon each creature or class of creatures its full and separate determination, its thisness or thatness through the eye of a conscious being. The name removes the residual uncertainty from the awakening world as a field of possibility almost realized. As the story continues, Adam itself was at that time not yet a man. In the context of the Genesis account, Adam seemed to be purely androgynous, the combination or melding of the feminine and masculine into a single earthling. The primal Adam is the source of all human possibility, male and female.

The act of removing Eve from Adam is not to claim, as many have, that she is derivative from him, but rather that *both* are emancipated as distinctive beings. The act of separation, here no different from the primordial and sequential separation of heaven and earth in the first chapter of Genesis, is the act of communication, of messaging, of bringing certainty and definition to the vague uncertainty or "superposition" of the primal Adam through the profoundly creative act of separating by naming "man" and "woman."

Naming means not only creation and separation but also communication and participation. The divine name given by God to Moses in the burning bush episode of Exodus 3, is traditionally rendered in translation as "I Am." Philosopher and theologian Martin Buber, dissatisfied by this static emphasis on the being of God, suspiciously a Greek rather than a Hebrew understanding, favors an alternative rendering of the Tetragrammaton, YHWH, as "I Will Be."[18] In the context of Moses' inquiry into the power and trustworthiness of the unidentified divinity whose voice he hears, Buber's suggestion makes sense. In the Exodus passage, Moses seeks assurance for the Hebrews that this god will be capable and steadfast, that Yahweh will be with them in trials that are sure to come. God's selection of the divine name decisively gives that assurance. By entering into this relationship, one that gives great emphasis not to the present but to future promise and anticipation, and is eventually sealed by the Sinai covenant, God self-objectifies and self-defines. Uncertainty (which god is this? will this god lead and protect us?) is replaced by certainty and commitment as communicated by God's own name.

Furthermore, the covenant is a primary case of interexistence, of Yahweh as the God of Israel and Israel as the people of God, a relationship (or coupled system) that literally constitutes or gives existence to the nation. Within this larger context, Israel, true to its name as "one who has striven with God" (Gen. 32:28), continues to respond to God through acts of its history, for better or worse, in a reciprocal give and take that continually tests the relationship.

God Is Different

Thus far, our account of the *imago Dei* is primarily a reiteration of categories found in a communication model as they apply to theology and anthropology. Given the structural similarities that make the *imago* possible, it seems that the only differences are those of degree. A person is a finite *kybernetes;* God is the infinite *kybernetes*. But this is not entirely true. Despite the application of the same model, certain absolute distinctions are present.

One major difference concerns divine personhood. We recognize that the notion of an absolute or infinite person may, without further qualification, be incoherent. Persons arise in consequence of engagement with other sentient *kybernetai* and to all the contingencies of their environment. The result is an embedded being who shapes and is shaped by its world, and one whose intimate and reciprocal connections with that world determine its life as a participating individual in a state of interexistence. Persons are determined by others as they, in turn, determine others. God, if understood as a

---

18. Martin Buber, *The Kingship of God,* trans. Richard Scheimann (New York: Harper & Row, 1956). See especially chapter 5, "JHWH and the Melekh," 99–107.

person, must in some real sense encounter others who determine God. But God, as creator, is ontologically prior to the creation and therefore must be more than simply a divine person.

This ontological priority is a second important difference. God is entirely self-creative, which is the same as self-sustaining. God's constant impartial survey of the *Pandemonium Tremendum* reaches to the very depths of its abyss and hence to its approach to nonbeing. The sovereignty of God is over both infinite variety and its negation in nonbeing asymptotically approached. Thus, God is not mortal, not threatened by nonbeing. All creatures are. This is an absolute distinction.

A third major difference between God and persons concerns God's privileged access to the *Pandemonium Tremendum*. Creatures work with immense but nonetheless finite variety. Much of it is already structured, that is, constrained, and determines the range of possible responses. The materials from which we self-construct are not always raw, and this limits our freedom. In contrast, God knows no such limits. The primordial chaos is unbounded and lacks any formal predisposition toward one possibility over another. It is constituted by elemental variety. By encountering and drawing upon the chaos, God suffers no limitation. Indeed, unlike the Platonic Demiurge or a human person whose freedom is severely compromised by the common need continually to wrestle with recalcitrant matter, God's freedom is guaranteed by the limitless contingency of the primordial chaos. Unlike creaturely persons, God is free to act in ways that would bring about any rationally coherent state of affairs, to actualize any conceivable world. This ability requires an internal source of potential, itself limitless. The primordial chaos provides this boundless contingency and guarantees the unrestricted freedom of the divine person that is reflected dimly in the finite human person in its restricted freedom.

A fourth and final difference between God and human creatures concerns the manner or mode employed by God to implement the divine will. Persons make decisions and move to effect them in the world as intentions. The actualization of the intention requires instrumental intermediaries—strategies and tools—to perform the labor and implement the desired end. God, however, carries through in a single unmediated step, the initial act of decision itself. The divine act of speaking out, of transmitting messages, is itself the act of creation. The divine word is the structured act, the declaration that brings about its own realization. Creatures are decision events carried out by God, as it were, face to face with the creation. Scripture is clear that God acts in history by using individuals and nations to carry out God's bidding. The "how" of this influence is, however, direct and unmediated:[19]

> For he spoke, and it came to be;
> He commanded, and it stood forth.
> (Ps. 33:9, RSV)

A being with complete or perfect power is qualitatively different from one with limited power, however immense. An almighty being will act with ease and grace impossible for creatures. There will be no striving, struggling, or grappling—merely effect. The Almighty will be invisible, hidden, or perfectly inconspicuous because it will never inadvertently draw attention to itself as cause, agent, or effector. The results of divine action will appear spontaneous or, more likely, as the consequences of lesser causes and powers. An omnipotent being will achieve its ends in no invasive or intrusive manner, for such a mode of action would mean having to overcome contrary powers, a position inconsistent with every concept of the Almighty. All this means that God, who seems to be the weakest of the weakest, achieves every aim without effort. This description of God's way resembles the way of the Tao in ancient Chinese religion. By achieving ends seemingly without striving, God is the epitome of *wu-wei,* or effortless action.[20]

HISTORY

The Historical Animal

A widely held supposition of contemporary theology is that the human species is irreducibly historical. This claim is difficult to understand as long as one defines history as merely a chronicle

---

19. The ambiguity of this account may be clarified by appeal to the earlier discussion of the world as God's body in chapter 7. We know that it is impossible to simply will one's nose to stop itching. Other urgent action is required. The hand becomes the intermediary, the instrument, itself directed by the will but accomplishing the urgent task indirectly for the sake of the will (and to the relief of the entire body, we suspect). In like manner, God mobilizes the components of God's body—individuals and nations—as agents to accomplish specific divine intentions. A prophecy from the book of Ezekiel provides a blunt example. God says, "I will deliver you [Israel] into brutish hands, those skillful to destroy" (Ezek. 21:31).

20. For example, see chapter 34 of the *Tao Te Ching.*

of human events in economics, politics, and individual lives to be studied retrospectively or relived in written or dramatized accounts. While history is what you find in history books, it is also much more. History is what people do with themselves when they build a world consisting of institutions, values, ideas, traditions, and relationships and then live in that created world as if it were objectively given. History is our second nature, a distinctively human element, similar to water for fish or air for birds, from which we take our bearings and define our lives.[21]

Our location in history shapes and determines our consciousness. We are postmodern rather than medieval in our beliefs and attitudes because this historical epoch is different from the medieval one. The highly questionable modern view is that social communities are the result of autonomous individuals negotiating a common contract whereby each participant voluntarily limits personal freedom for the general welfare and common good. The ideal is that societies are intelligently designed artifacts (e.g., the social contract model of John Locke). What this philosophy neglects is the fact that no freestanding and independent witness who can think, design, plan, and implement social structures can exist without his or her own mind being the conditioned result of a previous social environment. We are defined by our times and traditions, shaped by them, even as we try to transcend their influence to shape us. The image of individuals standing outside the influences of their historical period is a simple contradiction. This, then, is the meaning of the claim that the human species is irreducibly historical.

The Self-inventing Species

History determines and liberates. As I look backwards into my biography, I easily detect the prevailing influence of others on my thoughts, attitudes, and action as well as the influence of events and broader cultural circumstances. My immediate impressions are that my fate was essentially set by the permanent impressions of these powerful historical circumstances. I had little choice in major matters of my own life. But as I look forward in anticipation of my future, I envision a full range of possibilities that are constrained only partially by the insidious influences of my past. The present moment, then, is the place where the trajectories of my past history

---

21. For a lucid discussion of history, see Christine E. Gudorf, "The Basic Problem with Natural Law: History," in *Body, Sex, and Pleasure: Reconstructing Christian Sexual Ethics* (Cleveland: Pilgrim Press, 1994), 70–74.

meet with my imagined futures, a place where I engage in the act of inventing myself.

Self-reflection toward the future is the imagination generating a field of possible action. The field is narrowed by decision processes based on many personal and social forces that limit this field to those options that are realistic and preferred. Subsequent actions are guided by this foresight and intended to bring the valued goal into reality. By anticipating our future, we engage in acts of communication. A field of possibilities is narrowed by constraint. Messages are sent and received through internal deliberations, conversations within, and uncertainty is relieved. The results are externalized, projected into the real world, where they are tested by trial and error to be reinforced, modified, or canceled by the feedback of experience. Each of us is an individual lifetime project, while communities and nations are corporate projects, but dynamic systems.

This emphasis on humankind as the self-inventive species is delightfully expressed by Spanish philosopher José Ortega y Gasset:

> Life in the zoological sense consists of such actions as are necessary for existence in nature. But man arranges things so that the claims of this life are reduced to a minimum. In the vacuum arising from the transcendence of his animal life he devotes himself to a series of nonbiological occupations which are not imposed by nature but invented by himself. This invented life—invented as a novel or play is invented— man calls "human life," well-being. Human life transcends the reality of nature. It is not given to man as it is given to a rock to fall and to the animal its rigid repertory of organic acts—eating, fleeing, building a nest, and so on. He makes it himself, beginning by inventing it. Is human life in its most important dimension a work of fiction? Is man a sort of novelist of himself who conceives the fanciful figure of a personage with its unreal occupations and then, for the sake of converting it into reality, does all the things he does—and becomes an engineer?[22]

With the ongoing revolution in genetics and the emphasis on sociobiology, the pendulum has swung somewhat, away from

---

22. From José Ortega y Gasset, *History as a System;* reprinted in Carl Mitcham and Robert Mackey, eds., *Philosophy and Technology: Readings in the Philosophical Problems of Technology* (New York: Free Press, 1972), 296.

Ortega y Gasset's near dismissal of the influence of biology to increasing recognition of its prevailing influence on who we are as historical creatures. Still, Ortega y Gasset's point is valid. The human species must deal consciously with "the disquieting strangeness of the case" that each of us is an entity "whose being consists not in what it is already, but in what it is not yet, a being who consists in not-yet being." We are "aspirations," creatures whose lives consist in finding "means and ways of realizing the program that we are." He concludes, "My life is pure task. It is not given to me as a present; I have to make it." The openness and uncertainty of this task convinces him that "I am a drama, if anything."[23]

The drama of a life lived in self-invention may not be as existentially open and unencumbered as Ortega y Gasset contends. Each of us is the constructive outcome of a series of decisions that specify us as individuals. The set of possibilities from which these decisions are drawn becomes increasingly restricted as life proceeds and the original variety is consumed. In this information-specifying process, constraint is introduced over time. The concrete person I become is the result of movement from unconditioned possibility to conditioned actuality.

But there is another side. My experiences contribute to a growing store of variety in my brain and mind. By increasing over time, this variety compensates for the variety that is lost in the irreversible narrowing of life's passage. This inner variety funds my imagination with new possibilities and increased competence to bring them about. In one sense, my history has shaped me and closed many doors; in another sense, it has given me a store of fresh variety that liberates. I am an open and centered human system, constrained and yet free.

The Milieu of History

The human *kybernetes* swims in the element of its own making. This fact alone testifies to the truth of Ortega y Gasset's witness to himself as "drama." The misdirected quest to discover "covering laws" of history that would serve the same predictive logic as laws of nature do for planets, galaxies, and falling rocks has proven futile. While the future is predictable, it is so only within a range of possibilities. This range represents constraint on the series of events

---

23. Ibid., 298.

we call history, not in a severe and uniform way, but in terms of likelihood. There are patterns in history that arise when societies settle in to well-defined conventions and habits, where the social worlds they successfully construct through imagination, selection, and externalization become constraining environments in themselves. But these predisposing regularities are far more plastic and amorphous than the fully determinate laws of physics and chemistry.

Another way of expressing the fact that we live in a historical milieu is through the notion of system. History is systemic in that it can be described as a dynamic whole that influences its participants. To coin a term, history is a "complexus" of action and influence to which the individual contributes and from which he or she receives. Historical systems fall within a spectrum of stability. In unstable ones, individual power is significant, for a single person may provoke a disturbance that tilts the system toward new possibilities while closing off others. In more stable systems, such influences are readily absorbed. In either case, however, the meaning of action is to be found in participation in the historical complexus, in the whole. In other words, meaning is belonging.[24] This is true not only for established historical systems but also for anticipated ones. That is, meaning for an individual may be centered in a total allegiance to a historical situation that is yet to be realized. The revolutionary is a citizen of a kingdom yet to be.

Algorithm and Story

Another perspective emerges in the comparison of algorithmic compressibility and Ortega y Gasset's fertile suggestion that we are novelists composing meaningful lives. The former idea is found in the work of Gregory Chaitin and described with admirable clarity by Paul Cilliers. Chaitin defines randomness not in terms of unpredictability but as "incompressibility." A series of signals is compressible if a program shorter than the series can be written that describes it completely. Cilliers offers this example:

> Consider a sequence of numbers of significant length, say a thousand. If this sequence consists of threes only, it is clearly possible to write a simple computer program, referred to as an algorithm, to generate it. Something like:

---

24. For a complete discussion of this idea, see Wolfhart Pannenberg, *Theology and the Philosophy of Science,* trans. Francis McDonagh (Philadelphia: Westminster Press, 1976), 129–35.

Step 1. Print "3."
Step 2. Repeat step 1 a thousand times.[25]

There is no randomness in this series since the program generating it is far shorter than the series itself. However, if the series of numbers is not so simple—for example, the results of tossing a pair of dice a thousand times—the program describing the series must be as long as the series itself. In such cases, compressibility is impossible and randomness is at its maximum. A series that resists compressibility must be in a state of great entropy.

Chaitin's account of randomness in terms of algorithmic compression has important implications for understanding complex systems and communities of systems. Current research into the complexity of such phenomena reveals that neither the events of evolution nor those of human history lend themselves easily to complete descriptions by abbreviated formulas. Even the development and behavior of individual complex systems can sometimes be described only by an itemized account of the novel events of their novel histories. Such systems generate their own unique states that are difficult to classify, if by "classify" we mean to encompass in an algorithm that applies to all similar systems. Any such attempt would result in a program that would repeat each state in the series. If the essence of a system is its potential for inclusion in an algorithm, and its existence is the absence of such potential, then perhaps philosopher Jean-Paul Sartre was right in ways he would not have imagined in his declaration that "existence precedes essence."

Similar points can be made through an analysis of stories. A story is a factual or fictitious narrative account with characters and events that combine in an ordered and dramatic direction to give a plot and integrity to the whole. A story progresses; the conflict or adventure develops and moves (in most cases) toward some end or resolution. The listener or reader senses the movement, at times predicting subsequent events on the basis of preceding ones. At other times, however, anticipation is impossible and surprise results. In any case, a story is not often amenable to algorithmic compression. While repetitive elements are not missing (in tragedies, for example, heroes repeat their faults time and again until they fall), the dramatic situation unfolds in novel ways. Repetitive elements give rhythm to the narrative, but they do not dominate. And if they

---

25. Paul Cilliers, *Complexity and Postmodernism: Understanding Complex Systems* (New York: Routledge, 1998), 9. See also G. L. J. Chaitin, "Randomness and Mathematical Proof," *Scientific American*, May 1975, 47–52.

did, then an algorithm would be an effective way of making a long story very short.

Stories may be likened to music. Both combine flexibility and novelty with order and constancy. Variations on major themes are possible. Unpredictability as stylistic variation or improvisation leads to uncertainty and prepares for surprise. Music is the proportional balance between complete constraint (one does not hear a constant tone) and the absence of constraint (one does not hear a cacophony of discordant notes). Likewise, in a good story the reader is subjected neither to a trivial repetition of situations nor to completely disconnected events that lead nowhere. Extensive algorithmic compressibility foreshortens aesthetic experience, while its complete absence reduces it to a series of atomic events.

This discussion carries over into theology. The *Deus ex machina* is credited with writing the programs, the algorithms guiding the great cosmic machine. This must be so or science, the discipline dedicated to reading these programs, would be impossible. In this picture, the *Deus* programs the world, a closed system, to unfold in a deterministic way toward an assigned destiny that represents the completion of the program, or toward a fixed set of repeated events based on the simple instructions ("repeat steps X through Y, N number of times").

The alternative is for an active, engaging God to act continuously toward the creation as an author acts toward a work in progress. This God-telling of the cosmic story does not lack algorithmic compressibility, but the regularity and repeatability emerges from the composition itself, from the author engaging the entire narrative and from the characters being developed and developing themselves. Because of God's steadfast provision of boundless variety, the course of history is thus experienced as sequences of contingent events and regularities. The major point, however, is that the future of the entire composition is entirely open.

Individual and collective histories are often "mythologized," rendered larger than life through the discovery or invention of internal themes that transcend a mere chronicle. The process represents an alternative to algorithms for giving order to a complex series without rendering it trivial. The so-called romantic school of mythology, of which Joseph Campbell is the most famous representative, includes the principle that personal and social histories must be mythologized if life is to realize its full meaning. An autobiographical account consisting only of haphazard episodes and disconnected events that, when taken together, tend in no direction and reveal no overall arrangement, usually indicates a confused individual with minimal autonomy and few coherent plans.

Autobiography is a constructive project. Through self-reflection, a person tells his or her story, and in the process retrospectively invents or discovers connections and direction. The classic *Auto-biography of Malcolm X* illustrates this point well.[26] Malcolm sees his life as a series of roles defined by the characters he played in the stories dictated by others, primarily the white man and the Black Muslim movement. Malcolm's liberation comes when he realizes that Allah was actually composing his story. Then and only then is he capable of expanding his limited perspective toward universal inclusiveness and accounting for his life with integrity and self-transcendence.

A life story may also be given meaning through identification with the similar stories of others within the context of some larger epic story. American history traditionally has been interpreted through the biblical history of the Israelites, their emancipation from slavery and their journey through the desert to a homeland of milk and honey. The American frontier was both the wilderness and the promised land, guaranteed by God and expressed in the nineteenth-century theological and political doctrine of "Manifest Destiny." Membership in a larger community means, in this rubric, sharing a common story, the mythic telling and retelling of a common history, which contributes to social and cultural solidarity and guides future decisions. In both Malcolm X and the American epic, the central image is God as the author of history giving order and coherence to its episodes. This image offers a concrete vision of a whole in which one can believe and to which one can belong with total commitment.

Symbols as Subsystems

Living myths and symbols are crucial components of a systems-informational account of the dynamics of history. Talcott Parsons, a sociologist who emphasizes systems theory in his approach, understands a society as a self-regulated cybernetic system.[27] He locates the regulating circuits in the cultural values—especially religious

---

26. Malcolm X, with the assistance of Alex Haley, *The Autobiography of Malcolm X* (New York: Ballantine Books, 1965).

27. See Talcott Parsons, *Social Systems and the Evolution of Action Theory* (New York: Free Press, 1977). For an insightful analysis of Parson's ideas for theology, see Christopher S. Queen, "Systems Theory in Religious Studies: A Methodological Critique" (Ph.D. diss., Boston University, 1986).

values—as these are incorporated into institutional subsystems. Parsons's theory is suggestive. Myths and symbols function as these regulating mechanisms, as filters inserted in decision processes where they trigger responses. Primary stories and images inhibit or amplify action by providing an abundant source for relevant patterns and variety. For example, religious symbols often carry an abundance of meaning because they are "polyvalent," that is, they signify multiple themes, events, or interpretations. In Christianity, for example, the symbol of the fish is replete with significance. Cyril Richardson lists several:[28]

- Jesus is the savior revealed in river Jordan in baptism.

- The miracle of the Loaves and Fishes prefigures the Eucharist.

- The Leviathan, the sea-dwelling monster, is served up as the main course of the Heavenly Banquet and conveys the eschatological message that chaos is conquered when the Kingdom comes.

- The fish is the sign of Jonah and thus a symbol for the Resurrection.

- In Jesus' promise to make his disciples "fishers of men," the command to bring the gospel to all people is highlighted.

Each of these symbolic contexts carries a particular prescription for directed action in ritual or contributes to establishing the reign of God. Without such concrete imperatives, it is difficult to see how the Christian tradition could be sustained.

A single image stores an enormous variety of messages that can be used to inform personal and corporate action. Symbols can liberate by removing existing constraint through the infusion of the variety they carry. Or they may impose constraint by guiding decisions in a specific direction. In either case, an account of human persons as systems of centered openness is incomplete without an understanding of the important role of symbols and myths in decision processes.

28. Cyril Richardson, "The Foundations of Christian Symbolism," in *Religious Symbolism,* ed. Frederick Ernest Johnson (New York: Institute for Religious and Social Studies, 1955); quoted in James C. Livingston, *Anatomy of the Sacred,* 3rd ed. (Upper Saddle River, N.J.: Prentice Hall, 1998), 77–78.

CONCLUSION

The categories for the interpretation of history and symbol are the same ones we have used throughout this essay. They are metaphysical accounts derived from communication and systems theory. They are not themselves historical, but they are compatible with the claim that history is a conspicuous feature of creation and especially important for human creatures. Therefore, while history is not the paradigm for the interpretation of all reality, it is decisive for the interpretation of human reality.

In parallel with the sequence of events that unfolds in the Genesis account, we have explored the primordial chaos first, then God, then creatures, and finally, human creatures. With the interpretation of the human person as *kybernetes* in this chapter, we complete the circle back to the *Pandemonium Tremendum* and God through the link of the *imago Dei*. In doing so, we also complete the discussion of God's nature that we began in chapter 6, especially in the section "Theogony." As the original posit or declaration, God self-oriented and then coalesced around that aboriginal decision. But that was insufficient. God becomes fully determinate only by speaking out to bring about the creation to which God then relates through give and take. The divine *kybernetes* takes precedent but also takes notice.

This taking notice may be further discussed in terms found in traditional theological discourse. Our intention in the next chapter is to examine the doctrines of divine providence, judgment, and revelation to assess their correspondence to the communication model.

– 10 –

The Joyful Noise of Providence, Judgment, and Revelation

DIVINE PROVIDENCE, JUDGMENT, AND REVELATION cluster nicely into a larger topic. Each is actually a special category of a larger movement of God to speak out intimately and bridge the gap between heaven and earth. The acts of God are nothing less than God acting by communicating. Just as the dancer and the act of dancing are inseparable, so God the speaker and the act of speaking are inseparable. Just as the pronouncement of the lover to the beloved "I love you" is a self-reflexive declaration that carries the lover along with the utterance to the beloved, so God's declaration "I will be with you" carries Yahweh along to the Israelites. Or, in other words, the *Logos* of the first chapter of the Gospel of John has the Word both residing originally in God and yet given by God to the world. Divine providence, judgment, and revelation are, consequently, all acts of God speaking out intimately to bring about a preferred relationship. In the communication model, the *logos* of the divine speaking out constitutes the creation and determines God's relation to it. In this chapter we will explore in some detail how this is the case.

PROVIDENCE

The Rationing of Variety

As recipient of the immodest yet apportioned deluge of nurturing variety, the creation is enabled to take up the continuing task of creating for itself. Creatures co-respond in the creative process of *opus ornatus*, of self-elaboration into countless species and unique individuals whose numbers are beyond tally. Yet, it would be wrong to conclude that God's acts in the creation end with these tasks of originating the world and providing gracefully the material for sustenance and self-organization. God also acts to bring about a preferred state for the world to achieve. The unified harmony of the divine "willings" constitutes the ideal telos for the creation. In the tradition, this directed care for the world exerted by God to shepherd it toward fulfillment is known as providence. An associated variant of providence is provision. In providential acts God provides for the creation with the intention of graceful and benevolent guidance. In terms of communication theory and the divine function as *kybernetes,* God guides or steers the world through the continuous but controlled and varying release of chaotic variety. The amount or power of this flow is determined by the divine intention. So, in addition to the continuous variety required to sustain the world in its bounteous being, there also is a secondary (but no less important) release for the sake of directing or correcting the creation.

The release of variety into the world is exclusively through God as the channel of its flow. The effects of this flow are proportional to its intensity. In essence, the quantity or degree of intensity corresponds to both the divine willing or intention and the subsequent effect on the creation. A minimal flow is required to sustain the world in its existence and requisite diversity. An increased flow provides gratuitous variety for the task of creaturely self-construction, a joyful noise to be arranged into the life ways of individuals and communities and given back to God, as the traditions say, "in glory." Indeed, "glory" itself may be understood as this splendorous noise initially given by God for the purpose of being returned eventually to God as the fullness of phrase, a composition arranged and performed by the grand orchestra of creation that is itself constituted by this noise.

Through acts of providence God apportions or rations the injection of raw variety into the system of creation as a whole or to specific components within the system. This rationing is the optimal road to a flourishing creation. The organization of creaturely systems in their environmental contexts is sustained in a reliable and continuous way through the divine allowance of incessant and infinitely adjustable variety.

The divine rationing of the primal chaos is itself an act of providential benevolence. Without this regulation of variety, the fundamental order and integrity of the creation would be constantly threatened. God protects the creation from prodigal variety just as "he assigned the sea its limit, so that the waters might not transgress his command" (Prov. 8:29). The very source of order in the world begins with the divine shield set between chaos and cosmos—the initial act of separation. The book of Job reflects a similar role for God as guardian of the vulnerable creation. This passage occurs in the famous chapter where God, reversing Job's interrogation, puts Job in the dock and asks several questions, including,

> "Or who shut in the sea with doors
> when it burst out from the womb?—
> when I made clouds its garment,
> and thick darkness its swaddling band,
> and prescribed bounds for it, and set bars and doors,
> and said, 'Thus far shall you come,
> and no farther,
> and here shall your proud waves be stayed'?"
>
> (Job 38:8–11)

The question is, of course, rhetorical; God commands the turbulent sea, encircling it with bounds. In like fashion, God's impounds the *Pandemonium Tremendum* to the benefit of all creatures, who otherwise would be engulfed by its tides.

The controlled release of variety is a gift reckoned for all creatures. After prophesying how the owl and kite, birds of prey, will inhabit the ruins of desolated lands, Isaiah describes how God has gathered them in pairs, a suggestion of divine keeping: "Not one of these shall be missing; none shall be without its mate" (Isa. 34:16). "He [God] has cast the lot for them, his hand has portioned it out to them with the line; they shall possess it forever" (Isa. 34:17). How the land becomes desolate in the first place is a question we will take up momentarily under the topic of judgment.

Isaiah's visions continue in chapter 35 with an account of a new paradise where healing of persons and the land is complete. The blind, deaf, lame, and dumb are restored, and the land, especially, receives the blessing of water from the wilderness.

> For waters shall break forth in the wilderness,
> and streams in the desert;
> the burning sand shall become a pool,
> and the thirsty ground springs of water;
> the haunt of jackals shall become a swamp,
> the grass shall become reeds and rushes.
>
> (Isa. 35:6–7)

God restores the land by providing an abundance of water. Gratuitously, God delivers water sufficient for the greening of the desert, and even more, for the flooding of the grassland and the creation of wetlands. The scene is symbolically suggestive of the release of variety from the "deeps" of the *Pandemonium Tremendum* to accomplish the same divine purpose of abundant blessing.

Rationing and rationality derive from the Greek *ratio*. Since reasoning is a process that values logical proportionality, the connection between rational thinking and rationing is a natural one. In the divine function as the benevolent *kybernetes,* God reckons the flow of variety in prudent and measured response to the requirements of specific situations in the creation.[1]

Logos and Dabar

This effecting of the divine willings through relevant proportional release of elemental variety is strongly suggestive of the *logos* in Greek and Christian thought. In various contexts *logos* signifies the rational principle inherent in both the world at large and human rea-

---

1. We should recognize that, for the moment, we have departed from Shannon's theory of communication based on the message selection as the generation of information for an alternative mode; we have moved from the digital model to the analogue model. Analogue computing and communication is based on continuous variations rather than discrete ones. The now obsolete slide rule, replaced by the digital handheld calculator, is analogical. The scales on one ruler or slide are marked the same way as inches on a length ruler and are proportional to the scale on an adjoining ruler. As the two rulers are aligned when calculations are made, the results can be read from the correspondence of marks on the two scales. Since the scales are continuous, like a number line, the results must be read precisely. The degree of precision is a matter of eyesight and judgment. Analogical communication does not rely on a set of messages but rather on the intensity with which a single message may be sent for its discrimination of meaning. A solo performer, a stand-up comic, for example, will receive feedback from the audience in terms of boos or applause. This simple message set contains all the variety, two possibilities or one bit, that is required to give the performer complete certainty with respect to the question "How did I do?" In another situation, where more civility reigns, a classical solo pianist will have uncertainty relieved concerning the same question, not with the either-or of boos or applause, but with applause alone. This time, however, the applause may vary continuously in intensity from faint and restrained to loud and enthusiastic. Faint applause, or very faint applause, is the near equivalent of the single distinctive message delivered by boos. Loud applause is the same message of confirmation for both the comedian and the pianist. Messages sent in the concert hall are fundamentally different from those sent in the comedy club. They are of a single form and vary continuously within a range of intensity. The problem that arises from this analogical form of communication is ambiguity. How does the pianist interpret applause that is too loud to be faint and too faint to be loud? The message is mixed. Uncertainly is not always relieved. For a perceptive discussion of analogical forms of communication, see Paul Watzlawick, Janet Helmick Beavin, and Don D. Jackson, *Pragmatics of Human Communication: A Study of Interactional Patterns, Pathologies, and Paradoxes* (New York: W. W. Norton, 1967), 60–67.

soning. It also signifies "word." In his study of Hebrew thought in comparison with Greek thought, Thorleif Boman draws several interesting parallels between *logos* and the Hebrew equivalent, *dabar.* *Logos* is derived from *lego,* "to speak." The primitive meaning of the root *le* is "to gather." But this is a very specific understanding of gathering, "not to gather pell-mell, but to put together in order, to *arrange.*"[2] *Logos* is found in moderate reasoned thought for the purpose of calculating an ordered state of affairs. The emphasis of Hebrew thought is very different. *Dabar* signifies the energetic thrust of speaking instead of a static arrangement of that which is spoken.[3] A verse from the book of Jeremiah dramatically confirms these emphases:

> Is not my word like fire, says the Lord,
> and like a hammer that breaks a rock in pieces?
> (Jer. 23:29)

Both concepts convey the understanding that words have power and that utterances in the mind or through the mouth have consequences. Nonetheless, whereas the Greek focused the power of *logos* to bring about a balanced, structured outcome, the Hebrews emphasized the dynamic dimension. This distinction is hardly novel. Ever since Plato raised the philosophical consciousness to the dimensions of "being" and "becoming," Western thought has wrestled with their apparent incompatibility. In the communication model, the *logos-dabar* distinction lends itself to straightforward correlation even as the tension between them remains. The *logos* resides with God from the beginning in the primordial acts of separation and gathering and remains effective in the divine rationing of the primal variety as the sustenance of creation. *Dabar* is also an important aspect of the divine life. The *Pandemonium Tremendum,* the blazing caldron of chaos, is the very stuff of creation whose presence is felt in the vitality of the world both in the birth of order and its perishing in a universal condition that Buddhism refers to as *anicca,* "impermanence." *Dabar* signifies the dynamic transmission of variety into the world as messages with varying degrees of constraint but with animating power and potential.

---

2. Thorleif Boman, *Hebrew Thought Compared with Greek,* trans. Jules Moreau (New York: W. W. Norton, 1970), 67.

3. Ibid., 65.

JUDGMENT: THE PLUMMET OF CHAOS

Variety as the Instrument of Divine Wrath

The Bible, especially the Hebrew Bible,[4] is replete with images of divine reckoning carried out as acts of wrath and judgment; God determines that something has gone wrong and then moves to set it straight through acts of cosmic retribution. The *logos* of the retributive act is based on the divine character as moral will, so prominent in Hebrew thought. God "determines," that is, calculates the kind and degree of the transgression (they tend to be grave) and then "determines," in another sense, to move against the transgressor. This second sense of "determines" corresponds to the notion of *dabar* as dynamic and energetic word and vectored will. We interpret it as the divine utilization of the primal chaos, the *Pandemonium Tremendum*, to rectify the skewed situation. Isaiah expresses this double "determination" of *logos* and *dabar* as the divine "plummet of chaos" (Isa. 34:11). The plummet is a plumb bob, not an unusual image in Hebrew prophecy, symbolizing that God takes the measure of Israel's sins and promises to respond accordingly. The "plummet" is the Mosaic covenant from which this measure is decided. The "chaos" is God's retribution.

God's employment of the chaos to bring about intended consequences through an act of judgment takes several forms. Easily the most frequent is regulating the release of variety so that destruction results. Once again, the image of water or the watery chaos is central:

> If he [God] withholds the waters, they dry up;
> if he sends them out, they overwhelm the land.
>
> (Job 12:15)

This passage is profoundly succinct in its summation of the strategies available to God for the instrumental employment of the *Pandemonium Tremendum*. God might choose to withhold the stream of variety altogether, with predictable catastrophic consequences. Or, equally catastrophic, God might choose to release a deluge of unrestrained noise into the creation and the results would be, as one might expect, pure chaos. Either case would constitute the utter destruction of the world and its reversion to the original primordial state. The primordial chaos would reclaim its own.

---

4. The New Testament also contains substantial passages about judgment, especially with respect to apocalyptic prophecy. Most of these, however, reflect theodicies established in Hebrew scripture.

In the first strategy, where divine judgment is carried out through the instrumentality of the incessant stream of variety, God withholds the essential nourishment of variety. "I reduced your rations," Ezekiel reports God saying (Ezek. 16:27). Things, left to their own, disintegrate from the depravation. "The gladness of the earth is banished" (Isa. 24:11). And the land withers. God acts even when God does not act, because divine nonaction has consequences just as damaging as action. Judgment may be applied through God's willful neglect of corruptive systems as they hasten irresistibly toward their own fall.

In the second strategy, where the flow of variety into the world is increased massively, the consequences are dire. Primal variety, the material stuff of generation, becomes the stuff of devastation. The divine rage is vented furiously against city and nation. The consequence is nothing less than conflagration.

> And the streams of Edom shall be
> turned into pitch,
> and her soil into sulfur;
> her land shall become burning pitch.
> Night and day it shall not be quenched;
> its smoke shall go up forever. (Isa. 34:9–10)

What remains is devastation. Stirred by disturbances borne on the winds of unleashed variety, all order has gone to pieces. Isaiah imagines the desolation: "The city of chaos has broken down" (Isa. 24:10). "For you have made the city a heap, the fortified city a ruin" (Isa. 25:2).

Unleashing of massive variety means that certain concrete systems in the creation are overwhelmed as from storm, earthquake, flood, or even by human implements. The blaring trumpets of the Israelites encircling Jericho signify the unleashing of variety sufficient to bring down the city's walls. Most dramatically, God rebukes by releasing torrential variety in annihilating proportions. The Noachian flood is the extreme example. This is an inundating and devouring chaos, the stuff of divine wrath.[5]

But God's strategies can be less violent and often carry different aims. The etiological myth of the Tower of Babel is a wonderful ac-

---

5. By far the most extensive threats and condemnations are to be found in the book of Ezekiel. In page after page, this angry prophet describes the effects of the divine wrath in certain terms: "I will pour out my indignation upon you, with the fire of my wrath I will blow upon you. I will deliver you into brutish hands, those skillful to destroy" (Ezek. 21:31–32).

count of God frustrating a project by injecting unstructured variety as noise to confound communication and scatter the ambitious laborers in all directions (Gen. 11:1–9). The event of Pentecost in the New Testament is an interesting reversal of this strategy (Acts 2:1–13). As the infusion of variety, the Holy Spirit descends like tongues of fire, and the members of a small congregation in the upper room find themselves talking in various tongues readily understood by pilgrims from different lands as they pass in the streets below. While the strategy is the mirror image of that employed at Babel, the intentions are far different. Babel resulted in the scattering of peoples; Pentecost is the initial step in gathering them again through the missionary activity of that small group of Christians who were now capable of taking the gospel to the nations in their own languages. Divine intention and historical context both count in a complete understanding of any particular instance of the infusion of excessive variety.

In the end, the outcome of God either withholding or unleashing the chaos is complete desolation. God literally uncreates a portion of the creation by razing it to the ground, leaving only rubble, or abandoning it to its inherent process of decay. The place returns to wilderness and ruin. The city or the land reverts to the primordial state of chaos, becoming "without form and void."

Clearly, this portrait of divinity gives radical emphasis to a God who "is clothed with terrible majesty" (Job 37:22, RSV), for "when he utters his voice there is a tumult of waters in the heavens" (Jer. 51:16). The one whose divine wrath is poured out upon the creation and requited through acts of retributive justice is the massive, determined deity of Rudolf Otto's *Mysterium Tremendum* who evokes foreboding, dread, and ominous prophecy, appropriate responses to a deity who commands the primordial chaos.

Creaturely Systems as Instruments of Divine Wrath

The surges of chaos released by God do not always come as lightning bolts from the sky, although some sudden catastrophic events, including floods and earthquakes, are easily characterized in this language of calamity. Time and time again the Hebrew scriptures identify creaturely systems as the instruments of divine judgment. The book of Job describes God as scattering his lightning about him and covering the roots of the sea, "For by these he judges the people" (Job 36:30–31, RSV). And the book of Psalms reports, "You make the winds your messengers, fire and flame your ministers" (Ps. 104:4). Creaturely instruments would also include individuals and nations. Great empires are raised by God as the swords of divine retribution. The total devastation remaining in the wake of invasion and conquest was known only too well by ancient Israel, given its experience with a series of conquests by Assyria, Babylon, and Rome. The four horsemen of the apocalypse—pestilence, war, famine, and death—represent the range of agents and events in the creation that may be marshaled into service by God in the focused release of massive pulses of primordial destructive variety.

Demonic Systems

Retribution is often associated with the conquest of evil, either in a punitive way or as an act to set things straight through the elimination of the agents of evil. Evil is known by its fruits, which are always and finally destructive. Because it connotes lack of structure and violent, agitated disorder, chaos is traditionally identified as evil. The primordial chaos, especially, is the power or state standing against God's plans to construct a "very good" creation. So, according to the traditional account, to do good God must first overcome and dispense with its opposite, the chaos. Furthermore, the creation is susceptible to the inherent weakness of reverting to chaos on its own. Where evil appears as violent destruction and chaos (unless the violence and chaos are directed against evil beings), the inevitable conclusion is that evil things have taken place.

But the primordial chaos, the *Pandemonium Tremendum,* suffers the undeserved reputation of being evil. Evil is to be located primarily in the character of systems that generate destructive chaos, the chaos that does not liberate but obliterates. Tillich refers to such systems as "structures of destruction," and includes them in his discussion of the "demonic."[6] Structures of being are characterized as "demonic" not through any association with demons or satanic influence. Rather, the term signifies the distortion of being, of things that have gone wrong in some fundamental ontological way in violation of principles of goodness and well-being.

In an analysis that parallels Tillich's, theologian H. Richard Niebuhr refers to similar structures or closed centers of value and loyalty as "henotheistic," and includes the absolute nation-state and certain historical manifestations of the institutions of the church and science as examples.[7] By "henotheistic," Niebuhr means that

---

6. Paul Tillich, *Systematic Theology,* 3 vols. in 1 vol. (Chicago: University of Chicago Press, 1967), 3:102–6.

7. H. Richard Niebuhr, *Radical Monotheism and Western Culture* (New York: Harper & Row, 1960), ch. 4.

such institutions tend to subordinate all outside centers of value to their own, declaring them either as false, derivative, or dependent, or instrumentally employing them to serve the purposes and absolute values of the insulated community. By constructing an entirely closed and idiosyncratic worldview, consisting exclusively of extremely specific relevantial information,[8] the demonic structure hopes successfully to transcend the relational universe altogether and occupy a self-constructed reality in which its members live, move, and have their being. Theirs is a pathological gnostic program whose intention is to move away from the world, possibly in order to move against it, in a unilateral project to replace the event-centered relational universe with a static one that has relevance only in terms of fixed values. Such is the goal of all passionate ideologies.

Demonic systems are those that distort both order and variety. They are closed in the sense that they take their bearings not from God, community, or the natural order—that is, from others in a state of mutually fulfilling interexistence—but from themselves alone. They are closed systems with sealed internal values to which all other values are subordinated. These systems of distortion move outward to dominate. Their use of the variety available to them is then either unrestricted, the violence of abandoning any principle of ratio or proportion, or that ratio is determined exclusively with respect to their absolute values. Demonic systems are self-deifying. They turn the *logos-dabar* dynamic to their own ends. In the modern era, sovereign nation-states sadly represent the unrestricted ambitions of such systems. Highly organized engines of power—for example, massive military establishments—are used to overwhelm and conquer others for the sake of domination or ideology. They reject relevant context by moving to complete their project of becoming the unrestricted and determining context for the world about them, a context of bondage.

In addition to retributive judgment, God may engage in similar acts of rescuing judgment that are especially pertinent to this description of demonic systems. Divine intervention is necessary in situations where distorted and demonic systems move to enslave and destroy others. Judgment inflicted upon such systems results in the rescue of their captives. Massive variety is withheld from or released into the world to relieve the burden of creatures dominated by demonic systems. In this way God does not rescue creation so much from chaos as through chaos.

---

8. See the discussion in ch. 1 of this volume.

REVELATION

Two Kinds of Revelation

Acts of divine judgment and rescue are instances of divine revelation, broadly defined as the disclosing of something that was previously concealed, in that they imply something about the nature of God and the content of the divine will. Western traditions have generally agreed that God cannot be discovered apart from divinely initiated or unilateral acts of self-disclosure. Beyond this concurrence, however, there is much contention about the divine strategy for self-disclosure. One position is to deny that any direct knowledge of God is available to humans apart from an authoritative and definitive act of history: the law given to Moses at Sinai, the coming of the Messiah in Christ, or the dictation of the Qur'an to Muhammad. From these exclusive and telling instances, other subtler and universal signs of the divine presence or hints of the divine character may be detected or deduced. But, without the primary events as paradigmatic instances of divine disclosure, called "special revelation," we would have no clues, no comparative standards for judging what is or is not revelation at other times and in other places.

Many theologians, however, emphasize a more universal picture of revelation, called "general revelation." Knowledge of God is available through a proper inspection of the nature of the creation, traditionally known as "natural theology." The premise is that somehow the creation resembles and reflects the divine character. Since knowledge about the creation is available to reasoned human inquiry, discoveries concerning nature and human life potentially disclose something about the divine nature. Here the confirmation process is reversed. General knowledge of God derived from evidence found in the creation provides universal standards for judging claims of particular revelatory events.

A Communication Model of Revelation

Karl Barth insists that revelation is not merely data. His concern is that objective information would inevitably be manipulated and abused by the sinful proclivities of fallen creatures. Revelation is transformation, a constitutive act that sustains a creature in its being or offers the gift of new being.

A communication theory of creation confirms these claims. Creation and revelation are the transmission of messages by God. This interpretation is a return to the ancient understanding of the role of words in primal and oral societies, for whom spoken words are utterances of power. Through declaration they alter states of the world. They proclaim and resolve. In Native American societies, ceremonial pronouncements were often followed by the declaration "I have said it," which gives the statements authority, finality, and meaning.[9] Revelation is far more than the disclosure of information that removes ignorance and satisfies curiosity. It is power.

Elsewhere, Barth describes the Trinity as God the Father sending a message, God the Son, to be received by the world as God the Spirit.[10] God's messages are not propagated through some neutral medium that bridges the gap between heaven and earth. The messenger, the message, and its reception are one single movement of three phases—the three in one. In the communication model, the *Pandemonium Tremendum* is the primordial side of the divine life. Without this dimension of infinite potential, God would not be God, and the creation would be impossible. The pure sustaining variety released into the world is God the creator and sustainer of all creation. It is the medium of divine immediacy and qualifies as general revelation. The more fully specified messages of history displaying constraint and redundancy are God the *Logos* and qualify as instances of special revelation. In both cases, reception of variety by creatures constitutes them at their very depths. It is for them the life-giving spirit, the power of being itself. In this twofold movement, God is the source, sender, and context of the constitutive fabric of the creation.

The communication model of revelation is not without paradox. With respect to the *Pandemonium Tremendum* alone, the infinite field of variety, any particular message has a probability of zero. It would never be expected. Creaturely uncertainty about God is therefore absolutely maximal. And the nature of a message that would relieve such great uncertainty is probably incomprehensible, undifferentiated from pure noise, and no less than an encounter with the *Mysterium Tremendum*. No finite creaturely mind, regardless of its information capacity, is capable of receiving and assimilating the immense amounts of information required to "know" God. A loving God therefore restricts the infinite field of variety to some smaller set of potential revelatory signals for the sake of creatures. Despite being severely constrained and more manageable, even this

9. From "Opening Prayer of the Sun Dance" of the Teton Sioux: in *American Indian Prose and Poetry: An Anthology,* ed. Margot Astrov (New York: Capricorn Books, 1946), 123.

10. See Karl Barth, *The Humanity of God* (Richmond: John Knox Press, 1960).

smaller set remains too great for complete human comprehension, and mystery is still present.

General revelation is the exuberant, incessant, and everlasting stream of variety, the steady speaking out of God without moments of silence. Simply to be is to be told; or, more accurately, to be is a continuous telling, a continuous act of communication. The meaning is spiritual and existential—the immediate grasp of the precious gift of life and the intuition that God is all about. General revelation is the communication of God through the blessing of creative and sustaining variety in all of creation.

Special revelation takes place within the context provided by this continuing stream of variety. It is *krisis* in the sense that the message is unexpected and requires a response of judgment (which is what *krisis* means) and action. As the transmission of variety, such messages recapitulate general revelation,[11] but since they must be taken from constrained or limited variety (limited with respect to the *Pandemonium Tremendum,* the infinite field of variety), they represent a different approach of God to the creation. Special revelation pertains to specific instances and constrained messages that both transform and constitute the recipients. The giving of the law at Sinai transformed a group of disoriented slaves into a people and constituted their existence as a nation.

Revelation, Surprise, and Faith

How are acts of God in history and nature perceived within human experience? Perhaps as awesome or astonishing events that seem to bring about outcomes favoring retribution and rescue. These instances appear to make sense within the expectations of tradition. So, on the one hand, they are hoped for, and, on the other hand, they come as surprise. Messages, loudly sounded, are like that; they are anticipated, yet, they come to relieve uncertainty and are therefore surprising. This combination of hope as expectation and surprise as the resolution of uncertainty is a hallmark of the theory of communication.

Information, in the form of messages, comes as a surprise in one of two extreme situations: when uncertainty is great or when certainty is great. Great uncertainty on the part of a receiver signifies that the receiver is completely unsure about which one of a set of messages will be sent because the set is large or all of the messages

11. Schubert Ogden, *On Theology* (San Francisco: Harper & Row, 1986), 86.

are equally probable. When a roulette wheel is spun and the ball settles on any number, the situation is settled for that turn. Considerable uncertainty is resolved, and surprise as joy or consternation is evoked in the player. In the case where certainty is great, surprise may result from the appearance of the unexpected when the expected was taken for granted.

The appreciation of a single event as an instance of revelation is based on the absence of constraint (when uncertainty is great) or on the presence of constraint (when certainty is great). In either case, there is no precedent on the basis of which the surprising event may be confidently predicted.

Of course, revelation may arrive right on schedule in satisfaction of confident prophecy. Still, it is in the very nature of special revelation to be "special," that is, distinctive, where "distinctive" is understood to mean highly unusual with respect to the regularity of the background circumstances out of which it appears. Something breaks into history to fulfill both hope and promise, but in ways unanticipated outside the sight line of faith. While acts of God may be anticipated in hope generated through faith, they arrive unexpectedly and come as genuine surprise.

Miracles are often instances of Revelation. A miracle is sometimes defined as an unusual or improbable happening with consequences of rescue or healing. In this way, the onerous character of traditional miracles as violations of the laws of nature is avoided. The most important instances of this weaker form of miracle as improbable events are those that are anticipated in hope and faith. The crossing of the Reed Sea (a tidal estuary on the Mediterranean rather than the Red Sea of tradition) by the Israelites just before an incoming tide resulted in frustration, and worse, for pursuing Egyptian forces whose chariots became mired in the muck. This natural but unlikely event, with its great timing and favorable consequences, was not expected as such, but hoped for in an attitude of trusting faith. It came as a surprise, but within the context of greater faith in a God, Yahweh, whose very name signifies a steadfast promise to protect.

Faith has this character, because the Lord of history is absolutely sovereign or free. Given the source of divine communication, the infinite field of variety, God decides not on the basis of precedent but anew with each message. There are no inherent preceding limits on the divine will. Hence, one essential characteristic of special revelation, even when anticipated in hope and trust, is surprise. Revelation is always new.

Revelation as Incessant Communication

For general revelation, however, constancy is as important as surprise. Theists perceive the goodness of God as revealed in the very uniformity of constitutive patterns in the cosmos. The patterns are the regular constraints imposed upon the *Pandemonium Tremendum* by God, limits set upon a much larger set of possibilities. As God communicates consistently, over time creatures gather experience about the patterns abiding in their environment and respond to them. Since evolution presupposes not only the play of chance but also necessity, complex living systems would never have been possible without this abiding constraint. Trustworthiness is the theological equivalent of this reliability in the experience of the world.

The model of divinity undergirding general revelation is not based on the craftsperson image of the creator in which God constructs the world as an architect designs and builds a house. Since the builder is omnicompetent and omnibenevolent, the building has a structural integrity respected and admired by its inhabitants, and thankfulness is the appropriate response. However, in the communication model, the integrity is defined as ongoing, sustaining divine activity. God speaks through the incessant stream of variety, both raw and constrained. The redundancies upon which all creatures depend are the states of the world generated by God's constant discourse. As we gather experience about these enduring states, our uncertainty about God's will diminishes. Based on precedents, God is predictable and the creation is reliable. God's actions could be otherwise. The potential of world-speaking, given the storehouse of the *Pandemonium Tremendum,* is without limits. Other worlds are possible, or simple arbitrary communication, a destructive babble, is also possible. The divine constancy must therefore be located in God's *hesed,* or steadfast loving kindness of nurture and nourishment.

Selective Expectation

There is one sense, however, in which revelation is relative. To some extent, the reception of messages depends on the state of the receiver. What is a message for one may be noise for another; communication is in the ear of the receiver. Two persons engaged in conversation in the presence of a musical performance are likely to find the music interfering. For someone else standing nearby, however, the conversation, not the music, is interference. "Noise" is the presence of disorder that contaminates order. It is the static that drowns out the broadcast. What is identified as noise, however, depends partially on the interests of the receiver, on what is expected or desired in the message.[12]

A noisy world is not necessarily a fundamentally chaotic world. It may be a world of various orders, of complex systems that constantly clash, with noise emerging from the resulting discord. This sort of second-order chaos has given rise to religious philosophies that interpret the world as an undesirable and very noisy place, the realm of *maya,* or illusion. The ultimate goal of human life in such philosophies is to take every conceivable action to become liberated from the cacophony.

The realm of *maya* is an extreme case. In theism the problem is how to distinguish the order of revelatory communication from the pervasive noise of competing message sources in the creation. Here the redundancy, the patterns perceived in the constraints applied to previous messages, is useful. Revelation may be that which is genuinely novel, unexpected, and surprising, but it may not be recognized as revelation unless the receiver is sensitive to the patterns that may be weakly present in the noise. Revelation is often a matter of judgment about what constitutes revelation. This is not to say that revelation is validated by reason alone, but that precedents are established through experience so that what counts as divine revelation is heard in terms of these precedents. The question is not one of recognition but of expectation. Hindus expect something different from Buddhists, and Buddhists yet something different than Christians.

These observations provide a platform for pluralistic universalism in revelation. Various traditions predispose their participants to anticipate that future revelatory events will satisfy particular criteria that were set by events in their sacred history, especially as these are expressed in symbols and iconography. These preparatory experiences allow them to distinguish signals from noise while at the same time granting that other traditions may have tuned into far different signals from the same noisy transmissions.

---

12. This selective interest applies to more than conscious judgment. Instinctive behavior qualifies, as do the mechanisms of the body as they sort out what is necessary and replenishing from that which is toxic or simply irrelevant. William James recognizes the importance of paying particular attention for the very content of consciousness: "Without selective interest, experience is in utter chaos...without it the consciousness of every creature would be a gray chaotic indiscriminateness, impossible for us to conceive" (*Principles of Psychology* [New York: Macmillan, 1886], 381).

CONCLUSION

While theological terms are employed liberally throughout this book, it is only in this chapter that we allow theological concepts to dictate and guide the discussion. God lovingly provides the fundamental infrastructure or environment for the nourishment and flourishing of creatures. But God also moves actively to shape the direction of that development in ways that are consistent with the divine intentions. These actions speak for themselves, but they are also speech acts. Thus, providence, judgment, and revelation may be treated under a single image of divine speaking out, and that, in turn, lends itself well to an accounting of each based on communication theory.

– 11 –

Evaluating
the Model

WE BEGAN OUR SYNOPTIC SURVEY with the thesis that electronic technology, as represented by the computer, is a window to the whole of things, inclusive of the things of heaven as well as of earth. As an instrument for expanding the horizons of our own self-understanding and as a research tool revealing novel dimensions of dynamic complexity in nature, the computer surely qualifies as a transformative machine. Beyond this impressive impact, however, it also prefigures deity by providing us with a theoretical framework for exploring new models of God. Since this framework is congruent with the deep structure of things, or so we suggest, we have not shied away from pursuing its consequences even to the point of expressing metaphysical conjectures as propositions about realities that are not only beyond purely rational demonstration but also quite nearly beyond the imagination. Since our sensate culture simply cannot fathom such thoughtful intangibles or appreciate why anybody would want to, we are burdened with justifying their pursuit.

In chapter 3 we discussed three criteria (there could be others) against which metaphysical proposals may be tested: internal coherence, mundane relevance, and pragmatic application. By way of concluding this study, it may be instructive to apply them to our systems-informational account.

The first criterion, *internal coherence,* is the most difficult to satisfy. We have identified several weaknesses in this system either as inconsistencies or lingering, inadequately answered questions. One concerns the ontological subordination of God to the *Pandemonium Tremendum.* The answer given to the cosmological question—why God exists—has the deity arising from the chaos as a spontaneous posit, the primordial decision that determines God. In addition to the puzzling bootstrap character of this account, there is the more

difficult problem of explaining the persistence of this initial determination. How is it possible for the primordial chaos, over an
eternity of turbulent mixing, to give rise to an enduring entity or
ordered state capable of fending off the destructive scouring of the
chaos? Also, is this divinity, the firstborn of this unbirthed and eternal core, true to monotheistic expectations for God and worthy of
worship?

A second problem has to do with the causal joint, the point
of contact between God and the creation that is necessary for
"mighty acts" of continuing creation, providential guidance, and
retributive justice. We proposed that God, the divine equivalent of
Maxwell's demon, disburses measured quantities of variety under
various degrees of constraint as messages or material for messages
in the composition of creatures. As the stuff of the *Pandemonium Tremendum,* variety is a metaphysical element, not a physical
or worldly one. Its equivalent in the world is information. This
means that for variety to become effective it must somehow generate information. Despite the appeal to decision processes to
carry out this transformation, it is unclear how variety becomes
information.

The promise of a complete accounting of some smooth and continuous movement from the *Pandemonium Tremendum,* through
God, into the creation remains unfulfilled. Seams do exist, especially at the crucial point of contact, the long-sought causal joint
between God and world. It is as if the muscular deity of Michelangelo's Sistine Chapel scene of the creation of humankind never quite
touches the outreached fingers of the drowsy Adam. An ontological
gap remains between God and world.

Final comments about the first criterion have to do with vagueness. Any reduction of vagueness in an abstract metaphysical system
is laudable. But its complete removal is impossible, particularly in
theological metaphysics. The nature of God includes irreducible
mystery. Speculative metaphysics grapples with this mystery when
its intentions are to make the reality of God clear and distinct.
Encounter with mystery and tolerance for it are not to be confused
with vagueness, loss of nerve, or with the presence of a gap in the
system (although sometimes appeal to mystery masks such gaps).
Our replacement of the *Mysterium* in Otto's *Mysterium Tremendum*
with *Pandemonium* should not be taken as any decision to eliminate
essential mystery. This is in appreciation of the wisdom of Tolstoy,
who, according to Norman Cousins, once said that it is a terrible
thing to watch someone who doesn't know what to do with the

incomprehensible, because generally, such a person winds up with a toy named God.[1]

With respect to the criterion of *mundane relevance,* the systems-informational account holds up well. It rides the crest of a gathering wave of theoretical advances in a number of interdisciplinary sciences that have to do with the dynamic systems aspects of the physical and biological worlds. By generalizing from the principles and discoveries of these sciences, it is entirely possible and certainly permissible to construct a fruitful worldview with metaphysical foundations whose general categories account synoptically for the kinds of things we find in the world.

Also, the overwhelming number and variety of creatures in all their intricate and novel detail is a very important fact about nature that has been neglected by science in its efforts to discover universal principles that govern all phenomena. But diversity is not a hoax or the lingering mirage of ignorance yet to be removed by further scientific inquiry seeking a "theory of everything." The testimony of the mighty throng of creatures is not to be suppressed but celebrated, and what's more, recognized for what it is, a fundamental truth about reality richly suggestive for theology and science alike.

In terms of *pragmatic applicability,* it is simply too early to determine the success of a systems-informational metaphysic in postmodern culture. We have argued that, insofar as the information revolution is transforming thinking and behavior, a philosophy built upon its basic axioms has consequences for our understanding of ourselves in the world. Indeed, it would be irresponsible not to provide some potential contribution to an emerging worldview, if only to catalyze discussion about God, nature, humankind, and the character of the relations between them.

Since the intention of this study is to offer a model of God that is in keeping with the foregoing expectations, some assessment of the *theological fruitfulness* of the model is important. To what degree is the God who manages the *Pandemonium Tremendum* for the sake of generating, sustaining, and directing the creation by the outpouring of variety the God of Abraham, Isaac, Jacob, Jesus, and Muhammad?

The strengths of the model appear to lie in several emphases. One is communication. This is an out-spoken God who sends the Spirit into the world for the world's sake. A second is relational-

---

1. Norman Cousins, comments in "Symposium," in *A Spacefaring People: Perspectives on Early Space Flight,* ed. Alex Roland (Washington, D.C.: Scientific and Technical Information Branch, National Aeronautics and Space Administration, 1985), 25.

ity. God and world carry forth together as a coupled system with
constant exchanges that result in a profound state of interexistence.
This emphasis may be too strong for those who prefer a monologue
that gives priority to God's fluency while the creation remains relatively silent. Still, it is important to understand that the conversation
was initiated by God, whose very words constitute the responding
creation. A third and final strength is the attention given to divine
sovereignty by the model. God's absolute freedom is grounded in the
infinitely fecund primordial chaos. Where else would it be? We have
argued earlier that God's love is the only reason for the creation and
that the logic of love requires a beloved. The theological claim that
God loves cannot be derived from any model (and certainly not this
one), because it arises from the experience of divine love in the lives
of creatures and in history. The model works from the givenness of
divine love. But the fact that an absolutely sovereign God chooses
to express the divine life in terms of the selfless giving of abundance
to the dependent creation is a reason for celebration and worship
as well as thought.

Finally, there is an issue of specificity. The axioms from which
the notion of God is derived do not lead necessarily to monotheism,
much less to particular monotheistic traditions, to Judaism, Christianity, or Islam. With some modifications, the system could apply
further afield, to oriental religions—Buddhism and Taoism come
readily to mind. Moreover, there seems to be no inherent limit to
the number of deities that the model could support, although this
unnecessary multiplication of gods seems arbitrary and violates the
prohibition against superfluous or unduly complicated explanations
in science, philosophy, or theology. Perhaps God could be eliminated
altogether—the atheistic option—in which case the *Pandemonium
Tremendum* would bear exclusive responsibility for the creation.
Unless, however, our basic concept of a dynamic primordial chaos
that consumes its own offspring worlds is drastically altered, this
position has little viability. Also, Whitehead's principle of concretion applies. Given the character of the primordial chaos as absolute
indeterminateness, how does the ordered and concrete (i.e., specific)
world arise? A decisive entity is required. God satisfies this function.

Most conspicuous is the absence of references to Christ or
any attempt, for that matter, to incorporate Christology into this
systems-informational ontology. Admittedly, it is difficult to construct a full-blown theological system, even in a study as sweeping
as this one. The intention was to focus on a model of God derived
from an account of the primordial chaos. It is therefore theocentric,

or perhaps "xaocentric." The model would support a Christology, but that work remains to be done.

These concluding remarks would be incomplete without some consideration for the metaphorical, rather than isomorphic, image of God that this model suggests. Evidence for a loving and generous God is found in the nurture of the incessant flow of sustaining variety. The act of providing nourishment out of one's own body, the maternal Eucharist, is an act of grace and love. The image of the infinite field of variety, the *Pandemonium Tremendum,* as that aspect of the incomparable vastness and potential of God, is one of the bounteous mother, whose children, all creatures, are born of her womb and feed from her bosom. This characterization of the divine creatrix balances the image of God the Maxwellian deity, the *logos* of structure and system, whose decisions are decidedly of the rational sort. At the risk of gender profiling, it should be noted that fathers also love. Their forms of nurture characteristically come from the provisions they bring from their labors—in this case, a supply of constrained and requisite variety. The images are complementary, but not in conflict or opposition since the intentions are identical: lovingly to sustain the creation.

Ironically, the *Pandemonium Tremendum* is the instrument of this divine love. The illegible chaos—a strange and mysterious mix of random elements conveying no meaning, no significance—is also the stuff of creation. God attends to the chaos, draws upon it at will and sends it into the world in measured proportion for the good. Creation is quickened by this release and receives its potential from the message.

Because it is illegible, the original chaos eludes all direct comprehension and must be explored in highly metaphorical and metaphysical ways based on hints taken from human experience of its residual presence in the order of creation.

Recognizing them leads to an assessment that is itself mixed. As an exercise in metaphysical theater, perhaps any attempt to discover invariance in the infinitely and irreducibly various *Pandemonium Tremendum.* is bound to eventual frustration. Still, along the way much that is instructive may be discovered.

Index

a se, 61
Abelard, 47
Abraham, 43, 221
Acts, 209
actualization, 12, 14n, 35–36, 73, 106, 109, 115, 118, 124, 134, 172, 177, 184, 187, 189, 191
actus purus, 117, 141
Adam, 156, 185n, 187–89, 220
Advaita, 44
aesthetics, 46, 69, 76, 171–72, 184, 198
Agennetos, 137
agnosticism, 61–62, 65, 185
algorithm, 80, 124, 196–98
alienation, 2, 30, 32, 172
Alpha, 124, 126
anarchy, 86, 90, 97–98, 134n, 136
anicca, 82, 123, 206
Anselm, 27n, 46
anthropology, 25, 31–32, 62, 182, 185n, 190
anthropomorphism, 37, 58, 179
apocalypse, 207, 210
Aquinas, Thomas, 25n, 35, 43, 153, 155
arche, 134, 136
Aristotle, vii, 11, 34–35, 87n
Ashby, W. Ross, 71–75, 104n, 123–24, 144n, 180
Assyria, 33, 210
astronomy, 9, 17–18, 33, 38
asymptotes, 98, 114, 131, 191
atheism, 35–36, 222
atoms, 7, 12, 20, 33, 36, 38, 81, 119, 144, 166, 170, 198, 200n. *See also* electrons
Augustine, 167–68
automata, 5
automobiles, 1–3, 5, 6, 13, 80, 86–87
autopoiesis, 39, 87n
Ayer, A. J., 47–48

Babylon, 33, 210
baptism, 200
bara, 154–55
Barbour, Ian G., 54, 64–65
Barth, Karl, 27, 58, 61, 136–37, 155, 212–13

Bateson, Gregory, vii, 70, 106
Beavin, Janet Helmick, 183n, 205n
Beer, Stafford, 102n, 170–72
Berdyaev, Nicolas, 105, 137n
Berger, Peter, 30n, 99
Berry, Thomas, 38
Bertalanffy, Ludwig von, 7n, 83n, 179, 181–82
bêtes machines, 29
Bhagavad Gita, 107n
Bible, 26–27, 36, 43n, 99, 119, 137, 199, 207. *See also* scripture
big bang, 113n, 132, 165
biology, 10, 13, 17, 19, 38, 55, 83, 86–89, 162, 176, 182, 184n, 194, 221
black holes, 115
Blake, William, 164
Boer, Pieter Arie Hendrik de, 133n
Bohme, Jakob, 105
Boman, Thorleif, 206
Bonino, José Míguez, 32n
Bosch, Hieronymus, 165n
Brahma, 134
Brahman, 44, 137
Brahms, Johannes, 68
brain, 1, 67, 69–70, 144n, 160, 179–84, 195
Brown, Frank, 64–65
Browning, Elizabeth, 169
Buber, Martin, 189–90
Buddhism, 82, 123, 132, 206, 217, 222
Bynum, Terrell Ward, 7n

Callicott, J. Baird, 8–10, 16, 21
Calvinism, 163
Campbell, Jeremy, 78n, 150n, 164n, 173n
Campbell, Joseph, 198
Camus, Albert, 98n
Capra, Fritjof, 83n
cars. *See* automobiles
Cartesian dualism, 29
causa sui, 133
causality, 10, 13, 20, 43, 97, 116, 120, 133, 140, 142–47, 154, 171n, 176, 220
cells, 67, 86, 147

ceremony, 53, 213. *See also* ritual; worship
Chaitin, Gregory, 196–97
Chandler, Stuart, 97n
chaos, ix–x, 18–19, 39, 67n, 73, 76, 83, 89–91, 96–99, 101–6, 109–10, 114–37, 141–43, 151–57, 159–63, 167–72, 175–76, 181, 186, 191, 200–201, 203–11, 217, 219–23
chaos theory, 39, 160. *See also* nonlinearity
China, 70n, 192
Christianity
    creation and, 128–29, 137, 154–55
    judgment and, 209–12
    metaphysics and, 43, 49, 51, 56n
    revelation and, 212, 217
    theology and, 23–29, 34–35, 185n, 187, 199–200, 205, 221–23
Church. *See* Christianity
Cilliers, Paul, 85n, 196–97
civitas, 16
classification, 5, 11–12, 15, 35, 197. *See also* taxonomy
Clayton, Philip, 126
closed systems, 82, 94–95, 150, 161, 175, 198, 211
coincidentia oppositorum, 114
communication, vii–ix, 4, 9, 14n, 39, 59, 65, 97, 102, 125–28, 133–43, 164, 171, 173, 176–79, 183–201, 202–6, 209, 213–17, 222–23
    in communication theory, vii–ix, 60–61, 66–95, 105, 108–9, 115, 117, 137, 147–58, 160, 169, 182, 203, 212, 218
Communion. *See* Eucharist
complementarity, 64, 159, 223
complexity, 18, 20, 39–41, 66, 73, 82–94, 148, 159, 162, 168–74, 180–85, 197, 219
compressibility, 196–98. *See also* incompressibility
computers, vii–ix, 1–11, 16–21, 39, 66–69, 87, 93n, 128, 160n, 164, 171n, 180, 196, 219
constraint, 37, 72–79, 82, 86–90, 94–95, 103–4, 114, 118–22, 125, 136–37, 141–45, 149, 152, 155, 159–64, 168–70, 176–77, 191–96, 198, 200, 206, 213–17, 220, 223
contingency, 54, 60, 89–90, 130, 136, 152–53, 157, 183, 190–91, 172, 196, 198
Copernicus, 17, 35

cosmology, ix–x, 10, 13n, 22–43, 45, 47, 51, 54, 59, 65–66, 107, 113n, 120n, 129–38, 151–58, 186–87n, 219
cosmomorphism, 58
coupled systems, 87–88, 92, 94, 186n, 190, 222
Cousins, Norman, 220–21
creatio ex nihilo, 101, 126–27, 132, 136. *See also* emptiness; nothingness; void
Creation. *See* cosmology
Cronon, William, 30n
cryptology, 67
cybernetics, 5, 11n, 67, 71, 75n, 87n, 91, 93, 104n, 123n, 172–74, 180, 183, 188, 199. *See also kybernetes*
cyberspace, 4, 14–16

dabar, 187–88, 205–7, 211
Dante, 161
Darwin, Charles, 17
Davies, Paul, 54–55
Decalogue, 35
deconstruction, 4, 9, 31, 133n
Deep Blue, 128
deism, 36, 42, 44, 144
Demiurge, the, 34, 105n, 123, 128, 137n, 191
demons, 16n, 150–51, 210–11, 220
Descartes, René, 44, 110
determinism, 12, 20, 39, 198. *See also* indeterminism
Deus ex Machina, 42, 198
Deuteronomy, 100
Deutsch, Eliot, 44
disorder, 72–82, 97, 124, 160–61, 172n, 176, 210, 217. *See also* entropy
ditheism, 101
divine sovereignty, 117, 122, 125, 127, 135–38, 222. *See also* omnipotence
divinity. *See* theology
DNA, 67. *See also* genetics
doctrine, ix–x, 23, 31, 35, 51, 53, 61, 101, 112n, 126–27, 155n, 158, 185, 199, 201
dualism, 29, 38, 43–45, 117n, 168, 185. *See also* Cartesian dualism
Dyson, Freeman, 17, 21

Eckhart, Meister, 105, 133, 137
ecology, 8, 10, 13, 24n, 30, 62–63, 70, 88, 91, 94, 106n, 147n, 166n, 171, 186n, 203
Edda, the, 82
Edom, 100, 208
Egypt, 33
Ehrenfels, Christian, 116n

Eigen, Manfred, 89
Einstein, Albert, 17, 54–55, 110, 112
electrons, 64, 165–66, 171n. See also
    atoms
Ellis, George F. R., 187n
emanation, 147, 149–50
empiricism, 6, 27–28, 46–48, 51–56,
    59, 106, 110, 113n
emptiness, 97n, 100–101, 108, 115,
    131. See also creatio ex nihilo;
    nothingness; void
energy, 5, 7, 18, 33, 38, 78, 80–82,
    101, 113, 119, 150–51, 162, 173
engineering, 5n, 67, 85n, 87, 178, 194
Enlightenment, the, ix, 8, 27, 31
entropy, 77–82, 95, 104, 150–51, 157,
    161, 164n, 170, 197. See also
    disorder
environmentalism. See ecology
epistemology, 7, 48, 65
equilibrium, 78–82, 92–93, 150–51,
    157, 163, 169, 171
eschatology, 200
ethics, 35, 184n, 187n, 193n. See also
    morality
etiology, 33, 134, 208
Eucharist, 200, 223
Euclid, 112n
Eve, 156, 189
evolution, 13, 16–18, 20, 31, 39, 82,
    87–90, 129n, 145n, 162, 169,
    171n, 176, 181–88, 197, 199n,
    216
existentialism, 13, 30, 70–72, 108, 159,
    173, 214
Exodus, 189–90
Ezekiel, 192, 208

faith, 2, 19, 24–26, 28, 31–32, 36, 43,
    46–51, 53, 61–62, 72, 129, 154,
    214–15
feedback, 77, 82, 87–88, 91–95, 180,
    183–84, 187, 194, 250n
Feuerbach, Ludwig, 58
flood, the, 208
forms, x, 11, 24, 45, 51, 63, 73–75, 82,
    85, 88, 104, 106–9, 118, 120n,
    140, 145, 160, 164, 167, 169,
    174, 185n, 205n, 207, 223
Frankenberry, Nancy, 156n
Franklin, Benjamin, 37
frequency, 9, 72–75, 85, 160n, 162–63
Freud, Sigmund, 17, 58
functionalism, 62

Galileo, 17, 35
Gasset, José Ortega y, 163, 194–95

Genesis, ix, 89–90, 95–96, 99–102,
    123, 129, 132, 134, 154–55,
    188–90, 201, 209
genetics, 13, 31, 67, 88, 145n, 194
geometry, 111–13, 120
Gilkey, Langdon, 28, 43
Gilson, Etienne, 43n
Girardot, N. J., 96
Gleick, James, 18
gnosticism, 15, 64, 172, 211
God. See theology
Godhead, 133–34
Gott, 137
Gottheit, 137. See Ungrund
Greek thought, viii, 7, 11, 20, 25, 34,
    37, 49, 54, 87n, 91, 111–12, 119,
    137, 166, 169, 173, 189, 205–6
Greene, Brian, 167n
Gregersen, Niels Henrik, 87n
Gregorios, Paulos Mar, 166n
Groothuis, Douglas, 4n
Gudorf, Christine E., 193n
Gustafson, James, 184n

Hall, David L., 134n
Hartshorne, Charles, 103, 116n, 147n,
    168
Haught, John, 129, 171
heaven, vii, 28, 32–35, 44, 51, 65, 100,
    154, 165, 169, 188–89, 200, 202,
    209, 213, 219
Hebrews, the, 54, 100, 119, 121, 154,
    187, 189, 190, 206–9
Hefner, Philip, 105n, 137n, 188n
Heidegger, Martin, 46, 119n
henotheism, 210–11
hermeneutics, 25, 32
Herrick, A. R., 144n
Heschel, Abraham, 156
hesed, 216
Hesiod, 132n
heterostasis, 91, 93
Hick, John, 163
Hinduism, 44, 82, 132, 134, 137, 217
historicism, 25
homeostasis, 91–92
homo sapiens, 91, 185n
Hopkins, Gerard Manley, 99
Hopkins, Jasper, 112n
Huchingson, James E., 83n, 147n, 148n
Hume, David, 26, 47, 119
hydrodynamics, 173

imagination, viii–ix, 4–5, 17, 24, 32,
    38, 48, 50–51, 55–63, 95, 98,
    101, 109–14, 118, 120, 132, 139,
    143, 146, 150, 180–83, 189,
    194–97, 219
imago mundi, 179, 185

immanence, 45, 97, 149, 157
incompressibility, 196. *See also*
  compressibility
indeterminism, 89, 97–98, 105, 109,
  121, 131, 143, 145, 148, 222. *See
  also* determinism
individualism, 2, 15–16
information theory. *See* communication
  theory
in medias res, 187
interexistence, 88, 90, 175–76, 182,
  186n, 187, 190, 211, 222
internal coherence, 52, 219
Internet. *See* cyberspace
intuition 7, 26–27, 54, 56, 109–11,
  118, 135, 139, 166, 214
Irwin, Lee, 33n
Isaac, 221
Isaiah, 100, 158, 187–88, 204, 207–8
Isis, 34
Islam, 44, 112, 156, 199, 221–22
isomorphism, 6–10, 19–20, 59–68,
  75, 83–84, 111, 113, 140, 147,
  149–50, 169, 185, 223
isos, 7
Israel, the people of, 133n, 156, 190,
  192n, 199, 202, 207–8, 210, 215
Italy, 73–74

Jackson, Don D., 183n, 205n
Jacob, 221
James, William, 217
Jantzen, Grace, 147n
Janus, 134
Jeeves, Malcolm A., 28
Jeremiah, 206, 209
Jericho, 208
Jesus. *See* Christianity
Job, 100–101, 119–20, 204, 207, 209
John, the Gospel of, 49, 202
Jonah, 200
Jordan, the river, 200
Judaism, 43, 51, 129, 221–22. *See also*
  Hebrews
judgment, x, 172, 180, 183–84, 201–18

Kabbalah, 129
Kant, Immanuel, 26–27, 47
Kasparov, Gary, 128
Kaufman, Gordon, 24n, 49–50, 62,
  90n
kenosis, 129, 187
Kepler, Johannes, 54
Kierkegaard, Søren, 58, 179
Kliever, Lonnie D., 23n
krisis, 214
Kuhn, Thomas, 17
Küng, Hans, 50, 56n, 89

kybernetes, 91, 171–73, 179, 182,
  185–87, 190, 195, 201, 203, 205.
  See also cybernetics

Laplace, Pierre Simon, 36
Laszlo, Ervin, 83n, 84n, 88
Leibniz, G. W. von, 46
Leviathan, 101, 161n, 200
Lewis, C. S., 167n
Lindberg, David C., 112n
linearity, 18, 90, 176
linguistics, 8, 24, 62, 67, 85
Livingston, James C., 200
Locke, John, 117n, 193
logic, vii, 25n, 27, 32, 35, 48n, 51,
  55–56, 59, 82, 109–10, 113–15,
  147n, 160, 195, 222
logos, 25, 34, 56, 134–35, 157, 202,
  205–7, 211, 213, 223
Lonergan, Bernard, 166
Luhmann, Niklas, 71

machines, vii–ix, 1–21, 28–29, 32, 36,
  38, 42, 44, 79, 81, 84, 94, 128n,
  139, 198, 219
MacKay, Donald M., 81, 117n
MacQuarrie, John, 25
magic, 33, 58, 130, 139
Malcolm X, 199
Marduk, 34, 161n
Mark, the Gospel of, 128n
Maruyama, Magorah, 11–14, 16, 21,
  173
Marxism, 2, 32n
materia prima, 175
materialism, 44
mathematics, vii, 6–7, 18–20, 35, 54,
  64, 67–69, 78–79, 85n, 110–13,
  118, 126, 156, 160, 167, 197
matrix, 106, 175–76
matter, 5, 20–21, 29, 34, 44–45, 99,
  106, 113–14, 123, 150, 156, 162,
  166, 172, 175, 191
Maurer, Armand A., 111n, 141n
Maxwell, James Clerk 17, 150–51, 220,
  223
maya, 44, 217
McFague, Sallie, 24n, 61–63, 147n
mechanism, 9–10, 20, 28–33, 36–39,
  42–43, 47, 82, 84, 156, 171n,
  176, 200, 217n
Mediterranean, the, 215
me-on, 105, 115, 131
metaphysics, viii–x, 20–22, 27–28, 33,
  39–65, 75, 91, 95, 102, 106–7,
  109, 111, 113–15, 123, 129, 132,
  137, 142n, 146, 219–21
meteorology, 9, 18
Michelangelo, 73–76, 87, 155, 183–84

microscope, 17–18
microstates, 79, 81, 123, 125–26, 131, 151, 161
Middle Ages, the, 34
Míguez Bonino, José, 32n
miracles, 36, 42–45, 58, 80, 143–46, 167n, 176, 200, 215
Moltmann, Jürgen, 175
monism, 43–45
monotheism, 32, 101, 132, 147, 152, 186, 210n, 220, 222
morality, 2, 30, 40, 47, 51, 184n, 187n, 207. *See also* ethics
More, James H., 7n
morphe, 7
Morse, Samuel, 75
Moses, 35, 156, 189–90, 207, 212
Moyer, Linda L., 181n
Muhammad, 221
Mumford, Lewis, 5
mundane relevance, 52, 219, 221
Murphy, Nancey, 18n, 187n
music, 68, 70, 76–77, 85, 90, 140, 161, 198, 216
Mysterium Tremendum et Fascinans, 105, 137, 209, 213, 220
mysticism, 35, 52, 65, 108, 133, 137n, 164
myth, 17, 33–34, 56, 79, 82, 102n, 123, 129, 134, 137, 139, 153–54, 161n, 170n, 198–200, 208
mythos, 34, 56

naming, viii, 97, 100, 137, 188–90, 215
Native Americans, 33n, 213
naturalistic, science as, 28, 48
Neo-orthodoxy, 27. *See also* Barth, Karl
Neoplatonism 111, 172
neuroscience, 18, 29
Neville, Robert Cummings, 47n, 120
Newtonian worldview, 9, 36, 39, 60, 110
Nicholas of Cusa, 112n
Niebuhr, H. Richard, 210
nihil. See void
noise, 76, 115, 123, 131, 134, 169, 175–77, 180–81, 202–18
nonbeing, 12, 14, 105, 115, 131–32, 137, 142, 168, 191. *See also* nonexistence
nonexistence, 103, 133. *See also* nonbeing
nonlinearity, 18–19, 39
nothingness, 96, 100, 115. *See also creatio ex nihilo;* emptiness; void
Novalis, 181
Nozick, Robert, 103
nurture, 127, 149, 156–57, 169, 216, 223

Ogden, Schubert, 50–51, 58, 119, 214n
O'Leary, Stephen D., 4n
Om, 134
Omega, 124, 126
omnibenevolence, 128n, 216
omnipotence, 119, 124–30, 144, 146–47, 156. *See also* divine sovereignty
omniscience, 60, 122, 124–25, 146
ontology, viii, 12, 24, 43, 46–48, 57n, 59, 66–67, 86, 97, 108, 116, 120, 129, 141, 145, 152, 161, 167–68, 174–75, 181, 183n, 185n, 188, 191, 210, 219–23
open systems, x, 77, 93–94, 169, 174–75, 179–80, 184–85
opus distinctionis, 153, 155
opus ornatus, 153, 155, 202
Ortega y Gasset, José, 163, 194–95
Osiris, 34
Otto, Rudolf, 105, 137n, 209
ouk-on, 115, 131, 137
Owen, H. P., 130n

pan, 166
panentheism, 147–48
Pannenberg, Wolfhart, 45n, 50, 56–57, 196n
pantheism, 33, 45, 126, 144, 147
paradox, 97, 109, 112, 154, 183n, 185n, 205n, 213
Parsons, Talcott, 199
particle accelerator, 17, 114
Peacocke, Arthur R., 18n, 133n, 145–46
Pentecost, 209
Peters, F. E., viii, 20n, 129, 145–46n, 171n
phenomenology, 105
philosophy, viii, 2–37, 163, 166, 168n, 189, 193–94, 196n, 206, 217, 221–22
physis, 87n
Pirsig, Robert, 164, 166
Plato, vii, 11, 34–35, 46–47, 104, 123, 134, 165, 191, 206
pleroma, 115
polis, 47
Polkinghorne, John, 48n, 163
polytheism, 14–15
polyvalence, 200
postmodernism, 8, 31, 85n, 197n
potentiality, 5–6, 11–12, 18, 35, 48, 68, 71, 73, 75, 78, 90, 98, 101, 104–6, 109, 115, 117, 120–22, 125, 137, 141, 151, 153, 171, 173–76, 182, 191, 197, 206, 212–13, 216, 221, 223

power, vii, ix, 1–8, 11, 14–20, 23, 26, 31–34, 38, 40, 45, 49–50, 55–65, 68, 70n, 72, 75–76, 78, 84, 88, 90–91, 98, 101–4, 110–32, 135–36, 139–47, 150, 152–58, 164, 169, 171n, 175, 182–86, 189–93, 196, 203, 206, 210–13
pragmatic application, 52–53, 219
praxis, 26, 31–32, 40
predestination, 163
predictability, viii, 12, 18–19, 38, 69–79, 90, 104, 122–23, 159–62, 172, 195–96, 198, 207, 215–16. *See also* unpredictability
Prigogine, Ilya, 93
probability, 69. *See also* statistics
prophecy, 26, 83, 158, 192, 204, 207–9, 215. *See also* Ezekiel; Isaiah; Jeremiah
Protestantism, 2, 8, 27, 50
Proverbs, 203
providence, x, 43, 81n, 87n, 144, 146, 201–18
Psalms, 100, 178, 192, 209
psychology, 29, 67, 182–83, 217n
Pythagoreanism, 35, 172

quantum mechanics, 17, 39, 110, 114, 132, 145–46, 160
Qur'an, 212

Rad, Gerhard von, 100n, 154n
Rahner, Karl, 154
randomization, 72–73, 76, 79–81, 97n, 98n, 103, 105, 111n, 118–19, 124, 128, 141, 151, 160–61, 176n, 196–97
ratio, 205
rationality, 6, 12, 34, 36, 42–43, 48, 51–59, 122, 127, 131, 141–43, 167, 183, 191, 205, 219, 223
Receptacle, 34
Red Sea, 215
reductionism, 29, 48, 83–84
redundancy, 72, 75, 100, 161–63, 213, 216–17
Reese, William, 116n, 168n
relational universe, 12–13, 174–75, 211
relativism, 30–31, 47, 64
relativity, 110, 112–13, 147
relevantial universe, 13–15, 173
Renaissance, the, 8, 35, 74
revelation, x, 1, 25–28, 32, 36, 49, 51n, 61, 71n, 201–18
Richardson, Cyril, 200
Riedl, Rupert, 89–91
ritual, 53, 65, 200. *See also* ceremony; worship

Rome, 34, 134, 210
Rosnay, Joel de, 83n, 93
ruach, 100–102
Russell, Bertrand, 29, 130, 156n
Russell, Robert John, 18n, 145–46

Salmon, Wesley, 80n
salvation, 1, 14–15, 24–25, 200
Sartre, Jean-Paul, 197
Schleiermacher, Friedrich, 27–28
scripture, 4, 25–27, 32, 40, 49, 53, 99–100, 119, 121, 154, 156, 187, 191, 207, 209. *See also* the Bible
semantics, 50
sensorium dei, 60
Shakespeare, William, 98
Shannon, Claude, vii–ix, 59, 66–69, 72, 75, 77–78, 173, 205n
Shiva, 82
Sigma, 124–26
Simon, Paul, 137n
simulation, x, 6–7, 19, 164
Sinai, 156, 190, 212, 214
sociology, 18, 30n, 40, 67, 99, 199
soul, 1, 4, 34, 53, 105, 161, 179, 181, 188
space-time, 106, 110–11
spirit, 29, 33, 100–101, 133n, 156, 178, 186, 209, 213–14, 222. *See also ruach*
statistics, 67, 79–80, 160n, 166n, 184n. *See also* probability
Stavans, Ilan, 37n
subsystems, 86–87, 145, 148, 157, 170, 174, 199–200
Swimme, Brian, 38
symbiosis, 32, 87, 90
symbol, 2, 9, 19, 60, 63–64, 97, 99, 120, 142, 182, 199–201, 205, 207, 217
systems theory, ix, 39, 66–95, 179, 199–201

Tao Te Ching, 97, 137, 192
Tao, the, 97n, 108, 132, 134n, 137, 170, 192, 222
Taoism. *See* the Tao
taxonomy, 5–6, 11, 165, 187–88. *See also* classification
techne, 87n
technology, 1–6, 8–11, 16–17, 21–22, 66–68, 83, 119n, 163n, 194n, 219
tehom, 100–102, 105, 109, 161n
Teilhard de Chardin, Pierre, 86, 185n
teleology, 34–35, 91, 134, 140, 173–74, 183, 203
telephone, the, 67–68, 117n
telescope, 17–18
television, 67–68, 70

telos. *See* teleology
Ten Commandments. *See* Decalogue
Tetragrammaton, 190. *See also* Yahweh
theism, 33, 40, 42–45, 50–51, 61, 112,
    129–31, 139–47, 217
theodicy, 128n, 163, 207n
theogony, 129, 132, 201
theology, 10–14, 17, 21–42, 45–46, 83,
    96, 103n, 116–17, 129n, 133–37,
    145–47, 163n, 171n, 174n, 182–
    87, 192, 196–99, 210n, 214n,
    221–22
    Christian, 35–37, 50, 137
    classical, 94, 124
    constructive, vii–x, 1–4, 21–24, 56,
        64
    dialectical, 27. *See also* Barth, Karl
    liberation, 31–32
    metaphorical, 24, 49–65
    metaphysical, 91
    natural, 103, 140, 212
    philosophical, 50, 196
    process, 13, 147
theoria, 26
theos, 25
thermodynamics, 78–81, 150–51
Thomism, 117–18
Tiamat, 34, 161n
Tillich, Paul, vii–viii, 14–16, 50, 60,
    64, 90, 91n, 115–17, 135, 137,
    141–42, 174, 182, 210
tohuwabohu. See void
Tolstoy, 220
tools, 1, 5–6, 16–17, 20–21, 39, 49,
    62, 64–65, 97, 160n, 180, 191,
    219
Tower of Babel, 208–9
transcendence, vii, 1, 23, 28, 35, 45–46,
    62–64, 97, 146–49, 156–57, 172,
    185, 194, 199
Trinity, the, 213
tsimtsum, 129
Tsu, Lao, 97n. *See also* the Tao
Turner, Charles Hampton, 182n, 183n

Ultimate, the, 14, 142, 167n
uncertainty, 38, 69–74, 78–82, 94–95,
    104, 108–9, 118n, 124, 149, 151,
    155, 158–61, 164, 169, 189–90,
    194–95, 198, 205n, 213–16
Ungrund, 105, 118, 132, 137, 170
Unmoved Mover, 94, 117n,
unpredictability, 19, 28, 38, 76, 90,
    122, 159–60, 198. *See also*
    predictability
Urgeschichte, 89n, 131

vectors, 117–18, 207
via negativa, 96
void, 43, 100–101, 109, 115, 119,
    123, 125, 131, 147, 209. *See
    also creatio ex nihilo;* emptiness;
    nothingness

Waldrop, Mitchell, 18n, 90–91
Watts, Alan, 176
Watzlawick, Paul, 183n, 205n
Whitehead, Alfred North, vii–viii, 13–
    14, 17, 20–21, 60, 104, 106–7,
    120n, 125, 130–31, 143n, 186n,
    222
Wieman, Henry Nelson, 174–75
Wiener, Norbert, 67, 91, 172–73
Williams, Terry Tempest, 165n
World Soul, 34
worship, 4, 29n, 53–54, 62–65, 156n,
    220, 222. *See also* ceremony; ritual
wrath, 207–9
Wuste, 105, 121
wu-wei, 192
Wyschogrod, Michael, 129

Xaos, 170

Yahweh, 137, 156, 190, 202, 215
YHWH, 190. *See also* Yahweh

Zaleski, Jeffrey, 4n
zeitgeist, 56
Zeno, 112
zero, 76, 112, 133, 161, 171, 213